MANAGING

COLLECTIVE INVESTMENT FUNDS

Ekaterina Alexeeva, Sally Buxton, Christopher Gilchrist and Mark St Giles

Published by  Cadogan *Financial*

MANAGING COLLECTIVE INVESTMENT FUNDS

Published by  Cadogan *Financial*

19 Buckingham Street, London WC2N 6EF, England
Email: cadogan@dial.pipex.com
Website: www.cadoganfinancial.co.uk
Telephone: 020 7976 2500 Facsimile: 020 7930 7402

Cadogan Financial ©2000

Printed and bound in the United Kingdom.

Design by October of the United Kingdom.

British Library Cataloguing in Publication Data.

A catalogue record for this book is available from the British Library.

First published 2000

ISBN 0-9538086-0-2

Acknowledgements

This book results from many years of working with clients in developed and in emerging markets worldwide. Much of the expertise contained in it was acquired through work on technical assistance programmes sponsored by the UK Department for International Development, the World Bank and the International Finance Corporation, whom we would like to thank for their support.

We also thank all those who worked with us on these projects and our many clients in Africa, Asia, Europe, Latin America and the United States, with whom we have enjoyed working and from whom we have learnt much. This work would not have been possible without the help of the many organisations that have provided us with information and guidance over the years, including the British Venture Capital Association, the UK Association of Unit Trusts and Investment Funds, the UK Association of Investment Trust Companies, the European Association of Investment Funds and Companies (FEFSI), the UK Financial Services Authority, the US Investment Companies Institute and the US Securities and Exchange Commission.

Last – but not least – we would like to thank our colleague Angela Burgess for co-ordinating the production of the book.

Contents

A business worth entering

1.1 The role of collective investment funds

Making money from managing other people's money is what operating collective investment funds ("CIFs") is all about. The main elements are attracting money from people who currently have spare cash and putting that money to work by investing it in a range of assets such as shares, bonds and money market instruments. Fundamentally, therefore, collective investment funds intermediate between savers and borrowers.

Investment funds intermediate savings

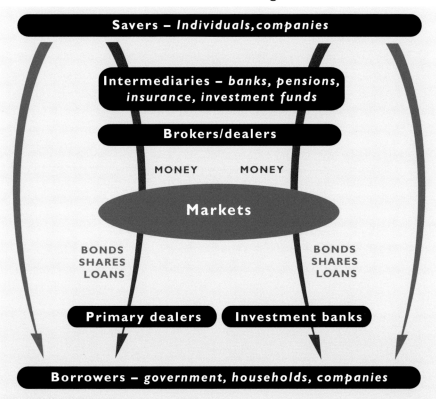

1

1.1.1   Building a successful CIF Management business is not simple

The key to building a business managing CIFs is consistently to give
CIF investors a good return; ideally this return should be competitive
in relation to other savings products and relevant indices, and should
outpace inflation. Since those who operate CIFs – fund management
companies ("CIF Managers") – make their money by charging fees
which are related to CIF values, they have a strong incentive to
increase the value of fund assets and thus to both enhance returns to
investors and fees paid to themselves. Also, the happier investors are
about their investment returns, the greater their readiness to invest
more money with those same managers.

This may sound simple; but it is easier to describe than to achieve.
Consistently making money from CIF Management involves rather
more than simply getting customers and choosing investments. If such
a business loses clients as fast as it gains them, or only gives them
poor returns, it will fail.

The focus of this book is building a successful CIF Management
business based on the operation of "collective investment funds"
(explanations of this and further technical terms are given in the
glossary), in which investors participate by buying a unit or share or
participation in a CIF. The book does not seek to cover the operation
of life assurance or pension funds, where the rights of the participant
are defined by the specific contractual terms of the particular
assurance or pension scheme with the individual concerned. The
rights of CIF investors derive, quite simply, from the purchase of a
share or unit or participation, each of which brings their holder equal
proportionate rights to returns achieved by fund investments.

1.1.2   Understanding the basic principles

A description of how funds work and the part played by different
organisations is given in Chapter 2; while the implications of different
CIF structures for developing a CIF business are described in Chapter 3.

1.1.3   Factors in decision-taking in developing a CIF business

The development of a successful CIF Management business has to be seen in the context of governing law and regulation, whose implications are outlined in Chapter 4. Fiscal and accounting regimes have a major influence on how effectively funds can operate, and are covered in Chapters 12 and 13.

1.1.4   Several activities must combine effectively

There are three main strands of activity within a CIF Management business and they must all interact effectively and efficiently for the business to be optimally profitable. They are:

- administration – operating funds and servicing their investors

- investment Management – investing fund money

- marketing – the creation, promotion and sale of funds

These subjects are covered in Chapters 5 to 11.

1.1.5   Everything has to be brought together

Any business has to have clear objectives and to co-ordinate its activities to achieve these objectives; if necessary, adjusting its strategy and activities along the way. It is worth noting that many of the most successful fund Management businesses have been built by an individual who has strong personal beliefs which permeate every part of the operation of that company. Examples include the Johnson family, now led by Edward C. Johnson III, which has built the famous US and international mutual fund group, Fidelity and whose family's net worth, as a result, is tens of billions of dollars; and Jack Bogle, creator of the equally renowned no-load, mutually owned Vanguard Group of the US. The function of overall business Management, planning for profitability and related budget issues is explored in Chapter 14.

1.2 How CIFs work

CIFs seek to attract money from investors, who receive shares or units or participations in the CIF, proportionate to their contribution to the total invested in the CIF. Each investor has a right to the income and capital growth achieved by the CIF, in the same proportion as the value of their holding within the total value of the CIF (which, if they held one of a hundred shares, would be one hundredth or one per cent). The CIF pools together large numbers of investors' contributions and invests that money on their behalf. The investments are chosen and managed by professionals, usually employed by the management company that promotes and manages the CIF, in line with the stated investment objective of the CIF; investors therefore do not have day to day control over how their money is invested.

How a CIF works

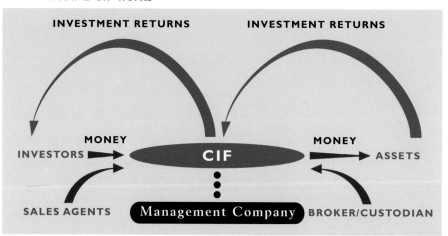

INVESTMENT RETURNS   INVESTMENT RETURNS

MONEY   MONEY

INVESTORS ▶   CIF   ▶ ASSETS

SALES AGENTS   Management Company   BROKER/CUSTODIAN

1.3   Why enter the business

1.3.1   CIFs: From small beginnings to over $8.6 trillion under management

CIFs originated more than a hundred years ago in Britain in the 1860s. One of the earliest funds to be created was the Foreign & Colonial Government Trust. Its launch document offered "the investor of modest means the same advantages as the large capitalist – by spreading the investment over a number of different stocks". This fund still exists today, as do several others launched in the UK in the following decades.

While the essential features of the CIF offer have not changed since that time, the scale of the business has: by the end of 1998, over $8.6 trillion ($8,600,000,000,000) was invested in over 30,000 open ended CIFs worldwide. This figure excludes the many hundreds of billions invested in closed ended funds, in the many "offshore" CIFs and in the so-called "hedge" funds. It also excludes funds from many emerging markets such as the countries of Central and Eastern Europe, Russia and Central Asia, which have increasingly been developing domestic investment funds.

Market share by country: value of open ended CIFs worldwide

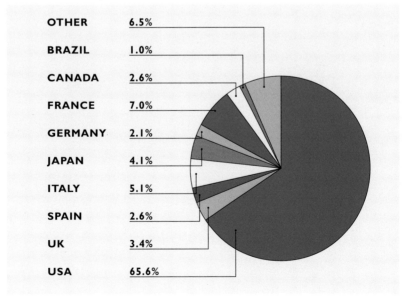

OTHER	6.5%
BRAZIL	1.0%
CANADA	2.6%
FRANCE	7.0%
GERMANY	2.1%
JAPAN	4.1%
ITALY	5.1%
SPAIN	2.6%
UK	3.4%
USA	65.6%

1.3.2   CIFs have become mainstream investments

In the last decade the collective investment funds industry has undergone a transformation. In the domestic markets of developed countries, CIFs have taken on a much larger role in the channelling of individual savings.

Formerly, CIFs were the smallest of the three groups of institutional investors in the developed markets, being considerably smaller than life assurance funds and pension funds. But a number of factors have encouraged an increase in the market share of CIFs relative to these other institutions. Probably the most important have been: the simplicity of CIFs compared with contractual life assurance and pension plans; relatively low costs and charges; convenience and ease of access; and, in developed countries, effective regulation resulting in a 'clean' public image.

The globalisation of world markets has also had major effects on CIFs. Though the vast bulk of assets under management in any one country are still typically domestic deposits, bonds or equities, the rate of growth in non-domestic assets under management has been even faster than domestic growth rates in the developed economies. Cross-border consolidation of CIF Managers into giant firms managing assets of over $100 billion apiece has begun.

1.3.3   CIFs are developing in emerging markets too

At the same time, CIFs have been recognised as a means whereby savings in emerging economies can be mobilised.

In some countries, mass privatisation of government-owned companies through vouchers which could be exchanged for participation in privatisation funds created a sizeable CIF market in a very short time. Though such privatisation funds have had problems – often they were set up under special laws which did not permit their evolution into properly-functioning CIFs – they have given the public in these countries some understanding of the idea of collective investment and a direct interest in its success. In other emerging markets, the early development of CIFs has been seen as a desirable component in developing capital markets. Both groups of funds have often had a difficult time: while in developed markets, the major expansion of CIFs followed long after the establishment of stock exchanges supported by a large body of individual investors, in emerging economies CIFs are playing a major role in the establishment of stock markets. Frequently, financial infrastructure is absent or weak – custody, registration, money transfer, for instance – and necessary legislation may be lacking, inconsistent or incomplete as well as being unevenly or poorly applied.

To some extent this is a consequence of the structure of these markets. Typically, they lack well-established long-term savings institutions (life assurance and pension funds) whose cash flow characteristically feeds developed financial markets. They may also lack a large affluent middle-class capable of acquiring financial assets or that class is just beginning to develop. In the developed markets, inherited wealth played a major part in the evolution of stockmarkets, but this factor has been far less relevant in former command economies. The appearance of a class with high disposable income, little knowledge of investment, and a need to save in the absence of state provision for retirement, provides an ideal environment for CIFs.

However, cultural factors may be as important as cash: some cultures are much more risk averse than others. Where risk aversion is strong, the establishment of well-regulated diversified CIFs can therefore play an important part in the mobilisation of savings.

1.4   Why CIFs are popular

Growth in assets in CIFs in selected countries

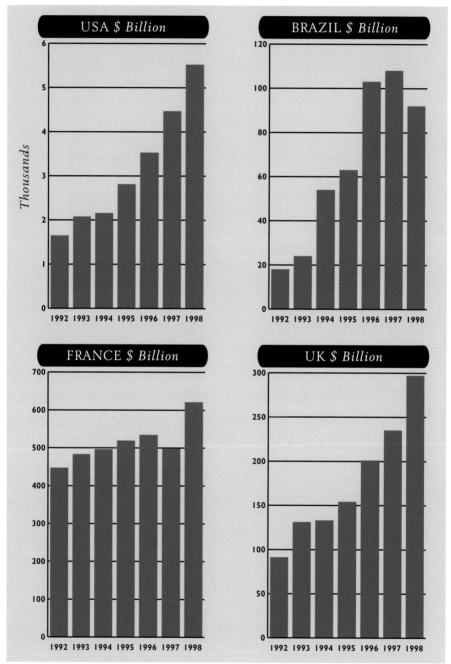

In the past decade, the rate of growth in CIF assets in developed economies has accelerated. At first sight this is paradoxical. One might expect that investors in mature markets would, as affluence and sophistication increase, be inclined to place a larger proportion of their wealth in individual securities – especially in view of the stringent policing of financial markets in developed countries today.

So the question arises: why do people in developed economies prefer CIFs to the direct purchase of securities? The answer is that investors find CIFs attractive because of the four factors of risk, cost, professional management, and regulation. These factors are as relevant to the prospects for CIFs in emerging markets as they are in developed economies.

1.4.1   Reduce risk

Investing through funds reduces risk:

- firstly, because funds usually invest in twenty or more different investments: mathematical studies show that the greater the diversification of a portfolio, the lower the risk in relation to the return (see section 5.2)

- secondly, because investing in higher risk securities does not necessarily generate higher returns

On the first point, once investors understand clearly that diversification pays – in that it lowers risk in relation to return – then they will value this diversification and seek it out. This is almost certainly the major factor in the recent success of CIFs in the US and Western Europe. It is even more relevant to emerging markets, where the risks involved in individual securities are usually higher, so that the advantages of diversification are greater.

Investors in securities also will become aware that securities whose perceived risks are high often do not produce correspondingly high returns. This contradicts the naive expectation of the novice investor that he can secure very high returns by finding the right high-risk securities. Essentially, the reality is that any investor with a small portfolio of risky securities is taking on far more risk in relation to return than he needs to. The experience of disillusioned investors in relation to high-risk, high-return investing in developed stockmarkets is probably a contributory cause of the rising cash inflows to CIFs.

From the perspective of the individual investor, diversification is valuable. It is worth paying for, because it reduces risk.

This diversified risk can also be taken through funds with a comparatively small amount of money – around $500 or $1,000 would be a normal investment; but to achieve a personal portfolio spread of 20 or more securities, most investors would need to have $100,000 or more.

1.4.2   Reduce cost

The second major factor in attracting investors to CIFs is cost. The details of the comparison will vary from one market to another, but the average 'small investor' will usually incur higher total costs by buying and selling a portfolio of individual securities than buying and selling a CIF.

The reason is that transaction costs in most markets have historically been related to the size of the transaction. The individual investor's transaction costs on small purchases or sales are typically five to ten times higher than those for institutional investors dealing in large quantities. The extent of the cost advantage this gives the CIF, as opposed to direct purchases of securities, will depend on the time for which the investment is held, the extent to which a portfolio is subject to changes, and the total charges levied by the CIF.

The cost factor is, as far as the individual is concerned, aggravated by risk. In order to reduce risk, diversification is necessary. Yet the greater the diversification, the greater the transaction costs: and the greater the relative advantage of the CIF.

1.4.3   Offer expertise

The evolution of developed markets has included a phase (ongoing in some cases) in which inadequate supply of public information gave possessors of 'inside information' a definite advantage. As regulation has reduced such imbalances, the possession and analysis of publicly available information has become the key to the selection and management of investments.

The volume and complexity of the information available mean that the scope for the amateur investor has become more limited. As developed markets show, there is a minority of people – often retired – who devote a good deal of time and energy to managing their own investments. But the majority of people lack the time, inclination or professional skills to do this. They are therefore inclined to delegate the task of selecting and managing investments to professional investment managers.

CIFs provide such full-time professional management in direct and simple form. This is valuable even in developed markets where information is widely available and financial markets are well regulated. It is even more valuable in countries where this is not the case.

1.4.4   Protect investors

The success of CIFs in many developed markets depends fundamentally on a framework of law and regulation, applied fairly and consistently. People must have confidence that their money is protected from fraud, theft and other abuses and that if these do occur, there are reliable means of compensation for those affected. In the absence of this confidence, individuals simply will not continue to buy CIFs in any volume.

In addition, tax law must put CIF investors in a position that is no worse than that of direct investors in securities. Failure to address this – often historic – problem has frequently adversely affected CIFs in emerging markets, where fiscal policy has often failed to keep pace with financial market development. Developed markets, recognising the contribution that CIFs make to mobilising the savings of ordinary people, often award them a favourable tax treatment, or create savings product "wrappers" that give tax exemptions to certain underlying assets, which may include CIFs.

This is a demanding agenda and one that has taken developed countries many decades to achieve. Specific regulation of CIFs did not really begin to take shape in the US or Europe until the 1930s, when funds had been in operation for seventy years or more. Even today, amendments continue to be made to aspects of tax law and CIF supervision and regulation in most jurisdictions, often associated with the development of new financial instruments or technological developments.

It is vital to appreciate that without a reliable regulatory system, the public will lack the confidence in CIFs that is crucial to the long-term development of a profitable CIF industry. Regulation may be seen as unnecessary by practitioners, but – if it is of high standard, is not unduly onerous and is consistently and fairly applied – it has considerable benefits to practitioners:

- it prevents creation of unrealistic expectations amongst potential investors by requiring proper and full disclosure of risk

- it creates barriers to entry which should reduce the likelihood of dishonest or disreputable players damaging the marketplace

- it sets clear rules, thus making competition more predictable and less expensive

- it referees the game, penalising malpractice and preventing its recurrence

It might be said that it is easier for developing countries to create regulatory systems, since they do not have a large existing body of financial sector and other law with which the CIF regulatory system has to be integrated, which is a source of problems in many countries. In many cases, emerging markets have a 'clean sheet' and can create a coherent system without the lengthy and complex adjustments often necessary in developed countries. Moreover, countries creating new regulatory systems can cut short the process that has taken many decades elsewhere by learning from the experience of others.

1.4.5   CIFs to suit different needs

CIFs offer both lower risk and lower cost than direct securities purchase
for most individual investors; in addition, they may be more tax
efficient. These are quantifiable benefits. In addition, CIFs offer the less
tangible benefits of convenience, professional investment management,
and (usually) less work in record-keeping and provision of information to
tax authorities than would apply to direct ownership of securities.

This proposition – lower risk, lower cost, professional management
and convenience – is the foundation of CIFs' success in every market.
Local factors, such as culture, taxation, regulation and the relative
stage of development of securities exchanges and markets, will shape
their evolution.

The majority of CIFs invest exclusively in money market instruments,
bonds or equities. The extent to which the four factors of risk, cost,
professional management and convenience apply to these different
types of investment varies according to the regulation, taxation,
quality of assets and level of competition within any one market.

For instance, in the case of money market funds versus deposits,
whether CIFs offer a reduction in risk to individual investors depends
on the nature of the banking system and the extent to which bank
depositors are protected by law in the event of bank failures. Indeed,
money market CIFs, due to their diversification, may even achieve a
higher credit rating than the banks or companies whose debt they
hold. CIFs of this type often flourish in cases where local regulation
sets a ceiling on interest rates on personal bank accounts, which CIFs
can beat by enabling investors to access the higher interest rates
available in wholesale money markets (as has been the case in the
USA and in France).

The reduction in risk provided by CIFs is more significant in the case
of bonds that are not of the highest grade, but it is most valuable in
respect of equity investments. The cost advantage of CIFs is also
greatest with equities where individual transaction costs are normally
higher than in bonds. Also the selection of equities through good

1

professional management can usually provide greater incremental returns than is possible in managing a portfolio of bonds.

In the long run, one might therefore expect equity CIFs to be the largest category of CIFs. However, individual investors start with portfolio preferences of their own in respect of the proportion of their assets they wish to hold in deposits, bonds and equities. Where investors can choose CIFs for each type of investment (as in the US), then the total assets in each type of CIF will reflect these portfolio preferences as well as the relative advantages of CIFs as compared with direct investment. Such portfolio preferences also account for the higher volumes of assets in bond CIFs than equity CIFs in most of the European Union, and for the higher volumes of assets in equity CIFs than bond CIFs in the UK.

Tax incentives attached to investing in different assets can also have a strong influence on investment preferences (see Chapter 12).

Different asset preferences: open ended funds by value – 1997

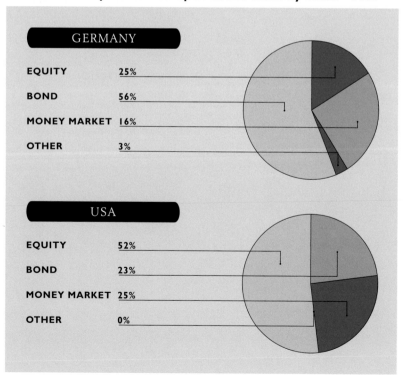

GERMANY

EQUITY	25%
BOND	56%
MONEY MARKET	16%
OTHER	3%

USA

EQUITY	52%
BOND	23%
MONEY MARKET	25%
OTHER	0%

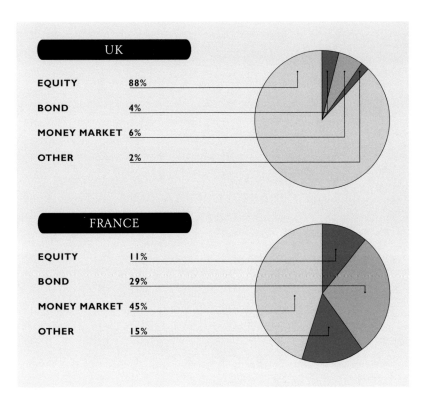

UK

EQUITY	88%
BOND	4%
MONEY MARKET	6%
OTHER	2%

FRANCE

EQUITY	11%
BOND	29%
MONEY MARKET	45%
OTHER	15%

The advantages of CIFs versus direct investment are even more pronounced when investing outside a domestic market, as people increasingly do in the interests of diversification of risk. Few individual investors could research foreign markets effectively for themselves, and dealing with the currency and other complexities of investing abroad – as well as the cost of this – is something few people would wish to take upon themselves. This is particularly true of investing in emerging markets, where there may be little information available on companies and no alternative to personal meetings with companies to "look them in the eye". This largely accounts for the recent rapid growth rate in CIFs investing outside their domestic market.

1.5 Who invests in CIFs

The majority of CIFs are designed to be marketed to ordinary people – though these funds may also attract institutional investors, such as pension funds or insurance funds, with similar needs. But there is also a substantial minority of funds specially designed only for institutional investors and for rich people (sometimes referred to as "high net worth individuals"). These funds are often designed differently from funds aimed at the public, with higher minimum investments and lower charges. They may be established in offshore centres which permit a wider range of investments to be made than onshore regulatory regimes, which are designed to protect less sophisticated investors; such locations may offer better tax treatment also.

Institutions may wish to use CIFs for many of the same reasons as individuals do. They may wish to achieve diversification of assets and to lower the costs of portfolio management. They may lack the expertise to invest in specialist areas but still wish to hold such assets.

Joint stock companies may also be investors in CIFs, as may charitable organisations, if such investment is tax efficient for them. Many countries have fiscal regimes designed to ensure that any advantageous tax status of funds is not abused either by companies or by individuals (see Chapter 12).

1.6   A future worth investing in

As this book will show, the many different types of CIF operating under different legal systems are based on a set of common principles.

The simplicity, low costs and ease of transaction offered by CIFs make them an easy choice for individuals wishing to invest lump sums or make regular savings from income. Where effective regulation provides the grounds for public confidence, CIFs can attract a significant share of national savings. In developed markets, CIFs are playing an increasing role in pension provision, as governments try to shift the burden of paying retirement benefits from the State to the private sector, a trend which is also true in emerging markets.

A common characteristic of emerging economies is that they have requirements for capital greater than their total domestic savings.

Foreign investment – direct investment and portfolio investment – can help to bridge this gap. In periods when foreign capital is easily available, governments may perceive little need to manage domestic savings flows. But when foreign capital is hard to come by, thus raising the cost of capital over the whole economy, there is a far greater incentive to channel domestic savings effectively into productive investment.

Recent experience shows that foreign portfolio investment into developing countries – whose stock markets are characterized by low liquidity – although in some respects desirable, can be problematic. This is because of the potential volatility of foreign portfolio investment which has a tendency to move from country to country as their attractions wax and wane. As a country is "discovered" by the international emerging markets specialists, large inflows tend to push the market up to unsustainable levels. When the investments are sold – because there is a new "hot" market, or because all emerging markets have gone out of fashion, or because of a flight to lower risk assets – the effects can be devastating, causing precipitous falls in share prices, market liquidity problems and the failure of local market participants such as brokers and banks. The development of a substantial domestic CIF sector can help stabilise the market at times of heavy pressure from international investors, because its investments will tend to be held for the longer term and are less likely to move en bloc than foreign CIF Managers.

Banks are a necessary means of channelling domestic savings but it is also important to provide sources of long-term equity capital for industry and commerce, a form of investment that CIFs are far better designed to produce than banks are. The provision of a well-regulated system permitting the establishment and promotion of CIFs can therefore play a significant role in economic development. Because of the factors cited above, it is certainly possible that as compared the recent growth of CIFs in the developed markets at a late stage of market evolution, CIFs' role in the emerging economies will prove far more significant at an earlier stage of development.

Understanding CIFs: key functions and roles

2.1 Key functions

2.1.1 Operational requirements

CIFs' fundamental purpose is to make money for their investors. Stated at its simplest, they do this by:

- the creation of a fund, promoting it so it attracts money, making sales, keeping investors informed (marketing)

- collecting money from many different investors, ensuring it is properly recorded and investment proceeds and information remitted to investors as appropriate (administration)

- investing subscribers' money in assets which align with the investment objective of the CIF and which it is anticipated will give a good return, and adjusting that portfolio as necessary (investment management)

These are the functions which must be carried out for CIFs to operate. However, two other key functions also are required, by regulation, to be undertaken.

2.1.2 Regulatory requirements

History has shown that it is not in the interests of the general public – or a country's economy, witness Albania – to permit the promotion of financial "schemes" to proceed unchecked. Large sums of money can be attracted from an overoptimistic public in a very short time, as the success of pyramid or Ponzi schemes worldwide constantly demonstrates. Over time governments will respond to scandals, and introduce legislation (the US Investment Companies Act 1940 and the UK Financial Services Act of 1986, are examples); or people become dissatisfied or distrustful of governments who fail to provide them with sufficient regulatory protection from such operations and elect a government which then takes the necessary action.

Thus CIF operators – in common with other financial product providers permitted to market their services to the general public – are subjected to a number of legal and regulatory requirements in return for governmental approval to offer financial services. These requirements are normally applied by a securities market or financial sector regulator, which may itself have a varying status and structure within different countries.

Such regulators are well aware that handling large amounts of money is a temptation to anybody; and for a person or company (ie, a CIF Manager) to have untrammelled access to such money is potentially asking for trouble. It is for this reason – basically, to prevent theft or misuse of CIF assets – that another function is required to be undertaken in relation to CIFs. This is "custody": the safekeeping of fund assets. This is required by regulation to be undertaken by an entity which is operationally separate from – or preferably wholly independent of – the CIF Manager, to reduce opportunities for collusion.

In order to deal with another temptation – not to represent CIFs' activities inaccurately – and to check that money is not being improperly siphoned off from CIFs, CIFs are also required by regulation to be audited by an independent and qualified auditor.

To summarise – while CIFs operate in different ways in different countries, all need the following activities to be undertaken in order for them to work effectively:

● marketing

● administration

● investment management

- custody

- audit

2.2   Key organisations

The form in which CIFs have developed around the world is largely a function of the particular environment within which they operate. Thus, while – as stated above – certain functions are key to CIFs everywhere, how these functions are carried out, by whom, and what rights and responsibilities attach to those who fulfil the functions, varies from country to country. The legal and fiscal frameworks of the countries concerned are usually key factors influencing the form CIFs take.

As discussed later (see Chapter 3), some CIFs are formed as:

- companies, whose directors are responsible to shareholders – ie, the CIF's investors

- trusts, with trustees who have duty to look after the interests of beneficiaries of the trust – ie, the CIF's investors

- contractual pools, where duties to CIF investors are specified in the contract between manager and investor

In essence, the corporate and trust forms of CIF are similar in that both establish a clear fiduciary duty to look after the interests of CIF investors either upon company's directors or the trust's trustee respectively. Contractual funds seek to replicate this fiduciary duty through the terms of the management company contract.

Each fund structure has an impact on the roles and responsibilities of the organisations involved in operating CIFs, which are also influenced by the requirements set by the domestic regulator.

In order to explore the details of these roles and responsibilities, a common allocation of functions to organisations is shown below.

CHAPTER 2

Typical CIF roles and relationships

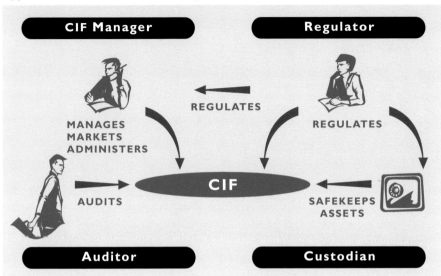

However, there are numerous variations on these themes which may vary within different types of CIF within each country, as well as between countries: these are explored further in Chapter 3.

2.2.1   Role of the CIF Manager

The duties which are carried out by the CIF Manager will vary from quite narrow (fund initiation and marketing only) to quite wide (all tasks except audit and custody), depending upon the structure of the CIF being formed. For the purposes of clarity, the functions listed below are those which, at a maximum, are carried out by the CIF Manager. In this book the terms "CIF Manager" and "CIF Management company" refer to the same entity.

2.2.1.1   *Marketing*

This is a broad title which at its most extensive, covers the following activities:

● market research

● creation of funds

2

- promotion of funds to potential investors, including general information provision

- sales of funds to investors

- communications with investors

Some of these functions may be subcontracted to other entities.

2.2.1.2 Administration

Administration includes two different areas of activity: the first being outward facing, which is servicing fund investors; the second, being inward facing, which is fund administration and accounting. At a maximum, these cover:

- outward facing:

- administering the flow of money into and out of a fund

- creating and maintaining individual accounts for fund investors

- confirming contractual details

- creating and maintaining fund registers

- recording all payments to and from investors

- inward facing:

- fund valuation and pricing

- dealing with reinvestment or distribution of dividends to investors

- advising fund managers of money available (or not) for investment

- recording fund portfolio transactions

- operating the accounts of the fund including income received and gains or losses realised

- liaison with the custodian and auditor

Again, some – or indeed all – of these activities may be subcontracted.

2.2.1.3   *Investment management*

Investment management will generally cover the following activities:

- research

- defining investment objectives and styles

- investment analysis

- portfolio selection and management

Here again, some – or all – of these activities may be sub-contracted.

Fund management companies have been started by a wide range of people and organisations, ranging from individual specialists such as lawyers, stockbrokers or accountants through to international financial houses and consumer brands.

2.2.2   Role of the custodian

The role and responsibilities of a custodian to a CIF will vary according to the legal structure of the fund: ie, whether the fund is constituted as a company, a trust or a contractual pool. It will also vary according to the duties placed upon the function in governing law and regulation. It is unfortunate that several different terms are used for functions which include that of custody; these are:

- "trustee": in this book this term is used only to refer to the capacity of a single trustee whose responsibility under a trust deed is to protect the interests of beneficiaries under that deed – ie the

2

CIF investors (it does not refer to multiple trustees of funds structured as business trusts in the USA or elsewhere, where the trustees are equivalent to directors of the fund and there is a separate custodian)

- "custodian": safekeeper of assets – used in this book to mean both depositary and custodian (except where central depositaries are referred to, see glossary)

- "depositary": broadly meaning the same as a custodian, therefore the term custodian is used throughout the book

Essentially the role of trustee or custodian can be classified into three parts, only two of which are linked to regulatory requirements.

2.2.2.1   Safekeeping of assets

Regulation requires the keeping of all the assets of the fund, whether cash or near cash, securities, title to real estate or other assets, by the custodian. Usually in a dematerialised system these assets are registered in the nominal ownership of the custodian, so the manager is unable to buy or sell assets without the assent and co-operation of the custodian. This is designed to prevent theft of CIF assets by the management company or by the directors of the fund.

2.2.2.2   Supervision of the conduct of business of the fund

Supervision of conduct of business of the CIF and its manager and its compliance with the trust deed, other founding documents and/or with regulation (referred to sometimes as "third party supervision") is another duty which may be imposed upon a custodian by regulation; alternatively it is a duty of a trustee under the trust deed. This supervisory role is not imposed on custodians of corporate funds, however, whose directors are responsible for such supervision. The supervisory role can cause conflicts of interest where the CIF is of contractual type, since it means that an entity contracted by a CIF Manager is being called upon to monitor the conduct of business of its hirer; this is why a duty placed on both CIF Manager and custodian to act only in the interests of CIF investors can be a useful clarifying measure.

2.2.2.3 Provision of additional commercial services

This third element of custodianship can be the provision of additional commercial services which may, or may not, be required by the CIF Manager to support the operations of the fund but which can conveniently be provided by the custodian if so desired. These would normally include money management services, such as currency management, and fund administration services such as registration.

The usual nature of regulatory requirements for custodians are summarised below.

Summary of varying roles of custodians by fund type

FUND TYPE	SAFEKEEPING ROLE	SUPERVISORY ROLE
Company CIF	required to be done by custodian	is the responsibility of CIF directors, not custodian
Trust CIF	required to be done by trustee, or custodian for whom trustee is responsible	is the responsibility of the trustee
Contract CIF	required to be done by custodian	sometimes required to be done by custodian, sometimes not

Some fund regulatory regimes require the appointment of a supervisory committee to a fund, whose task is to monitor the performance of the fund management company and sometimes the custodian, thus providing another form of "third party supervision". The effectiveness of such committees, whose access to information is dependent upon the management company and custodian, who are unlikely to voluntarily expose themselves to criticism, is perhaps questionable.

Trustee and custodian operations have been founded by a variety of individuals and organisations in the past. Today the increasingly global nature of the business, the technology investment needed and its transaction orientation has resulted in the majority of custodianship and trusteeship being undertaken by banks or banking subsidiaries. In addition, custody fits naturally alongside the other money management services that such institutions also offer.

2.2.3 Role of the auditor

The requirement that funds be audited by an independent and qualified auditor is standard to most regulatory environments. Such auditors may, or may not, be the same auditor as that which provides audit services to the CIF Management company. Regulation or accounting professional ethics generally require that the auditor must be independent of the funds and the management companies they audit.

The standards to which audits must be undertaken will be set by domestic accounting standards. Special accounting standards are usually set for CIFs, since their operation is not comparable with that of ordinary companies or other trusts. Chapter 13 gives more details of this.

Regulation may place on a CIF auditor the responsibility of reporting any discrepancies found to the CIF regulator, as an additional element of supervision.

2.3 Role of the CIF regulator

In this book, the role of the CIF regulator is taken broadly to mean the regulatory body:

● whose approval, registration or licence is needed prior to a CIF being publicly offered for sale

● whose licence or registration is required prior to a CIF Manager being permitted to seek approval for any CIFs it wishes to offer

● which monitors and supervises the operation of CIFs and of their managers

- which has powers to discipline those responsible for malpractice within CIFs, and to order compensation to be paid for any damage to CIF investors

The CIF regulator may, or may not, also regulate the conduct of custody business (which is sometimes covered by bank-related law or regulation instead); also it will regulate the conduct of CIF trustees. This regulator is often the regulator of securities markets in general, since fund units, shares or participations are usually defined as securities. References to 'regulator' or 'securities regulator' in the book refer to the regulator of CIFs.

2.4 Ability to delegate duties or responsibilities

It is noted above that CIF Managers may subcontract some tasks to other parties; as indeed may trustees and custodians. However, there is an international legal and regulatory principle that such delegation, while permitted:

- does not absolve the entity subcontracting the task from responsibility for ensuring that the task is properly undertaken by an organisation with the necessary regulatory status

- places upon the entity subcontracting the task a duty to ensure that any such task is undertaken in compliance with the governing law and regulation

- does not remove liability for any failure to complete subcontracted tasks properly and satisfactorily, except in certain defined circumstances (in such circumstances the contractor is expected to pay any damages and recover these from its subcontractor under breach of contract or other provisions)

Rules are usually defined to cover conflicts of interest potentially arising from the subcontracting of tasks to associates of companies or personnel of the entity subcontracting the task.

Implications of different CIF structures

3

The three different CIF legal structures – company, trust and contractual – have already been mentioned in the first two chapters of this book. In this Chapter the implications of different structures of CIFs, which have developed in different legal environments, are examined more closely.

The first CIFs, formed in the UK over 130 years ago, were formed both as trusts and as companies. Then, as today, the creators of the funds examined the legal structures available to them, and the relative merits of each structure in operational and tax terms, and chose what they considered to be the most attractive to potential investors.

The fundamental choices when creating a fund are:

● which legal structure – company, trust or contractual pool

● which operating structure – open, interval or closed ended

● which management structure – internal or external

● which category of fund – ie, what class of assets will it invest in

These are the terms used throughout this book for the different types of structures.

The range of structures which may be able to be used will depend on the law and regulation governing them, which will be individual to the legal framework of the country in which a fund or funds is to be created; and that of any other country into which it is planned to sell the fund. Some countries' legal frameworks will be more flexible than others; the most flexible often being found in the 'low tax' or 'offshore' domiciles. These may be countries or designated areas within a country, or sometimes islands (respective examples being Luxembourg, Ireland's 'International Financial Services Centre' in Dublin and Bermuda) which have made a strategic decision to create a legal and fiscal environment which is attractive to fund managers. 'Hedge funds' – which are usually created in one of the structures below, but which have a limited range of professional investors and need investment flexibility – are often created in these 'low tax' domiciles and use a variety of different fund structures.

This Chapter also briefly reviews the categories of fund which regulators may require CIFs to fall within which relate to the asset classes in which funds invest.

3.1 CIF legal structure

Corporate form CIFs are the commonest form in the world, often coexisting within countries with either trust or contractual funds. It is unusual to find trust and contractual forms coexisting, because usually a legal environment which will not permit formation of trust form CIFs due to a lack of the common law concept of trust will use the contractual form as an alternative. Contractual form funds are commonest in countries with a Civil Code tradition, though there are a few countries which have been influenced by British legal traditions where the concept of trust is applicable by reference to British precedent (South Africa, which has a primarily Romano-Germanic legal framework, being an example).

3.1.1 Company CIFs

CIFs formed as companies operate on the basis of company law in the country concerned, though they are usually subject to specific additional regulatory and fiscal provisions or exemptions (see Chapter 4 and Chapter 12 respectively) which distinguish them from ordinary companies. This is because CIFs are not ordinary companies, which usually seek to make profits from producing goods or providing

3

services: instead corporate CIFs aim to give their shareholders good returns from selecting and managing investments.

The practicalities of CIFs' operation, and their need to attract large numbers of investors, dictate that such companies must be:

- of the "open" and not "closed" company type, since "closed" companies require any shareholder who wishes to sell their holding to seek the approval of other shareholders prior to so doing. Seeking such permission clearly would not be feasible for funds which have thousands or tens or even hundreds of thousands of investors

- formed as limited companies: that is, the liability of their shareholders is limited to the amount paid to buy shares in that company; clearly unlimited liability would not be attractive to potential investors

As a company, a corporate CIF has a board of directors which is responsible to shareholders for the performance of the company in which they have invested. Such directors have a fiduciary duty to their shareholders, which essentially places a responsibility on them to treat shareholders' money as carefully as they would their own. The board is legally responsible for contracting the services of a CIF Management company, a custodian and any other provider of services to the fund, such as the auditor and monitoring their performance of their obligations.

It should be noted, however, that since it is normally the CIF Management company which stimulates the creation of new funds (which bring in more management fees), it is normally the management company that selects the directors of the fund, also. Regulation of fund directors to correct any biases thus created is strongest in the US, where a majority of CIF directors are required to be independent of the CIF Management company and where certain decisions must be made by those directors independently from the management company. This is generally considered to be good practice though not all regimes are so demanding.

The rights of corporate CIF investors are the same as investors in other companies, as shareholders, though they are often given additional rights and required to vote on additional issues to those required under company law. These usually include such matters as a change in investment objectives and an increase in fees charged to the fund.

Unusually as far as companies generally are concerned, corporate CIFs may be created with a defined life – generally of between 5 and 25 years – at the end of which they will be liquidated and assets paid out to shareholders. Limited life corporate funds can offer more complex share structures and guarantee type funds to be operated (see Chapter 11).

This fund form is the most common in the world, the largest group being the American open ended investment companies, commonly known as 'mutual funds'.

Relationship between corporate CIF and investor

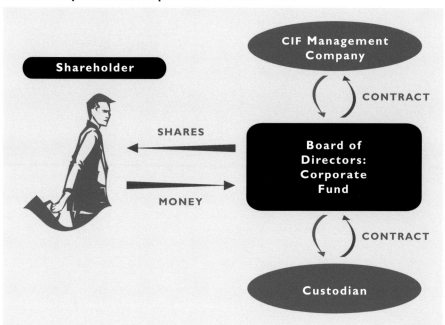

3.1.2 Trust CIFs

CIFs which take the trust form are most commonly found in countries whose legal system has been influenced by that of the UK: primarily the countries of the former British Empire and the USA (also referred to as "common law" countries). A trust, put at its simplest, is an arrangement recognised by law under which one person (the trustee) holds property for the benefit of another (the beneficiary).

CIFs formed as trusts are often known as "unit trusts". They are created by the signing of a trust deed by a CIF Management company and a trustee. The investor becomes a beneficiary of the trust upon subscription of money to the fund, in return for which he receives a holding of units.

The trustee of a unit trust is entitled, in the final analysis, to sack the management company if it fails to adequately perform its duties as required by the trust deed and by fund regulation. Thus the task of the trustee is as onerous in this form of fund as directorship of a corporate form fund, with approximately the same liability to fund investors.

Voting rights of unitholders are more limited than those of shareholders in corporate CIFs, though the issues upon which they are required to vote at a special meeting are similar to those extra matters on which corporate CIF investors must vote.

Relationship between trust CIF and investor

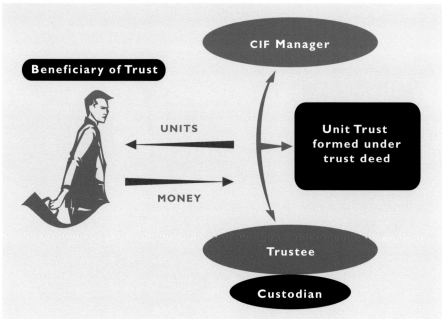

3.1.3 Contractual CIFs

This form of CIF is created by a contract between the investor and the management company to provide management of the pooled investment according to the contract and the founding documents of the fund (sometimes called fund rules). The management company is required to have a contract with a custodian to provide custody services to the fund, as part of the approval process of the fund by the regulator.

The participant's interest in the fund is proportionate to his contribution to the size of the fund. The rights of investors in such funds are defined by the contract with the management company, and by investment fund law and regulation, which often specifies requirements for the terms of such contracts. These rights are often weaker than those of shareholders in corporate type funds or beneficiaries of trust type funds; unlike them, contractual fund investors often have no vote on changes to the fund which substantially affect their interests (eg an increase in charges).

Relationship between contractual CIF and investor

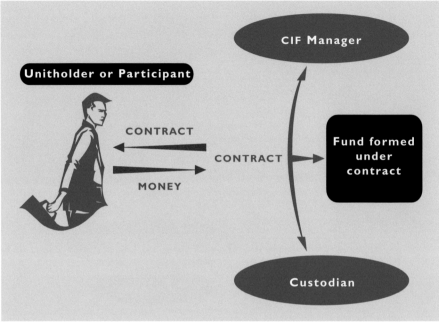

3.1.4   Partnership CIFs

Another form of fund is the partnership structure, which is not commonly used for CIFs offered to the public, but is often used for funds designed to attract only large scale, or professional, investors. Partnership structure funds can occur both in common law and Romano-Germanic countries: their operation is governed by the relevant legislation and by fund law and regulation. In this form, the management company is the general partner, offering partnerships to a relatively small number of investors who become limited partners.

These funds are most commonly formed in low tax domiciles, which often have more flexible regulation enabling a wider range of assets to be held.

Summary of the implications of the main legal structures

	CORPORATE FUND	TRUST	CONTRACTUAL
	Corporate fund	Trust	Contractual
Legal form	joint stock company (corporation)	trust	often not defined as legal entity: contractual pool collectively representing individual interests
Governing law	company law or commercial code, CIF law, stock exchange requirements if listed	trust law or precedent, CIF law	law of contract or civil code, CIF law
Issues	shares	units	units or participations
Rights over fund assets	the amount of each fund asset and of income from it proportionate to number of fund shares owned as % of total fund shares in issue	the amount of each fund asset and of income from it proportionate to number of fund units owned as % of total fund units in issue	collectively amongst all fund investors or each has rights over income and capital in proportion to ownership of the fund
Investor status	shareholder	beneficiary of trust (unitholder)	unitholder or participant
Voting rights of holders	as per ordinary shareholder plus those set by CIF law and regulation	as per trust deed plus those set by CIF law and regulation	none or those set by CIF law and regulation
Meetings of holders	Annual and Extraordinary	Extraordinary only	none or Extraordinary only
Fiduciary duty to investors (eg supervise manager)	fund directors	trustee	none unless specified in CIF law or contract with investors
Holder of fund assets	custodian	trustee or custodian on trustee's behalf	custodian
Assets registered in the name of	fund or custodian on behalf of fund	trustee or custodian on trustee's behalf	management company or custodian on behalf of fund
Founding documents	Memorandum and Articles of Association and equivalent eg Charter	trust deed	contract and rules of fund
Offering document	prospectus	prospectus	prospectus

3.2   CIF operating structures

CIFs, whether of company, trust or contractual type, generally operate
either in 'open ended' or in 'closed ended' form; some regulatory
frameworks also permit the operation of the 'interval' or 'clopen' form.

3.2.1   Open ended CIFs

An open ended CIF is one which has an obligation to issue (sell) and
redeem (buy back) shares or units regularly. As a general rule, most
open ended funds issue and redeem daily, but a different minimum
may be set by regulation – for instance, that an open ended CIF must
issue and redeem at least once every two weeks on the same day and
at the same time: it is important that this is done on a regular and
clearly stated basis.

This constant issue and redemption means that the capital invested in
the CIF varies from day to day as new investors arrive and other
investors leave the fund. This is why open ended funds structured as
companies are often referred to as 'companies with variable capital'.

These funds have to be able to create and cancel shares or units in the
CIF every day, which is sometimes very difficult to achieve under
ordinary company law. Open ended company CIFs therefore are often
inoperable unless special enabling legislation is passed.

A fundamental need of open CIFs, which have to be able to buy and
sell assets in their portfolios every day, is to be able to invest new
money or sell assets and pay out redemption proceeds easily. This is
why such funds are required by regulation to invest primarily in liquid
assets – assets which are easy to buy and sell quickly.

Open ended CIFs constitute the largest proportion of CIFs
internationally, their most attractive feature being that investors can
buy or sell units quickly and easily. Open ended funds operate in
corporate, trust or contractual form in most developed financial
markets, which provide them with the range of liquid assets they
need in order to operate fairly and effectively.

Relative size of open ended versus closed end fund markets

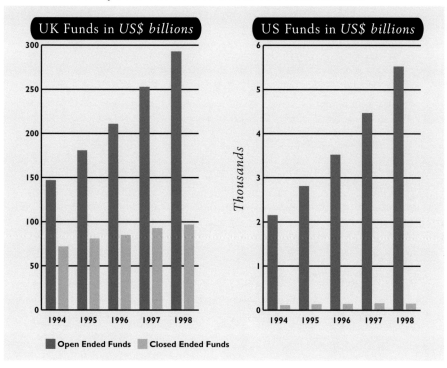

UK Funds in *US\$ billions*

US Funds in *US\$ billions*

Open Ended Funds   Closed Ended Funds

3.2.2   Closed ended CIFs

A 'closed ended' fund is one that, like a company, has a fixed amount of capital in issue, though closed ended funds can operate in company, trust or contractual form. These funds have an initial offer period and at the end of that offer, they close to further subscription: usually no further issues may be made unless existing holders agree. There is no duty on such CIFs to redeem – ie, to buy back shares or units from investors – so there are no demands on them to sell assets for cash. This also makes them more able to borrow or 'gear' (see section 5.2), since their capital base is more stable.

This fund structure is suitable for investing in illiquid as well as liquid assets and is commonly used to invest in emerging economies. Many countries' early CIFs were formed as closed ended company funds, since these fit more easily within laws governing companies than open ended company funds do, and since assets at that time were relatively illiquid. Closed ended funds continue to be formed in (and to invest in) liquid financial markets, however, since their form has other uses: in creating funds which invest in bonds and which guarantee a specified return to investors, for instance; or in creating corporate funds which issue shares with different rights (see section 11.6), which can enable a series of different investor needs to be catered for within a single fund.

3.2.3 'Clopen' or 'interval' CIFs

There is, in addition, a further variant; the so-called 'clopen' or 'interval' CIF. This is a CIF which opens for sale or repurchase on an occasional, though regular basis. The usual minimum requirement is that such funds must 'open' at least once a year. Some open monthly, and others quarterly.

These funds are really a half way house between closed and open funds; they have the advantages that:

- they can enable occasional redemptions at NAV, which is more attractive than closed ended funds whose shares or units can rarely be realised at NAV except upon winding up a fund

- they do not have to meet regular redemptions, so can invest in less liquid assets than open funds, which is helpful in emerging and transitional economies

To date, generally they have been more commonly used by professional investors than by ordinary investors.

3.2.4 Key differences between open and closed CIFs

The most important distinction between the operation of open and of closed CIFs is created by the obligation on an open ended fund to issue and redeem regularly.

An open fund, once it has finished its fixed price initial offer, issues and redeems shares or units every day and therefore has variable capital. At any one time, it therefore has to balance the interests of new investors buying, existing investors selling and ongoing investors continuing to hold, while contending with the fact that the value of assets which it owns changes from day to day. This change in value has to be taken into account, so that new investors do not pay too much or leaving investors receive too little, disadvantaging them; or that new investors do not pay too little and existing investors receive too much, disadvantaging ongoing holders.

The principle which is required by law and regulation to be applied to buying and selling shares or units in open ended funds is that of equality: a fund must receive in payment for a sale, or pay out for a redemption, the net asset value ("NAV") of the share or unit. This 'net asset value per share (or unit)' is calculated by taking the total value of the fund, less its liabilities (which is the 'fund net asset value'), and dividing this figure by the total number of units or shares in issue at the time of the calculation of the value. (A more detailed explanation of the importance of net asset value and how it is calculated is given in Chapter 5.)

An open ended fund can therefore have in issue an unlimited number of units or shares, which will all have the same NAV at any one point in time.

By contrast, closed ended funds have only a limited number of shares or units in issue, which are issued only within a specified period prior to a closing date (ie, they have fixed capital). Thereafter the owner of a share or unit in closed ended fund can only sell it if he can find a buyer for it. This is usually done through a secondary market such as a stock exchange or trading system: it is often a regulatory or fiscal requirement that closed ended funds' shares or units be listed or quoted – otherwise the chances of sellers being able to find a buyer would be low and the funds would, therefore, not be attractive to many investors. The price that the buyer of a share or unit in such a market will pay will depend upon the level of supply and demand for that share or unit. If few fund shares are available, but demand is high, prices will rise; where many fund shares are available and demand is low, prices will fall. Thus the price paid is rarely the same

3

as the net asset value of the share or unit; it could be more or – mostly – it will be less than net asset value.

The fixed capital base of a closed ended fund also makes it more able to borrow money which it uses to 'gear' or enhance its performance, through buying more assets. Open ended funds, whose capital is variable, are only permitted to borrow within narrow limits, due to the risk of sudden changes in capital.

Thus it is the fixed capital structure of the closed ended fund which creates its main differences from that of open ended, variable capital, funds. As a general rule, closed ended funds are cheaper to operate than open ended funds, since their portfolio and register are more stable.

3.2.5 Pros and cons of different operating structures for CIF Management companies

Each operating structure has implications for the way that the CIF has to conduct its business. For a CIF Management company, both open and closed funds have advantages and disadvantages. Open ended funds can be promoted consistently over time, and assets under management within a single fund can expand substantially; however, investors may leave in droves if fashions change or markets fall. Closed ended funds are usually only promoted once on the first issue and do not expand over time except in value of assets managed; however, if fashions change or markets fall investors can only leave if they find another buyer. Management fees on closed ended funds can therefore have a more limited downside; but also have a more limited upside.

Key characteristics of the two main operating structures

LEGAL STRUCTURE	OPERATING STRUCTURE	
Corporate	**Open Ended** • *variable capital* • *continuously issues and redeems shares* • *shares issued and redeemed at prices closely related to NAV, through the management company* • *not usually listed or traded* • *required to invest primarily in liquid assets* • *very limited or no borrowing powers* • *externally managed* • *the most common variety of open ended CIF*	**Closed Ended** • *fixed capital* • *after initial capital raising at fixed price, generally can only issue new shares or redeem existing ones with shareholder agreement* • *shares trade in secondary market; price set by supply and demand* • *usually listed or traded* • *may invest in liquid or illiquid assets* • *often wide borrowing powers* • *may be internally or externally managed* • *the principal form of closed ended CIF*
Trust	• *continuously issues and redeems units* • *units issued and redeemed at prices closely related to NAV, through the management company and/or trustee* • *not usually listed or traded* • *required to invest primarily in liquid assets* • *very limited or no borrowing powers* • *externally managed* • *commonest in countries whose legal system is affected by British traditions: often called unit trusts*	• *fund has power to issue more units but does not use it* • *units may be traded in secondary market; price set by demand and supply* • *may invest in liquid or illiquid assets* • *may have wide borrowing powers* • *may be internally or externally managed* • *rarer form of fund mainly used by institutional investors and based in offshore centres such as IFSC Dublin, Channel Islands, Bermuda*
Contractual	• *continuously issues and redeems units or participations* • *units issued and redeemed at prices closely related to NAV, through the management company* • *not usually listed or traded* • *required to invest primarily in liquid assets* • *very limited or no borrowing powers* • *externally managed* • *common form in Continental Europe and countries who have adopted Romano-Germanic legal frameworks*	• *has single issue of units or participations* • *units may be traded in secondary market; price set by supply and demand* • *sometimes listed and traded* • *may invest in liquid or illiquid assets* • *may have wide borrowing powers* • *may be internally or externally managed* • *rare form – may be found in Continental Europe and countries who have adopted Romano-Germanic legal frameworks*

NB: UCITS (Undertakings for Collective Investments in Transferable Securities) is the generic name used in European Union Law to cover open ended collective investment schemes which invest in transferable securities.

3.2.6   Pros and cons of different operating structures for investors

While both open and closed ended funds are designed to offer the same service to investors – essentially, portfolio management – the operational differences between them have some pros and cons.

Generally, investing in an open ended fund is more straightforward: the management company sells and buys back units and shares every day, at a price which is required by regulation to be based on net asset value (NAV); that is, the net asset value of the fund, divided by the number of units in issue.

By contrast, unless investors subscribe to an initial offer of a closed end CIF, if they wish to buy a holding in an existing closed ended CIF, they have to find an existing investor willing to sell. Prices of CIF holdings in the secondary market are therefore set by supply and demand, and do not necessarily relate to the value of the fund in which a holding is being bought. This can have advantages for investors though, since most closed ended CIFs' shares or units can be bought at a price which is lower than NAV (this being being known as being 'at a discount to NAV', the discount being expressed as a % of NAV – the reverse, where share or unit prices are higher than NAV, is referred to as being 'at a premium to NAV', and also expressed as a % of NAV). So an investor may pay 100 for a share which has a NAV of 120, which will pay dividends on 120, and not 100. Of course, the investor will face the same problem when he comes to sell his holding, which is that he may have to sell it for less than its value, too. Dealing in the secondary market may mean that the investor has to use a stockbroker, which some find off-putting.

3.3   Management structures

There are essentially two ways of constructing the way a fund is managed: known as 'internal' or 'external' management.

3.3.1 Internal management

Essentially, internal management is where the people who operate the fund on a day to day basis are employees of the fund, which meets the cost of their employment and functioning including office space, equipment, power and supplies. In other words, the fund which is internally managed operates as a normal company does. Funds which are internally managed are quite rare and are usually only of the closed ended corporate form. Technically it would be possible within a trust form for the trustee to employ a management team within a fund; but a contractual fund (whether open or closed ended) cannot be self managed, since it has no existence in law and cannot contract employees, sign leases, etc.

This is a relatively rare form of management structure internationally; this book therefore focuses, throughout, on the more normal structure – external management.

3.3.2 External management

External management – which is by far the most common arrangement – is where the people who operate the fund on a day to day basis are not directly employed by the fund, but by a management company contracted to provide services to the fund for a specified fee.

A variant, which is external management with a twist, is for the investment funds operated by a management company to own that management company. Such an arrangement may only be made if it is in compliance with investment powers permitted to funds (see section 5.2). A well known example of such an ownership structure is The Vanguard Group of the US.

How external management works: corporate fund

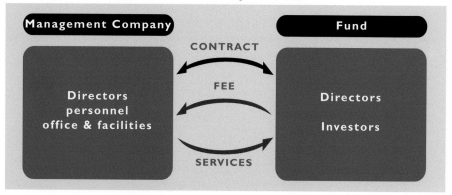

How internal management works: corporate fund

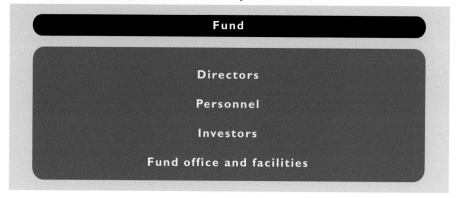

3.3.3   Pros and cons of internal management

Examples of internal management of investment funds are relatively few and far between. Most funds are created and operated by a management company, rather than internally managed, for the following commercial reasons:

- future value: fund management companies hold contracts for the management of funds, from which they derive a stream of revenue of between 0.25% and 3% of the value of the funds they manage. As such, a management company has a commercial value and can be sold. A management structure within a fund cannot be sold unless it is separately incorporated first; and anyway will only have a contract for a single fund, which is a much less attractive proposition – revenues from a single fund are vulnerable to its performance

- economies of scale: multiple funds contracting a single management company for services spreads the cost of the management company across a series of funds, rather than focusing all the costs of its operation within a single fund; lower costs will make their funds more attractive to investors

- diversification of revenue flows: a variety of funds to meet different needs can be provided by an external management company, ensuring that when one product is out of favour, another is in favour and so maintaining revenues; a single self managed fund cannot cater for a series of different investment needs or changes in the popularity of different forms of fund or fund investment objectives

- financing development: revenues from a series of funds managed under contract enables the management company to finance its development, eg investment in IT, more easily; single self managed funds clearly could have problems financing major investments of this kind and in building expensive investment expertise internally

In general, regulators are not particularly keen on self managed structures, either. Reasons for this include:

- operational considerations: the impossibility of operating an internal management company within an open ended fund structure is a major consideration – a fund which has varying capital could find that sustaining the costs of internal management of $250,000 – a normal cost of 2.5% of a fund of $10 million – can easily become a fee of 25% if the fund shrinks to $1 million, due to market movements or redemptions reducing the value of the fund on which management costs are levied. This would clearly adversely affect the interests of fund investors

- licensing considerations: withdrawing the licence of a management company for regulatory failures can be done relatively easily where that management is external – the management company can

simply be replaced by another licensed manager and the funds
continue to operate; but removing the management of a fund
which is internally managed would mean either having to take
away the fund's licence, so that the fund would have to cease to
operate or that its management would need to be changed: both of
which could adversely affect the interests of its investors

- cost control considerations: assets of a self managed fund can
  easily be eroded through excessive costs of operation which may
  be difficult to identify from outside; off balance sheet contingent
  liabilities can build up which can become problematic (employee
  contracts, leases, pensions). Contracts for external management
  specify what fees are payable and their payment from the fund to
  the management company is easily traced; identifying flows of
  money and levels of cost of operation within a self managed fund
  is much more difficult

- clarity of responsibilities and liabilities: contracts between
  management companies and funds clearly identify responsibilities
  and liability; if the management company makes an error or omits
  to act, it has to compensate for any loss. If an internal
  management team of a fund makes an error or omits to act the
  only sanction is against the individuals involved who are unlikely to
  be able to finance large sums

- valuation considerations: valuation of funds can become
  problematic if fixed assets are owned by the self managed fund
  which are not investments – eg office buildings

- lack of incentive to perform: there is a lack of incentive for
  internal managers to perform well, since their salaries will not rise
  or fall in line with fund net asset value; whereas external
  managers' fees will rise if the value of assets rises or fall if they
  fall, since their fee is a % of net asset value. Also, there is little
  downside for them in poor performance, whereas an external
  management company could be fired

- resistance to change: self managed funds will be resistant to takeovers or liquidation due to loss of jobs, so failing funds may continue in existence rather than being taken over or liquidated

So while there are some very successful self-managed funds, of high reputation, the self-managed structure is not the one most commonly adopted internationally.

3.4 Fund categories

Regulators generally require that when funds are submitted for their approval, they are categorised by the type of assets in which they invest. These categories usually include:

FUND CATEGORY	INVESTMENT OBJECTIVE TO INVEST WHOLLY OR PRIMARILY IN
securities fund	securities (equities, bonds)
money market fund	money market instruments such as certificates of deposit
futures and options funds	futures and options
property funds	land or buildings
warrant funds	warrants
feeder funds	another CIF, based in another domicile
fund of funds	other CIFs
umbrella funds	CIFs which have within them a range of sub-funds between which investors can choose and switch from time to time
flexible funds	may vary its portfolio over time to invest in securities or money market instruments

Sub-categories of funds also exist but are not usually defined by regulation; these are covered further in Chapter 11 on product development.

It should be noted that countries vary in their approach to fund categorisation. In some countries a separate set of legislation may apply to closed ended funds which invest in property, as opposed to those which invest in securities. An example is American Real Estate Investment Trusts (REITs), which are created under REIT legislation passed in 1960, rather than under the Investment Companies Act of 1940, which covers open and closed investment companies which invest in securities and money market instruments.

In general, management companies are not permitted by regulators to operate two funds whose investment objectives, structure and terms are very similar, unless they are destined for different markets and have other differentiating features. Reasons for this include the fact that a single, larger fund usually would be more cost effective for investors; and the conflicts that arise for management companies in encouraging investors to choose one fund or the other.

The regulation of CIFs

4

4.1   Protecting investors

Regulation of CIFs is designed to ensure that CIFs and their service providers operate according to the rules set up by legislation and regulation. Usually the Law nominates what agency (or agencies) will be responsible for CIFs regulations, usually a securities commission or one of its variants. The ultimate objective of regulation is to protect rights and interests of investors – clients of CIFs, because:

- the success of any market economy depends on the confidence and support of individual investors whose savings support economic growth

- investors, by providing for their own financial security, partially remove this burden from taxpayers and the state

In the most successful markets firm, fair and effective regulation of CIFs has been found to be in everyone's interest for the following reasons:

- the general public needs to be protected from misinformation, fraud and theft; regulation is designed to minimise the possibility of this occurring

- CIF operators and service providers know that their business is largely dependent on the public's confidence; they also have an interest in ensuring that their counterparts and peers act in an honest way

- the state wishes to have efficient and honest markets play an important part in the national's economic activity

4.1.1   Public confidence is an outcome of effective regulation

Effective regulation which both investors and CIF operators trust and understand creates a positive climate, where the public has confidence in CIFs and CIF operators can successfully market their funds. Under effective regulation investors know that there are clear rules governing the operation, management and finances of promoters and managers, and thus can rely on the regulator to curb abuses. If abuses take place, then they will be able to obtain redress and possibly compensation. The table below demonstrates what priorities both investors and CIF operators have under effective and ineffective regulation.

Comparison of effective and ineffective regulation

Public confidence is a public good. No CIF can have it unless all CIFs

	EFFECTIVE REGULATION	INEFFECTIVE REGULATION
Investors	Concentration on what funds to buy	Concentration on whether to buy funds or not
Operators	Concentration on winning in the competition with other participants by ● promoting investment objectives ● enhancing attractiveness of existing products ● and developing new ones	Concentration on attempts to ● establish public confidence or ● secure money to manage: by virtue of lobbying the government for special treatment, tax concessions and the like creating distribution cartels promising unrealistically high returns

have it. It is easily damaged. A major scandal in which individual investors lose money is likely to result in a loss of confidence it will take years of effort to repair.

The main characteristics of effective regulation are:

- consistency: when rules are internally consistent and do not contradict other regulations and legislation, including legislation and regulation not specific to CIFs (e.g. tax legislation)

- even application: every regulated entity has to comply with the same rules, and, in the event of non-compliance, everyone in breach is punished in the same way

- stability: the regulatory regime does not change too frequently

- enforcement: the regulator has to have enough powers to ensure compliance by regulated entities, and to compel those out of compliance to comply

- avoidance of unnecessary costs – cost of regulation should not lead to the bankruptcy of businesses, a deterrent to entry into the market or to making services more expensive for clients

4.1.2 Limits of regulation

For both Securities Regulators and CIFs, it is vital to be clear about what regulation can achieve and what it cannot.

For example, regulation cannot prevent fraud. It can limit the extent to which fraud is possible, and this is a desirable objective. But it must also be recognised that determined and ingenious individuals will always find weaknesses in any system so that frauds are likely to occur from time to time even in a well-regulated environment. So in addition to limiting the possibility of fraud, it is also vital to set in place methods of ensuring that investors who are defrauded by regulated entities can obtain redress and compensation.

4.1.3 Over-regulation versus under-regulation

A regulatory regime which is thought to be unnecessarily specific and restrictive is termed "over-regulated". Such a regime is often the result of a regulatory viewpoint, that public confidence is a function

4

of controlling activities of managers and operators through the right set of rules and operating procedures, which are more effective if they are very detailed and specific and contain large numbers of restrictions and limitations. The consequences of such a regime are:

- inhibiting the capacity of CIF operators and service providers to innovate

- higher costs imposed on operators by regulation almost always being passed on to investors. A heavy regulatory burden therefore means higher costs for investors

- longer time scales for decisions

- as the requirements are very specific, they tend to change frequently, which leads to uncertainty and extra cost in changing systems

Excessively relaxed rules and procedures and lack of regulatory control are the characteristic features of "under-regulation". Under-regulation is likely to result in fraud, scandal and loss of public confidence. Paradoxically the disaster caused by under-regulation is likely to give birth to over-regulation.

Although CIF operators and regulators genuinely regard public confidence as a desirable outcome, their views on means of reaching the goal are quite different. The CIF operators want Securities Regulators to do the least that is necessary to achieve this and the Securities Regulator usually sees much more need for its involvement in a wider and wider range of matters. This tension between Securities Regulators and operators is inevitable and can be balanced only through constructive dialogue.

4.2   The regulatory system

The regulatory system usually consists of:

- primary legislation

- the government department, executive agency or agencies responsible for regulation

- the set of rules lawfully promulgated by the Securities Regulator(s)

- the criminal and civil courts

- and any independent arbiters of consumer complaints such as ombudsmen or financial services arbitration tribunals

The regulatory systems in use around the world differ in many respects. In some, the primary legislation contains considerable detail while in others, all the detail is left to the rules made by the Securities Regulator. In some systems, the adjudication and enforcement mechanisms of the Securities Regulator are highly formalised, while in others they are largely informal. The civil and criminal courts may play a larger or smaller role depending on the penalties the Securities Regulator is able to impose under its own authority and on the adequacy of means available within the rules for investors to obtain redress without going to court.

The following sections outline the essential features of a regulatory system for CIFs, leaving open the issue of how they are achieved. They derive primarily from the ten key principles identified by the International Organisation of Securities Commissions (IOSCO) which were designed to apply to open ended funds. Many, but not all, apply equally to closed ended funds.

4.2.1   The legal framework

All regulation must have a basis in law. In some countries Presidential decrees or Resolutions of Ministers are regarded as an adequate substitute, although most would agree that an Act passed by the national Parliament provides a firmer judicial foundation.

The Law governing CIFs can also cover other areas, eg securities markets or pension funds and life assurance; the detailed rules for each are handled by regulatory bodies. Alternatively it can deal with CIFs only; in this case the legislation is likely to be a bit more specific but still detailed regulations and operational matters will be left to a Securities Regulator.

In most cases the Law does not usually contain very precise details but confines itself to general principles. This is because:

- principles do not change frequently, but market practice does

- sensible legislators do not want the law to be too rigid, but to allow for reasonable development of the industry

- laws have to have the approval of Parliaments and few members of Parliament are experts in the detail of financial activity

- once enacted, laws take a long time to change

The items normally covered in primary legislation specific to CIFs are included in the following table.

Elements of legislation on CIFs

1. Definitions	The nature of regulated funds is defined; some types of fund are excluded
2. Classification	Investment funds are grouped into categories. The most basic distinction is between open-ended and closed-ended. In countries which permit several different legal forms (corporate, contractual, trust) these too will be defined here
3. Management structure	The permitted relationships between managers, investment advisers and custodians/trustees are defined
4. Fees and charges	Charging methods are defined; upper limits for charges may be set
5. Registration and licensing	Requirements and procedures are laid down for obtaining a licence to form and operate a fund
6. Authority of the Securities Regulator	The Securities Regulator's authority is defined, as is the procedure for the Securities Regulator to delegate responsibility for specific functions
7. Affiliated persons	There are provisions to bar affiliates from occupying positions or carrying out transactions in which conflicts of interest arise
8. Investment and borrowing	Restrictions are set; for example, a fund may not be permitted to hold more than x% of its assets in any one security, or to hold more than x% of the issued capital of any one company
9. Capital structure	Where funds have different classes of shares, the rights of these are defined
10. Reporting	The content and frequency of reports to investors is defined
11. Records, accounts and audit	Content and frequency of records and the procedures for accounting are laid down
12. Custodian/Depositary/Trustee	The duties of the custodian, depositary or trustee are defined
13. Share/unit holders' rights	The rights of holders of shares or units are defined
14. Duties and legal obligations of Directors or Trustees	If a fund has directors, their legal obligations are laid down in general terms, although usually reliance can be placed on Company Law
15. Prospectus, publicity and marketing	The general principle is that funds, managers and advisers should not make misleading or inaccurate claims
16. Mergers and acquisitions	There are specific rules for fund mergers and acquisitions

The existence of a Law governing CIFs and their operation is vital, since:

- it is the Law, on the basis of which judges in the courts base their judgment: courts are the institutions of the last resort, where investors and CIF operators apply for protection of their rights

- it is the Law which defines what a CIF is and what it is not – this makes it possible to make all institutions which behave like funds be officially licensed and regulated; and to exclude companies which have been created for the purposes other then those of CIFs, but who would like to misuse CIF status to enjoy some benefits (eg tax privileges), characteristic to CIFs

4.2.2   Who regulates

The law usually contains a statement showing who will regulate particular activities. Much of the detail is normally found in the rules of a Securities Regulator authorised by the primary legislation. Such Securities Regulators may be of three distinct types:

- a Department within a government Ministry, usually the Finance Ministry or the Central Bank

- an agency created specifically for this purpose by the primary legislation, usually called a Securities Commission, Securities Board or Investment Board (and here referred to as the regulator or Securities Regulator)

- a self-regulatory agency or agencies, which consist of practitioners in the industry operating a voluntary regulatory function under the supervision of the government agency or ministry

Formerly, in many developed countries, Securities Regulators were of the first type. However, the speed of change in financial services generally makes this method problematical. Among the difficulties are frequent changes in personnel, as government officials usually move from one department to another, which results in a lack of senior expertise and management continuity; delays in adapting rules to changes in circumstances, because officials are remote from the market place; lack of communication between industry practitioners and officials; and lack of priority in updating legislation.

Consequently most developed countries now use agencies external to government departments to undertake the regulatory functions. While such agencies usually lay down the operational rules, other bodies may play a part in their implementation. These bodies may be self-regulatory organisations set up for the purpose or existing professional bodies, particularly those in the legal or accountancy professions. Such bodies may, for example, have the role of 'policing' their memberships delegated to them by a Securities Regulator; or may, in the case of auditors, have specific responsibilities to report breaches in the regulations by the funds or management companies audited by them to the Securities Regulator.

It is worth noting that the detailed rules and regulations outlined by the Securities Regulator can only change within the Law and can never contradict or change the principles in the Law. In the same way the rules and standards of self-regulatory organisations must conform with the provisions of regulation at a higher level (ie statutory regulation) or the Law.

An example of regulatory framework (not related to any particular jurisdiction) is demonstrated by the Chart on the next page.

Example of regulatory framework

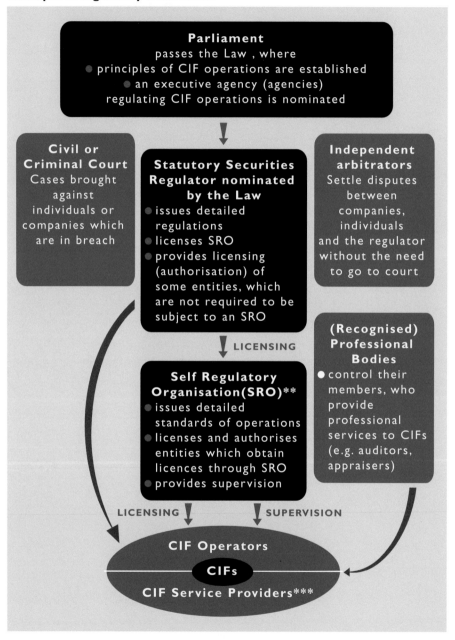

Parliament
passes the Law , where
● principles of CIF operations are established
● an executive agency (agencies)
regulating CIF operations is nominated

Civil or Criminal Court
Cases brought against individuals or companies which are in breach

Statutory Securities Regulator nominated by the Law
● issues detailed regulations
● licenses SRO
● provides licensing (authorisation) of some entities, which are not required to be subject to an SRO

Independent arbitrators
Settle disputes between companies, individuals and the regulator without the need to go to court

LICENSING

Self Regulatory Organisation(SRO)**
● issues detailed standards of operations
● licenses and authorises entities which obtain licences through SRO
● provides supervision

(Recognised) Professional Bodies
● control their members, who provide professional services to CIFs (e.g. auditors, appraisers)

LICENSING   SUPERVISION

CIF Operators
CIFs
CIF Service Providers***

**SRO – may or may not exist depending on characteristics of an operating regulatory system. If it does not exist, then the statutory Securities Regulator exercises licensing and supervision
*** Only some service providers may be required to be licensed and supervised by the Securities Regulator: some of them are not regulated and the others are regulated by regulators different from Securities Regulator. For instance auditors are usually not regulated by Securities Regulator. Also even if they have to be regulated by the statutory Securities Regulator, they may be members of SROs different from that of CIFs or have no SRO membership at all

4.2.3   Regulation by function and by institution

Regulation by function is where all financial services of a particular type - CIFs, for example – are regulated by a single body, regardless of the type of ownership involved or the type of corporate group of which it is a part.

Regulation by institution is where all the financial services (however 'regulated' financial services are defined) offered by a certain type of institution are regulated by a single body. Banks are the most obvious example, since it is an almost universal characteristic of Central Banks to wish to regulate all the activities of the banks where they ultimately have regulatory responsibility. The implications of both regulation by function and by institution are outlined in the table below.

Regulation by function and by institution

REGULATION BY FUNCTION	REGULATION BY INSTITUTION
CIFs, CIF operators and some service providers are regulated predominantly by the only regulator (The Securities Regulator) irrespectively of the type of institution involved	*The regulator is determined depending on the type of institution (or its parent) offering CIFs*
Large companies with many operations will have to obtain licences for each type of their operations (including CIFs operation) from different regulators and report to each of them in different ways	*Large institutions will have to get licences from and report to a single regulator with regard to all their operations.* *Although CIF operators can be part of large financial groups, they are usually required to be separate companies with CIF operation as the only permitted business. Therefore a CIF operator has to obtain a separate licence*
Same regulatory standards are applied to any type of companies operating CIFs	*Different regulatory standards may be applied to different organizations, operating CIFs – this may lead to double standards and regulatory arbitrage*
A number of functional regulators are less likely to see systematic fraud taking place in big companies, since each of them is aware of some types of operations, but not the others	*Single institutional regulator is more capable to spot a deep fraud in big companies, since it is knowledgeable about the whole picture as well as about separate operations*

Both regulation by function and regulation by institution have their advantages and drawbacks. Some countries have recently attempted to resolve the issue of institutional-versus-functional regulation by merging all forms of financial regulation, including that applying to banks, insurance companies, pension schemes and asset management, into one system governed by a 'super-regulator'. This may prove more or less efficient than a system of separate functional or institutional regulators: it is too early to judge.

There is no clear conclusion which type of regulation is better. Cost and efficiency factors favour a single regulation by function of CIFs. Much depends on the overall shape of the financial system, and the extent to which liabilities are removed from companies' balance sheets by insurance or other means. Also as far as CIFs are concerned, the greater the prudential role played by independent and financially strong custodians, depositaries or trustees (generally referred to throughout this book as custodians except where trustee is specifically meant), the less concerned regulators need to be about fraud and hence the weaker the arguments for institutional regulation.

Most of the detailed aspects of regulation of specific aspects of CIFs will be dealt with in the relevant following sections of this book. This section focuses on the principles underlying regulation and summarises the essential contents of any regulatory system.

4.3   Regulatory principles

Most governments give support to the development of collective investments, since they help to mobilise private savings in a constructive way. The State often gives CIFs and its investors some incentives, for example in the form of tax concessions. In exchange the State requires that CIFs are used for the purposes they have been originally created for, that investors are not defrauded and that privileged fund status is not misused by other non-CIF organisations, wishing to get benefits.

To achieve all of this different countries use a variety of mechanisms to govern CIFs. But thanks to the efforts of the International

Organisation of Securities Commissions (IOSCO), there is a set of generally agreed principles for the regulation of CIFs.

Whatever the form of the regulatory systems and the nature of the bodies involved, certain common principles underlie the rules and procedures.

The most important are as follows:

- custodianship of assets should be separated from management of a CIF and preferably undertaken by a non-affiliated body

- conflicts of interest should as far as possible be eliminated by barring certain relationships and transactions between managers, custodians, investment advisers and their affiliates

- valuation and accounting methods must be clearly laid down, consistently applied and universally adhered to

- the Securities Regulator must have powers to fine, ban, disqualify and suspend individuals, management companies, investment advisers, custodians or funds if they breach the rules

- the rules must clearly outlaw the publication or dissemination of inaccurate or misleading information to existing and prospective investors

- managers of CIFs who delegate responsibility for functions (such as investment advice and administration) must not be able to escape their responsibilities to investors

- investors' rights must be clearly defined and investors should have means of referring complaints to Securities Regulators

- prospectuses and other marketing documents should contain all the information an investor might reasonably require to make an informed decision

4

4.3.1 The key implications of regulatory principles

The 10 core principles have been developed by the International Organisation of Securities Commissions ("IOSCO") in order to create a useful framework within which legislators and regulators can apply the generic principles listed above. They are:

4.3.1.1 *Fund structures*

CIFs must conform to certain defined legal forms and structures. It must be impossible to set up or promote a CIF that does not conform. Investors must be certain of their rights. Funds must be clearly segregated and independent and where this is not the case – for example where a certain set of funds may share some liabilities, in the case of umbrella funds for instance – this must be made clear to investors. For detail, see Chapter 3.

4.3.1.2 *Custodians, depositaries and trustees*

The system should separate the assets of CIFs from the assets of management companies or other entities, and the assets of an individual CIF from all other CIFs. A custodian, depositary or trustee should hold the assets. This entity should be at least operationally independent of the CIF Management company and should be liable without limit to investors for any loss incurred by investors resulting from its failure to perform its obligations. The qualifying requirements for custodians, trustees and depositaries should ensure they have financial and management resources adequate for their obligations.

4.3.1.3 *Eligibility of operators*

The system should impose standards of conduct and minimum eligibility for CIF operators (managers) and custodians and depositaries. These should include capital adequacy, the integrity of directors (at a minimum through the proven lack of any criminal convictions), expertise and the ability to meet minimum standards for administration.

Some systems require authorisation both for the management company of a CIF and of a CIF itself. In others it is the CIF alone that is subject to authorisation (for detail see section 4.4).

4.3.1.4 Delegation

To ensure equality of protection to all investors in CIFs, the system must ensure that all duties which are laid on the operator of a CIF also fall on any delegate to whom the operator subcontracts any service provided to the CIF. Equally, the system must ensure that CIF operators cannot pass their own primary responsibility to investors onto any delegates (refer also Chapter 3).

4.3.1.5 Supervision

A single regulatory authority should take responsibility for CIFs within its jurisdiction. CIFs should be registered with or authorised by the Securities Regulator before the operator begins marketing activity. The Securities Regulator must have the power to investigate CIF operators and should have adequate powers to protect the interests of investors, including revocation of operators' licences, suspension of dealings, freezing of CIF or operators' assets, levying fines, withdrawing CIF authorisations, commencing civil proceedings and recommending criminal prosecutions (for more detail see section 4.4.1 of this Chapter).

4.3.1.6 Conflicts of interest

The system must recognise the existence of potential conflicts of interest between a CIF operator and its affiliates and investors. This may be dealt with by the definition of an operator's general 'fiduciary responsibility' to investors or by the adoption of specific rules (for more detail see section 8.5).

4.3.1.7 Asset valuation and pricing

The prime requirement is that the system of valuation and pricing must be fair to ongoing investors, incoming investors and outgoing investors. The price of an open ended or interval CIF must be related to the Net Asset Value of the CIF calculated on a regular basis in accordance with specific rules or accepted accounting practice (for further information see Chapter 5 and Chapter 13 respectively).

4.3.1.8 Limits on investment and borrowing

The system should place limits on the investment and borrowing capabilities of a CIF. These should serve the purposes of portfolio diversification, provision of liquidity to meet redemptions, and containment of risk within defined parameters (for more information see section 5.2).

4.3.1.9 Investor rights

The system should confer specific rights on investors, including the right to withdraw their funds from a CIF within a reasonable period of time or to be able to sell shares in a secondary market. Investors should have the right to participate in significant decisions affecting a CIF, or to have their interests protected by a Securities Regulator or other independent third party. Investors should be able to refer complaints to the Securities Regulator or an independent complaints arbiter (see section 10.5).

4.3.1.10 Marketing and disclosure

The essential requirement is that operators provide existing and prospective investors with all the information they need to make informed decisions and that this information should be neither misleading nor inaccurate. Detailed requirements should also be set for the regular provision of reports (including financial data) to investors on the management and operation of a CIF. Prospectuses should also comply with a required standard. Advertising should be required to be consistent with the prospectus. In addition, information on matters such as charges and returns should be provided in such a way that they can be quickly understood and that comparisons can easily be made (see Chapter 10).

4.4 Regulatory activities

4.4.1 Activities of the Securities Regulator

As was previously said the Securities Regulator establishes detailed rules and regulations governing activities of CIFs and their service providers. Apart from this, it also licenses and supervises activities of CIFs and CIF related entities like CIF operators, custodians, etc. The other function of the Securities Regulator is enforcement – a system of measures it undertakes to ensure compliance.

4.4.1.1 Establishing detailed rules and regulations

Depending on the regulatory system, the Securities Regulator issues more or less detailed guidelines on how to apply the law, in the form of regulations. Once regulations are issued and gazetted all subjects have to comply. Sometimes to avoid unnecessarily long and detailed regulations, Securities Regulators keep them short, but issue explanatory letters and legal opinions in relation to regulatory issues which can be interpreted dubiously. While drafting regulations, some Securities Regulators consult with practitioners or their trade associations.

From time to time Securities Regulators change regulations partially or fully. CIF operators must be aware of all changes and adjust their systems and procedures accordingly. Transitional provisions may permit gradual, rather than immediate, implementation.

4.4.1.2 Licensing and authorising

In most jurisdictions, the operator (manager or management company) of a CIF must be licensed independently of the licensing (or authorisation) of the CIF itself. Because CDTs (depending on the legal structure) usually carry the main responsibility for the protection of investors, they are required to be licensed, though some regimes do not require fund CDTs to be specifically licensed as such. The licensing of new CIF operators and authorisation of CIFs is a major responsibility of a Securities Regulator. In a few jurisdictions obtaining membership of SRO is equivalent of getting a licence.

A company's licence is the regulatory permission issued to the company to run a proposed business. The purpose of licensing can be defined as ensuring that those who obtain licences are honest, competent and solvent.

To obtain a licence an applicant has to demonstrate that it satisfies all the licensing requirements and also to pay a licensing fee which may be nominal or rather substantial.

Authorisation of a CIF constitutes regulatory approval for the CIF to be offered to the public.

4.4.1.2.a Setting licensing requirements

Regulatory systems will always set rules for the capitalisation of a CIF operator and sometimes for the custodian, depository or trustee (if they are banks, banking capital requirements may be relied on instead); they will also set qualification rules for their directors and senior managers. They may also require that management of CIFs is carried out by separate companies, not the departments of other financial institutions, and that operating CIFs is a sole and exclusive activity of such companies. In some jurisdictions a licence issued to a CIF operator also covers managing pension funds and investment management for life and non-life insurance companies and private portfolio management; in other words a full asset management licence. In other jurisdictions special licences are required for the management and operation of CIFs, separately from other asset management activities.

There is some debate about the convenience of granting licences to cover all asset management and investment advisory functions. What usually influences CIF operators to seek a specific licence to operate CIFs is connected rather with capital and other prudential and regulatory requirements than those of competence; it is in some ways convenient both for regulators and regulated to be able to define different activities precisely within different legal entities for these reasons.

Requirements for directors and personnel generally focus on:

- honesty: the individuals who are going to manage the activity should not be disqualified because of previous convictions for fraud or financial crimes, or because of previous failure to comply with regulations of the securities or other regulator. In some jurisdictions, Securities Regulators rely on an individual's declaration that he or she has no criminal convictions, on the basis that discovery of a false statement will result in immediate disqualification and other penalties. In other jurisdictions, the

Securities Regulator will make its own investigations through police or court records

- competence: directors should preferably have some relevant experience, if not in the management of CIFs then in other relevant fields such as securities markets, banking or commercial law. To ensure that individuals are competent to carry out the proposed activities, some systems require the test of competence by means of examination. In some jurisdictions a CIF operator and custodian cannot be granted licences unless members of their personnel have got individual qualifications

Where the character and qualifications of individuals are a factor in granting a licence, the Securities Regulator will normally keep a file of all such individuals, noting any regulatory transgressions. Fraud is almost invariably an individual matter, and in most cases it is preferable for Securities Regulators to deal with it by eliminating the rogue individual – preferably through a lifetime ban on any involvement in the business – rather than by withdrawing the licence of the operating company.

Requirements for companies generally focus on:

- competence: as in the case of an individual, a company should demonstrate that it is competent to carry out its business, which is tested by submission of organisational structure and business plan. This will not only show whether the company has adequate capital for its plans, but also whether it has a realistic grasp of the costs involved in the business, and whether it has put in place an appropriate management structure. Securities Regulators will be particularly concerned to see that the structure provides clear accountability for managers

- capital adequacy: the organisation must have sufficient capital to carry on the proposed business and to accept the risks of it, and would be capable of paying some compensation to clients, if required to do so

The amount of capital needed by a CIF operator and by a custodian or trustee is a much debated topic among regulators. There are three distinct approaches:

- a fixed amount of capital unrelated to the size of funds managed or to operating expenses

- capital expressed as a percentage of the market value of funds managed (in the case of CIF operators) or under administration (custodians/trustees)

- capital expressed as a fraction/multiple of operating expenses. Some regulators distinguish between the equity capital and available working capital

Which approach is preferable will depend on the legislative, regulatory and management environment. The most significant relevant factors are:

- the existence of custodians or trustees which are independent of CIF operators and which are themselves substantially capitalised

- the availability of insurance for professional indemnity, errors and omissions, and employee fidelity bonding

- the existence of an industry funded compensation scheme

If none of these three features is part of the system, then it may be necessary to require CIF operators to have substantial capital resources to underwrite potential losses to investors caused by negligence, maladministration, etc. In this case the second approach to capital requirement may be most prudent.

The greater the reliance that can be placed on alternative means of compensating investors, the less capital needs to be required of a CIF operator. Though regulators' instincts will tend to be to set capital requirements on the high side, such requirements can have damaging effects. They are likely to deter new market entrants, thus restricting competition, and possibly even resulting in oligopolies which become price cartels, resulting in investors paying unnecessarily high costs.

Once authorised, a CIF operator will normally be required to file accounts at regular intervals: the Securities Regulator can therefore easily spot any declining trend in free capital and take any necessary action.

As far as a custodian or trustee is concerned, here there is an obvious case for a substantial capital requirement and/or a requirement for the custodian or trustee to be a particular type of company, for example a bank, which itself provides further protection through the authorisation procedures required to obtain a banking licence. Some jurisdictions require the custodian/trustee to be separately incorporated from its parent and for the subsidiary to be capitalised according to the requirement of the regulator, while others are content to rely on the substantial capital required for banks.

The system will normally define means whereby CIF assets held by a custodian are to be distinguished from the custodian/trustee's own assets in the event of its insolvency. But most systems attempt to restrict eligibility as a custodian or trustee to organisations of the highest financial standing and reputation in order to minimise the risk. They also seek to achieve clear segregation of assets and isolation of risk by requiring the custodial operation to be a company (albeit possibly a subsidiary of a larger group) whose sole business is custody.

4.4.1.2.b The process of licensing and authorisation

The process of licensing is carried out by means of requiring the applicant to complete a set of standard application forms, which are designed to tell the regulator what he needs to know about honesty, competence and solvency of the applicant. Along with the forms usual submissions include:

● documents relating to the establishment of the enterprise – if a joint stock company, its directors, owners and founders

- specific information relating to the product or products to be offered by the licensed company – if an investment fund, the charter of rules, the prospectus

- evidence that the required capital has been paid in

- documents related to individuals, including certificates of passing of any required professional qualifications

- evidence that the licence fee has been paid

The Securities Regulator is usually entitled to ask for additional information from a company or individual, should he find it necessary for making a decision.

The time for considering applications is usually limited by legal and regulatory provisions. If the Securities Regulator makes a decision not to grant a licence, it informs the applicant and indicates the reasons for refusal.

In the case of both CIF operators and custodians or trustees, licences may be granted for a specific period or until revoked. Whichever is adopted, regulators usually undertake periodic formal reviews of an operator's fitness, and such reviews extend further than the operator's formal reports and accounts. If a licence is granted for a specific period of time, it has to be renewed after the stated period is over. While applying for renewal applicants should allow for some time during which the regulator considers the application.

To register a contractual fund or a trust, a CIF operator should usually submit scheme particulars (also known as fund rules) or the prospectus of issue, documentation related to companies which are proposed to service the CIF, contracts concluded between service providers and CIF (if the CIF is a corporate fund) and between CIF operator and other service providers (if the CIF is formed in contractual or trust form).

4.4.1.2.c Who considers the application for licensing

This is usually done by a department of the Securities Regulator, which can be responsible for licensing of all market participants or exclusively of those related to funds. After considering the application the department presents its view of the applicant's suitability to the Board.

4.4.1.2.d Need for an appeals procedure

The system should incorporate an appeals procedure so that the applicant may appeal against the Securities Regulator's refusal to grant a licence or against the withdrawal of a licence or the imposition of serious penalties. The more transparent such procedures are, the easier it is for the Securities Regulator to send signals to other applicants. Such open procedures can also play a major part in building public confidence in the system.

4.4.1.3 Supervision

4.4.1.3.a Monitoring

After all the necessary licences and authorisations establishing the right to carry out business activities have been issued, the Securities Regulator will continue to supervise the activities of the licensed entity in order to be satisfied that it continues to comply with the Law and the regulations. Exercising its supervisory functions, the Securities Regulator will require that a CIF operator:

- provides periodic reports – these will have to be filed with the Securities Regulator at regular intervals, monthly or quarterly; the regulator will check that the reports which the law requires to be submitted are received on time and are complete and correct. It will check the information in the reports to ensure that the law is being complied with

- seeks the permission of the Securities Regulator for changes in the recorded details of activities. Only important changes have to be approved by the regulator before happening – they are sometimes known as "clearance events"

4

- notifies the Securities Regulator about changes, which have already happened. This covers less important changes which do not require a preliminary approval, but the regulator should be aware that they have happened – these are sometimes known as "notifiable events"

- provides additional information on request. The Securities Regulator is entitled to ask for additional information or clarification at any time

The Securities Regulator may require information from all parties, providing services to a fund. This could include:

- additional reports from the custodian or trustee as well as notification in certain cases where there have been breaches

- audit reports – the statutory auditor is required to make a report to the regulator after the annual audit and at certain other times, and is sometimes required to verify that certain regulatory procedures have been complied with during the period under review

- complaints from the public – the regulator may also become aware of complaints by the public against a licensed entity, which are made directly to it

If through its routine monitoring the Securities Regulator spots minor or technical breaches, it will ensure that they are corrected. Usually the regulator sets up a deadline by which the breaches should be corrected.

If there is a suspicion that a breach is likely to have some damaging effect, this may call for further actions by the regulator – on site inspections or special investigations to determine the extent of the problem.

4.4.1.3.b Inspection visits

Routine inspections are normally carried out in a regular cycle, with each CIF operator subject to an inspection each year or over a longer period. Frequency of inspection visits can also depend on company's risk profile and company's track record with the regulator. Inspection usually involves a visit by a team to the offices of the regulated entity and a detailed examination of books and records. However the inspection cycle is usually not too regular, so that regulated entities do not come to expect a visit in a particular month and arrange their affairs accordingly.

Apart from routine inspections, inspection visits can also result from worrying evidence in companies' reports, when the Securities Regulator suspects that things are not in order; or from a specific complaint or referral from another regulator. Then the team will look closely at things, which it believes will indicate if things have gone wrong.

4.4.1.3.c Follow up communications

As a result of both routine monitoring and inspections the Securities Regulator will communicate with a regulated entity, pointing out errors and requesting that they be rectified; verifying at the time of the next report or inspection visit that they have. The regulator can issue a more generic "management letter", pointing out in detail the errors and defects of the reporting and in the overall compliance methodology with the request to rectify errors.

4.4.1.3.d Who monitors and inspects

Depending on the structure of the Securities Regulator, this may be the department which considered the company's application for a licence or a specialist department dealing with monitoring and inspections only.

4.4.1.4 Control and enforcement

4.4.1.4.a Investigations

Regulation can only be effective if it is properly enforced. To be able to enforce the Law and the regulations a Securities Regulator is granted authority to investigate and impose sanctions on those who are in breach of the rules.

4

If, as a result of monitoring and inspection visits, the monitoring department believes that the problems are greater than it is possible to resolve without a decisive action, it may pass on the case to the enforcement department of the Securities Regulator. Enforcement departments usually deal with enforcement issues related to all market participants and have personnel who specialise in different areas of market operations.

The enforcement department will either investigate the case using its own resources or can recommend the higher authority (the Board) to trigger full scale investigation procedures, which are normally carried out by the specially appointed team of investigators – often personnel of an outside specialist, like an audit or law firm and perhaps representatives of different departments of the Securities Regulator. An investigation may take several forms:

- a thorough inspection visit of longer duration with more detailed information being requested

- an investigation accompanied by a suspension of all activity

- taking over effective control until the problem is identified and a solution is found

In either case it is usual for the company being investigated to bear the cost of the investigation. The results of investigation procedure are usually made public.

A regulated entity under investigation, as well as any third parties, are expected to provide all the information required by the team of investigators.

As a result of its own information or based on the report of a specialist investigation team, the enforcement department will express its view of the situation to the top Board of the Securities Regulator and make recommendations about the appropriate course of action. It is the top Board which will make the decision about any disciplinary measures to be taken and ways of regularising the situation.

It is worth pointing out that given the cost of investigation has to be covered by the company under investigation, and also the inevitable damage to the company's reputation arising from the need for an investigation, that investigation is in its own right one of the punishments within a wide range of sanctions used by Securities Regulators for the purposes of enforcement.

4.4.1.4.b Dealing with errors

Given the scale and number of transactions undertaken by a CIF Manager, there is the potential for numerous administrative errors, which the regulatory system should find and require to be rectified. The severity of an error is measured by the scale of damage to investors – clients of the fund. The most significant errors are ones which lead to clients suffering quantifiable actual losses or opportunity losses, where they miss out on future profit or increases in value. The actual reasons for errors are numerous, but in general they can be categorised as follows:

- **incompetence** – bad or disorganised management or administration which leads to mistakes

- **arrogance** – belief by the regulated entity that regulations are an unnecessary imposition

- **deliberate fraud** – a systematic attempt to steal clients' money in a variety of ways

4.4.1.4.c Sanctions

The imposition of sanctions by the Securities Regulator has several objectives:

- to have investors losses (if occurred) covered at the expense of those who are guilty

4

- to exclude from the market or to limit the presence of companies who breach the rules

- to make sure that general public is aware of breaches made by a particular company

Depending on judgment as to the severity of the breach the regulator can, in ascending order of force:

- issue a private reprimand – which means a black mark on the file and potentially closer vigilance in the immediate future

- issue a public reprimand, which makes the black mark on the company's reputation widely known

- demand that the individual employees are suspended or dismissed. In many countries dismissed employees are not allowed to take up other jobs in the market, which means that they may lose their livelihood

- simply require that customers be compensated

- impose a fine and require the miscreant to repay losses to investors

- withdraw the licence – in effect putting the operator out of business

- inform the state prosecutor – the regulator can recommend starting court proceedings against the entity in breach, the result of which can be the initiation of criminal proceedings against directors, which might, if a guilty verdict is brought in, result in imprisonment

4.4.1.4.d Ensuring compliance

All regulated businesses, of which a CIF operator is one, have to ensure that all the systems required by the regulations are in place and operating efficiently as well as the internal systems, which ensure regulatory compliance. The word "systems" is taken to cover the whole complex of equipment, hard- and software, trained staff and clearly defined operating procedures.

To provide the means for internal compliance a CIF operator will form a compliance department, headed by a Chief Compliance Officer. A compliance officer, usually with a background of legal practice or of extensive practical experience, works closely with both the Securities Regulator and the executive directors of the company. The main task of the compliance officer is to ensure that internal procedures are likely to deliver full compliance with the regulations. He is also responsible for trying to ensure that senior management takes swift and decisive action to correct any errors which come to light and discipline or dismiss individuals who have inadvertently, carelessly or deliberately failed to comply with established internal procedures

4.4.2   The regulatory role of the custodian

As was already said, the separation of custodianship from fund management is a principal regulatory requirement, since it means that a fund manager has less chance to steal investors' money. In some jurisdictions the role of a custodian is not limited to safekeeping of assets, completing transactions and a range of commercial services. It may have broader function, one of which may be ensuring full compliance of funds' operations with regulatory requirements and letting the Securities Regulator know about any breaches made by the CIF operator in relation to CIFs.

4.4.3   The regulatory role of the auditor

The auditor has to check CIF's and CIF operators' financial reports not only to provide a true and fair view of their financial situation, but in many jurisdictions also has an obligation to run tests designed to verify whether any regulatory breaches have occurred. In most jurisdictions breaches must be reported not only to the senior management of the CIF Manager but also to the regulator.

4.5   Compensation

This is the issue of recompense for investors for any failure, fraud, mismanagement, etc on the part of operators or custodians, as a result of which they have suffered losses. For Securities Regulators, this lies at the extreme end of the regulatory chain, and because they concentrate on framing rules to avoid it happening, they can lose sight of the fact that to the public it is the single most important feature of the system. Speedy and effective methods of compensating individuals are vitally important to establishing public confidence in the regulatory system.

4.5.1   Use of insurance

In developed markets, it is usually possible for CIF operators, custodians and other financial service providers to purchase special insurance cover called 'professional indemnity' or sometimes 'errors or omissions' insurance. Claims can be made against the insurers if the insured party becomes liable to make payments to investors as a result of its own negligence, failure or omission. Insurers will only be prepared to issue such policies if they can place reasonable reliance on the effectiveness of regulation, the competence of the CIF Manager and on the legal system or other arbitration procedures to deliver independent and fair judgments.

4.5.2   Funding of compensation schemes

Many regulatory systems are underpinned by compensation schemes which are intended as the ultimate safety net. These schemes may be funded by governments from taxpayers' money or by CIF operators through a fund built up by regular contributions or by levies after the event. Most government-sponsored schemes are limited and often place quite low limits on the maximum possible compensation. The dangers of unlimited taxpayer-funded compensation schemes have been well illustrated, notably by the vast cost of the rescue operation for a large number of US Savings & Loan Institutions in the early 1990s. Such unlimited schemes create 'moral hazard' in that both operators and individual investors tend to act increasingly irresponsibly when they know they will not bear the costs of their own folly.

4.5.3   Use of ombudsmen

Some systems incorporate an independent complaints arbiter or ombudsman who deals with individual investors' complaints and arbitrates between them and CIF operators or custodians. Often such complaints concern maladministration. An informal, non-judicial system of this type can act quickly and is far less costly than action through civil courts. It can therefore be of advantage to CIF operators as well as individual investors. Arbitration decisions from a specialist body are likely to be more consistent than court judgments, providing clear guidance to operators and enabling them to forestall the whole procedure by settling with complainants if previous arbitrations show the arbitration is likely to favour them. To ensure that the system remains open, it is preferable for individuals to retain the right to pursue matters in the civil courts even after going through such a complaints procedure, though it is normal that the members of the arbitration or ombudsman scheme (CIF Managers, custodians) have to agree to abide by its decisions.

4.5.4   Need for prompt, speedy and efficient action

Whether or not individual complaints are dealt with in this way, major issues of fraud and mismanagement have to be dealt with by the Securities Regulator itself. As far as the public is concerned, information, speed and restitution are the important issues. Securities Regulators may derive satisfaction from instituting proceedings against CIF operators that result in them being closed down or disqualified, but the public will be unimpressed if they do not get their money back. Equally, even if the system enables individuals to receive compensation, they will not be happy if they have to wait years to obtain it.

In terms of public confidence, then, the regulatory system must authorise speedy action by the Securities Regulator and create mechanisms for forcing CIF operators and custodians to pay out compensation without long delays. Where such mechanisms exist, even major scandals can be dealt with without damaging public confidence in the industry as a whole.

4.6 Cost of being a regulated business

There is no doubt that being in a regulated business costs money. The list of the activities which may involve costs include:

- paying licensing fees

- satisfying licensing requirements for capital adequacy, maintaining required capital throughout the whole life of a CIF Manager

- establishing and maintaining systems required by the regulation and systems ensuring regulatory and internal compliance

- providing that a CIF is serviced by licensed service providers, such as custodian, trustee, registrar, appraiser, auditor, etc.

- hiring qualified employees or training them for necessary qualifications

- making sure that penalties and fines can be paid if necessary

- participation in compensation funds

- arranging for possible necessity to pay compensation to investors, if errors occur

- paying necessary insurance premiums

Anyone who plans the business of CIF operation should allow for such costs and budget for them. These costs may certainly defer the time at which the break-even point is reached and reduce the profitability of the business in the longer term, something about which CIF Managers always complain.

However all these costs form the price of maintenance of public confidence, on which the whole business development is dependent. The trade-off is that the government often provides regulated businesses with special favourable conditions (e.g. grants them tax privileges). In any event management of CIFs can be a highly profitable business for efficient operators, so most realistic managers regard regulatory costs as a price worth paying.

4.7   Regulation of CIF foreign activity

4.7.1   "Offshore" CIFs

CIF Managers will, in the attempt to attract funds, locate their CIFs wherever they can obtain an advantage which may attract investors. Offshore locations such as Bermuda, Luxembourg and Dublin's International Financial Services Centre offer both lower tax and more flexible regulation than applies to most onshore funds. Some investors are particularly attracted by the possibility of:

- tax evasion – investors simply wish to conceal assets from their domestic tax authorities or to distance wealth from a politically turbulent situation in their home country

- tax shelter or deferral – since funds in many offshore centres do not have to pay tax on income or capital gains, income received without deduction of tax at source plus any capital gains may be accumulated within the fund, and the investor does not need to pay tax until he sells the shares or units and repatriates the proceeds

- investing in unusual assets – many offshore jurisdictions permit investment in assets which would not be permitted for domestic funds in developed markets – investment in emerging markets, for instance

- structure – offshore jurisdictions often do not place limitations on the types of legal or commercial structure in which funds may be created, and thus greater flexibility is available

As long ago as the 1970s, the promoters of the infamous Investors Overseas Services (IOS) were able to attract hundreds of millions of dollars in subscriptions for their funds from places like Russia and Latin America from which it was, in theory, impossible as well as illegal to invest in such funds. No doubt many offshore funds today also attract subscriptions which are both illegal and, according to local regulation, impossible. Provided purchases of CIFs are intermediated by banks or others whose responsibility it is to ensure that the money paid has not been laundered, the promoters of offshore CIFs are unlikely even to know who or where many of their investors are.

In the long run, the only way to prevent the use of offshore CIFs for the purposes of tax evasion is through a robust domestic tax collection system. Both the US and the UK tax the domestic investor on income and gains regardless of the location of the individual's investments. The US goes further and seeks to look through any offshore arrangement. The individual's non-disclosure of relevant income or gains is subject to heavy fines and criminal prosecution which may result in imprisonment. Thanks to the efficiency of the tax authorities, it is believed that the amount of tax evasion through the use of offshore funds by US and UK citizens is relatively insignificant in terms of the total state revenues.

There are also valid tax reasons for the use of offshore locations. One is that some CIFs are set up for institutional investors who are themselves wholly or partially exempt from domestic tax. But in many cases domestic legislation does not permit the establishment of tax-exempt CIFs or, if it does, imposes restrictions on them. The result is that many CIFs designed for institutional investors are established in offshore centres.

There are also regulatory reasons why CIF Managers use offshore locations. Domestic regulations are designed to protect the average individual investor and for this reason often outlaw whole categories of investment, or funds using certain investment strategies. If there is a demand for such funds from domestic investors, then CIF Managers can only satisfy it by locating funds offshore.

In recent years developed countries have reacted to the loss of tax revenue and of business to offshore financial centres by reforming their own legal and taxation regimes to reduce any disadvantages suffered by fully domestic CIFs. In practice, therefore, most individuals or institutions will tend to prefer domestic CIFs, not only because the advantages of offshore CIFs have been reduced, but also because many countries seek to protect investors from the risks of buying less well regulated offshore funds and limit the marketing and sales of CIFs which are not authorised and licensed under domestic legislation. Some countries even go so far as to penalise the owners of shares or units in offshore CIFs by imposing a harsher tax regime on them than on the owners of shares or units in domestic CIFs.

Even within a common trading area such as the European Union, which has passed legislation which specifically permits the distribution of CIFs authorised by the proper authorities in any one member state in any other member state, differences in taxation of CIFs and specific tax advantageous savings plans which favour domestic CIFs mean that most individuals and institutional investors will be better off buying a domestically domiciled CIF.

4.7.2   Non-domestic CIFs

A question for domestic regulators is to what extent to permit the sale of non-domestic and/or offshore-based CIFs into their country. A number of approaches are possible:

● ban all sales of non-domestic CIFs

● permit sales of non-domestic CIFs only if operators obtain domestic licences and comply with all domestic regulations

● permit sales of non-domestic CIFs if operators are authorised and registered in another approved country and adhere to local marketing regulations

The first approach is frequent in developing countries, while the last is that used in free trade areas such as the European Union. The EU has one general law governing the establishment of open ended CIFs (the 'UCITS Directive') and a CIF established in one country may sell in another country provided it meets local marketing rules and that local investors will receive the same services as other investors in the same CIF, in their own language. This approach is only possible where all the countries within the relevant area have robust regulatory systems governing domestic CIFs.

Most countries impose some kind of restrictions on CIFs which are not domiciled in that country and not licensed by the domestic Securities Regulator, but few place any restrictions on foreign ownership of CIF operators which seek a full domestic licence and intend to market domestically and abide by local legislation and regulation.

While most countries wish to foster their own domestic CIF industries, it can also be beneficial to involve experienced CIF Managers from abroad. It is easy to make domestic licensing procedures so cumbersome for non-domestic institutions that none will actually enter the market (an approach partially used by Japan over many years) but in the long run, the creation of domestic cartels simply results in inefficiency and poor service plus high charges for investors. The best way to foster development of a strong CIF industry is competition within an effective system of regulation.

4.7.3   Sale of domestic CIFs abroad

The vast majority of CIFs are marketed to investors within the domicile where the relevant CIF is located. They are licensed and regulated according to the rules of the country of domicile.

However, there are trends which indicate that this will change:

● the establishment of many new CIFs in low-tax and low-regulation offshore centres, to be sold into other countries (as outlined in 4.7.1)

● the creation of common rules governing CIFs within trading blocs such as the European Union

Regulatory and tax treatment (if any) of cross-border business is an issue to many authorities. It affects domestic funds selling abroad, and foreign funds selling into the domestic market. The general principle on which regulators work is to assess the level of regulation in the domicile of the fund; if it is equivalent to that of the country in which the fund will be sold, then such sale may permitted, subject to certain requirements. For instance, within the European Union, any fund which meets the requirement of the UCITS Directive may be marketed into any other country of the European Union, subject to registration of such intent and compliance with the other country's marketing regulations. However, it is also a requirement that such CIFs must first register with their domestic regulator their intention to market in other countries, identifying those countries by name.

4.7.4   CIFs investing abroad

The ability of CIFs to invest abroad is not normally a function of fund regulation, but of currency exchange rules, commonly set by central banks. Such controls have reduced in developed markets, but are still common in emerging markets: they often completely prevent any foreign investment by CIFs.

If foreign investment is possible, it is normal for regulators to establish requirements for this, rather than leave such decisions to the discretion of individual CIF Managers. These requirements may be set by the regulator simply listing those markets which are considered eligible for investment (on the basis of their own assessment of eligibility), or by setting requirements which the securities must comply with (usually these are liquidity and transparency related) and leaving CIF Managers to decide if individual securities meet these requirements or not. Most commonly, open ended funds would be limited to investing in securities listed or traded on exchanges or regulated trading systems, while closed ended funds may be permitted to hold less liquid securities.

Foreign assets are required to be held by a custodian, which may be a foreign branch of the custodian or trustee of the CIF, or another organisation, known as a sub-custodian. The lead custodian will usually select the sub-custodian and will remain liable for any failure of the sub-custodian.

Valuation: the key to CIF operation

5

5.1 Why valuation is central to the operation of a CIF

This Chapter deals with the investments which CIFs can include in their portfolios, requirements for diversification, and the way those investments are valued. Subsequent chapters deal with the sometimes complex arrangements for translating the value of the pool of assets into a price per share/unit at which investors into the CIF can buy or sell; and with the end result of pricing – the issue and redemption of shares/units.

The chart below shows the relationship between the portfolio of assets held by the CIF and the investor, the price being the point where the two meet.

The investor meets the portfolio

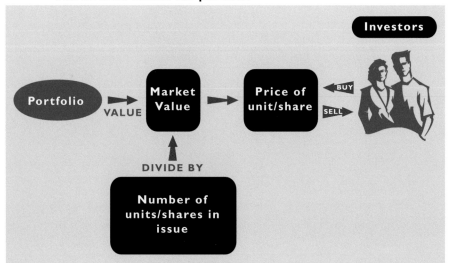

The type of assets that CIFs are permitted to hold is normally laid down by regulation, as is the maximum percentage of the portfolio that may be invested in the securities of any one issuer and the maximum percentage of any one issue that may be held. Borrowing by CIFs, except for closed ended types, is usually severely curtailed.

Valuation of fund assets and pricing of fund shares/units are central to the operation of CIFs. If investors are to entrust their money to a common pool, they must have confidence that the way in which the investments owned by that pool are valued and priced is fair and does not disadvantage them. Though this may seem obvious, the facts of market practice and behaviour mean that unless great care is taken in constructing and regulating valuation and pricing systems, investors can easily be disadvantaged either to the benefit of other investors or – more seriously – to the benefit of the CIF Manager, who may be able to gain in a number of different ways. In addition, since the net asset value of a fund is the sole means by which investors can judge the performance of a CIF Manager, any error in valuation or manipulation of prices on which valuations are based, may cause existing or potential investors to take investment decisions based on misleading or even fraudulent information.

It is therefore normal for Securities Regulators, in addition to specifying the type of investment considered appropriate for different types of CIF, to make specific rules covering the methodology of both valuation and pricing, and how they must be carried out. In particular, the way that the pricing of open ended funds is undertaken is usually subject to very precise rules. This is because where investors enter and leave funds daily, manipulation of, or errors in, valuation or in pricing can have serious implications for them, resulting in investors paying too much to buy shares/units or receiving too little when they redeem their holdings; most significantly pricing errors may dilute the interests of continuing investors.

In most cases, valuation and pricing are undertaken by either the CIF Manager or by a specialist third party administrator. In the case of open ended funds of a contractual or trust type, which do not, like corporate style funds, have directors to look after investors' interests, Securities Regulators often make the custodian responsible for ensuring that the CIF Manager properly applies the valuation and pricing rules. In addition the auditor will, in the course of the audit take samples of the pricing calculation and verify that they have been correctly and properly done.

Accurate valuation of assets is also important in ensuring compliance with investment and borrowing limitations on CIFs; fluctuations in the prices of individual assets held in the portfolio may, for example, mean that limits set for maximum holdings in any one issuer or asset class can be exceeded inadvertently.

5.2 The significance of permitted assets and borrowing rules and limitations

The type of assets which CIFs may hold, which affect how valuation may be achieved, is usually defined in legislation and regulation. Investments are normally confined to securities of different types and cash deposits. Some regulators permit real estate and other types of asset, such as precious metals, to be held, but this is unusual. Real estate is an important asset class in its own right, but is unsuitable for inclusion in open ended CIFs. The types of legal structure suitable for holding real estate is more likely to be a specialised vehicle of a closed ended corporate type (Real Estate Investment Trusts in the US and Property Companies in the UK). This Chapter does not therefore deal with real estate in any detail.

5.2.1 Open ended and closed ended CIFs have different characteristics

There is an important difference between open ended CIFs and closed ended CIFs. Because open ended CIFs are usually required to issue and redeem shares/units regularly at the wish of investors, typically daily in most developed markets, but occasionally less frequently, the ability to value the assets held in the portfolio of the CIF and more importantly the ability of the manager to buy and sell those assets in order to invest new subscriptions and to meet redemptions, is a high priority. Thus the majority of the assets held by open ended funds are usually required to listed on a recognised exchange or regularly traded on another type of market (bonds are typically traded in inter dealer markets for example). This requirement ensures that a market price can be established at the time of valuation and that there is sufficient liquidity for securities to be bought and sold in reasonable quantity at most times.

Less liquid assets, which are not regularly traded or not traded at all, are generally considered unsuitable for inclusion in the portfolios of open ended CIFs and the percentage of a portfolio represented by such assets is limited to a low figure, typically 10% or less. Closed ended CIFs which have no obligation continuously to issue and redeem shares/units, are much more suitable vehicles for holding illiquid assets, such as private equity or venture capital investments or securities in emerging markets, which, even though they may be listed, are often extremely illiquid. But even investors in closed ended CIFs, whose ability to buy after the initial issue or to sell is limited to their ability to purchase from an existing investor who wishes to sell or to sell to a new investor who wishes to buy, will want to be able to be able to determine the value of their assets per share/unit from time to time in order to be able to monitor the progress of their investment and to have a guideline as to what a reasonable market price for the shares/units should be, if they wish to buy or sell.

5.2.2 Borrowing by CIFs has its dangers

Borrowing by open ended CIFs is discouraged since the leverage or gearing created by the changing number of shares/units as well as the changes of the market value of the assets in the portfolio can cause unexpected damage to the share/unit value.

Even closed ended CIFs' asset value per share can be seriously affected by changing market values. This can be illustrated as follows.

Effect of borrowing and of changing market value of net assets of closed ended CIFs

	MARKET VALUE 1	MARKET VALUE 2	MARKET VALUE 3
Portfolio of assets	1,000	1,500	500
Borrowing	-500	-500	-500
Value of net assets (portfolio less debt)	500	1,000	0

Borrowing is beneficial if the value of the portfolio of assets rises (Market value 2) but catastrophic if markets fall sharply (Market value 3). Clearly the example is exaggerated in order to illustrate the point and it would be unusual for publicly offered CIFs, even of a closed ended type (but not perhaps for hedge funds) to incur such high levels of debt or for market values to rise or decline by such a large amount over a short period.

In the case of an open ended CIF the net effect of changing market values will be compounded by the changing number of shares/units in issue as the following example shows.

Effect of borrowing and of issue and redemption of shares/units for open ended CIFs

	MARKET VALUE 1	MARKET VALUE 2
Portfolio of assets	1,000	1,000
Effect of redemptions (outflow)	–	-500
Borrowing	-500	-500
Value of net assets (portfolio less debt)	500	0

Even though the value of the portfolio has remained unchanged, the redemption of shares/units withdrawal of money resulting from redemptions by investors, accompanied by no reduction in the level of debt, has destroyed the value for remaining investors.

5.2.3   Typical limitations for open ended CIFs

5.2.3.1   Types of asset

Legislation and regulations usually identify the categories of asset
which are suitable for inclusion in open ended CIFs, particularly those
which are offered to the general public. Specialised CIFs which are
offered only to institutional investors or wealthy private individuals
will not usually be subject to the limitations applied to publicly
offered CIFs. CIFs which are designed to include very esoteric assets
which do not wish to be subjected to any limitations on borrowing are
usually formed as offshore funds in jurisdictions which have relatively
liberal regimes, or as limited partnerships.

The assets permitted are generally selected for their characteristics of
liquidity (that is, able to be bought and sold easily at any time),
transparency (the terms of their issue and the rights of investors are
clearly defined and there is regular disclosure of information by the
issuer) and for the soundness of the issuer. Typically they would
include those outlined below.

5.2.3.1.a Cash and bonds

The assumption is that bonds and other types of debt instrument
listed below are relatively free of risk in when issued by good quality
issuers: such as sovereign debt of developed countries, deposits with
top international banks, municipal debt and top quality corporate debt.

Debt issued by countries outside the top ranks, however, has proved to
be anything but riskless. Regular defaults by a number of countries in
the categories "emerging" or "developing" have sounded warning signals
that even sovereign debt needs to be carefully considered by investors.

Liquidity is also a controversial topic. Many bonds trade infrequently
after their initial issue, even in developed markets. This poses two
problems for the managers of CIFs and Securities Regulators:

● the ability to ascribe a market value in the absence of frequent
trades which would establish a market price

- the inability to dispose of assets, if it becomes necessary to do so, at realistic prices

CIFs, which invest predominantly in bonds, and which are often sold to the public on a promise of a high return with relative security, often encounter difficulties for the above reasons.

A typical list of assets of the deposit or bond type considered suitable for publicly offered CIFs would be as follows:

- deposits with banks, sometimes limited to those banks which have top credit ratings

- certificates of deposit, commercial paper guaranteed or accepted by banks

- government bonds and short term paper

- debt issued by agencies of government and guaranteed by government

- municipal or regional government debt

- bonds or other debt instruments issued by multinational bodies (the World Bank for example)

- debentures and loan stocks issued by companies in any number of currencies in addition to the home currency of their country of domicile, sometimes with some limitation as to the credit rating of the issuer

- convertible bonds (which have both bond and equity characteristics)

Naturally there would be considerable variations in such a list from country to country, depending on the availability of particular types of deposits or debt obligations. Some countries' regulations are more restrictive than others, with the most liberal regimes leaving the problems of valuation and liquidity to the managers.

The types of asset described above will be used in different ways in different categories of CIF. The principle which underlies the price volatility of fixed income securities is "the longer the unelapsed time until maturity, the greater the price change up or down in response to a movement down or up in interest rates".

Money market funds, which aim to behave like a substitute for a bank account, will therefore invest almost entirely in paper which has short maturities (usually less than 90 days) and which is issued by issuers which have impeccable risk ratings; this means that, since price changes of the underlying investments are unlikely even in response to quite sharp interest rate movements, the price of the share/unit will remain stable at a price typically of $1 per share/unit.

The prices of CIFs which invest in longer term bonds will typically be more volatile, ranging from the most stable, which invest in the government bonds of countries with AAA ratings, to those which invest in "junk bonds", bonds issued by domestic issuers with low ratings or even those which are in technical default, and the bonds of emerging countries.

5.2.3.1.b Equities

The other main asset class in which CIFs are typically permitted to invest is equity (shares or stocks in companies). Here again the criteria are those of liquidity (ability to buy and sell assets easily at any time), transparency (provision of regular information to shareholders and clearly defined shareholder rights), and the status of the issuer. Again those framing the regulations face certain difficulties in defining the nature of permitted investments. The old criterion – listed on a recognised stock exchange – which passed the responsibility for supervising the quality of the companies listed, and the information that they provided, to the exchange itself, is harder to apply as trading has broken loose from traditional exchanges, which used to have a monopoly of organising trade in securities.

Despite the increased diffusion of trade in securities, it is still possible to define "recognised trade organisers", since even so-called OTC markets, such as NASDAQ, will not allow trade in shares of companies which have not met certain criteria. Most regulators would opt for giving a list of such trade organisers and then leaving individual stock selection to the discretion of managers.

Even with these safeguards the shares of smaller companies tend to be illiquid, and, in times of crisis, just when investors are most likely to wish to redeem, liquidity in larger companies can disappear too. Some regulators have attempted to meet this problem by requiring that CIFs which invest in certain types of asset should maintain a percentage of their portfolio in cash at all times, something which a prudent manager would do in any case. The danger of this approach is that the regulator may be inclined to set a high figure for the "protection" of investors, whereas, in a rising market, such a high cash proportion will act as a drag on performance.

A much more real problem is that of valuation. Who can tell what a correct market price should be for a share which has not traded for two or three weeks or even longer? The "synthetic" solutions, which are moderately satisfactory for bonds, cannot be used to value equities, as will be seen in the section on valuation.

There is no neat and tidy solution to this problem, so most regulators will set broad guidelines and leave it to the good sense and business judgement of managers to strike an appropriate balance.

5.2.3.2 Diversification

One of the often stated advantages of CIFs for investors in them is diversification, that is to say portfolios which are invested in a number of different shares or bonds and which thus avoid the concentrated risk of being invested in the shares of only one company. The question of how many different shares should be included in one portfolio to achieve optimal diversification is the subject of much academic and industry debate. The mathematically derived solution seems to suggest that between ten and fifteen different shares, provided that they represent companies in different industries, are sufficient, and that each incremental share added after that reduces risk very marginally.

5.2.3.2.a Ensuring an adequate number of different holdings in any one CIF

For CIFs a fairly standard solution, in developed markets, is to limit any one holding of shares to 5% of the total value of the portfolio – in effect requiring each CIF to have at least 20 separate holdings. In practice, it would be unusual for any one CIF to have as few as 20 holdings, since the business of monitoring percentages which were at the limits of what was permissible, and subsequently having to adjust the portfolio to stay in compliance, would be too time consuming.

In some less developed markets however, the 5% limitation is regarded as too low, if there are relatively few leading shares which represent a high proportion of market capitalisation; it is not unusual in some markets for the major oil and gas company or the telecom company to represent 15-30% of the market. In these cases formulae can be worked out to allow, for example, 40% of the portfolio to be represented by not less than three shares, with no single holding accounting for more than 20%; the balance of 60% should consist of holdings which represent not more than 5% of the value of the portfolio. In this way each portfolio will have to consist of not less than 15 different shares.

The exception to the diversification rule is the case of investment in government bonds; since there is theoretically no specific risk involved, diversification is unnecessary. Even here, however, funds are usually required to invest no more than 35% of the fund in any one issue.

5.2.3.2.b Avoiding excessive concentration in the securities of any one issuer

5.2.3.2.b.i Equities

CIFs are not designed to be "holding companies" or to exercise management control functions over the companies which they hold in their portfolios. Not only do their investment managers lack the skills to be able to manage industrial or commercial companies, but also the favourable tax environment which governments have often deliberately created to encourage savings in CIFs is not one which revenue services like to see abused by tax avoidance schemes designed for controlling owners of companies.

There is the additional disadvantage that large "blocks" of shares which represent substantial ownership of a particular company can be extremely hard to sell. CIFs are not designed to be investment banks or vehicles for the ambitions of affiliates; the temptations for investment banks and other owners of management companies to misuse the money in CIFs managed by them are great, and are fully discussed in section 5.3.3 and 8.5.

Large holdings controlled by the same group and its affiliates may also attract the attention of the authorities responsible for policing take-overs and mergers; rules of engagement may cause holdings in excess of a certain percentage to trigger a takeover bid.

Thus limitations are placed on the percentage of any issue of voting shares of any one issuer that may be held by any CIF; this percentage is often subject to aggregation of all holdings of the same security across the whole range of CIFs managed by any one management company. The limit will typically range from 5% to 25% or even higher. The higher limits will usually only apply in the case of CIFs set up specifically for privatisation or corporate restructuring, in which cases there is a positive wish on the part of the authorities to enable the CIF to exercise strong shareholder influence on companies.

5.2.3.2.b.ii Bonds

In the case of issues of bonds, there are different reasons why high percentages of the issue should not be held by any one CIF or a group of CIFs under the same management. Clearly liquidity considerations are common to both equities and bonds, but ownership of a high percentage of a bond issue does not confer any degree of voting control.

So the reasons in the case of bonds for not permitting a high percentage of an issue (or issues aggregated) by the same issuer are related more to concerns over manipulation. It would be tempting for any bank or investment bank, which advises corporate clients and helps them to raise money, to use the CIFs under management of its subsidiary or affiliate as "underwriters" or buyers of last resort for a sticky issue.

5.2.3.2.b.iii Deposits

Where there is any doubt about the solvency of the banking system, it is usual to require that not more than a certain percentage (10% might be a typical figure) of assets should be deposited with any one bank.

5.3   Key aspects of valuation

All CIFs value their assets at regular intervals. Usually a minimum frequency for valuation is established by regulation which also establishes that open ended funds are not permitted to set prices for issue or redemption unless a recent valuation has been undertaken. In the case of open ended funds investing in liquid assets of the types described above, such valuations are normally undertaken every day or at the very least once a week.

Closed ended CIFs normally value their assets less frequently and may do so only every month, or at intervals of three or six months. Interval CIFs may only be required to value their assets immediately prior to a pricing and dealing point. The central assumption however, in this section, is that daily valuation is the rule.

5.3.1   Frequency of valuation

The basic principle is that the more volatile the prices of assets in which the CIF invests, and/or the greater the volume of buying and selling of shares in a CIF, the more frequent valuations should be.

In the case of closed ended funds, the calculation of the Net Asset Value (NAV – that is, total assets of the fund less total liabilities) provides essential information for investors, who will want to compare the price at which the CIF shares/units trade in the secondary market to their NAV. But the CIF Managers are not generating revenue from sales of new shares/units in closed ended funds and are not generally required to value frequently by law, so they have no incentive to spend money on frequent valuations. Usually they will therefore undertake periodic valuations at specified dates and will publish a NAV at those dates. In between these valuations, investors can estimate the NAV by knowing what the CIF's actual investment portfolio was on the previous valuation date and adjusting for the changes in the market prices of the assets in the portfolio. In developed markets, brokers create models of closed ended CIF portfolios and publish their own estimates of their NAVs on a daily basis as a guide for investors.

Open ended CIFs investing in money market instruments, equities and bonds normally value on a daily basis.

Securities Regulators often require the valuations to be verified by a third party such as the custodian, particularly in the cases of CIFs of a corporate or contractual type, where the CIF itself does not have its own independent directors.

Many Securities Regulators also require the auditor to take samples of valuations and prices of the previous year during the course of the annual audit, and to verify that these were carried out according to the established procedures and were mathematically accurate.

The use of independent valuers is much more relevant in the case of real estate than in the case of securities, for which they are unlikely to be able to establish a realistic market value to a higher degree of reliability than the manager or the custodian.

5.3.2 Liquidity

Where a CIF invests only in securities which are frequently traded on an active and regulated stock exchange or on a dealer market which has a system for regular disclosure of prices and volumes of trades, which is immediately accessible in physical or electronic form, valuation is relatively simple. But many CIFs hold other types of asset where an up to date market price does not exist or cannot be relied upon. Accordingly, definite principles for the valuation of various types of asset are required. These may be set by Securities Regulators or the rules may leave it to custodians or CIF directors to agree such principles with CIF Managers.

Examples of valuation problems frequently encountered in both developed and developing markets (more frequently in the latter) are:

- bonds which trade infrequently or not at all

- shares or bonds, which have traded in the past, but in which trade dries up

- unlisted securities of all sorts, if permitted

- trades which take place "off market" between broker/dealers and which are not reported

Liquidity is the key factor in determining which valuation method should be applied. The greater the liquidity – the greater the regular volume of unconnected transactions in an asset – the greater the confidence that can be placed in being able to sell or buy the asset at that price. The less the liquidity, the less confidence can be placed in the ability to buy or sell at that price and the greater the adjustment that needs to be made for this uncertainty in the valuation process.

5.3.3   Scope for manipulation and abuse

The less liquid the asset, the more important the principle of independent valuation becomes. Unquoted securities are a prime example. A number of abuses are possible unless specifically banned by regulation:

- the directors of the CIF Manager or other connected individuals may be substantial shareholders in unquoted companies in which a CIF holds shares. It will be in the interests of these investors to ensure that the valuation placed on the shares is as high as possible when the CIF is buying

- an investment manager employed by the CIF Manager may have a financial interest in unquoted securities which conflicts with that of the CIF investors

- an investment manager may use artificial values of unquoted securities to generate a rise in the CIF's NAV, thus creating an impressive performance which attracts investors to buy shares/units in the fund at an inflated price – and increasing management fees

Valuation of such assets therefore requires special care. There are several principles which can be applied by a Securities Regulator:

- ensuring that the methodology and process of valuing non-traded or infrequently traded assets is standardised and allows as little scope as possible for individual variation

- in the case of both equities and bonds requiring that assets which have not been traded, and for which no realistic brokers' quotations can be obtained are written down to a price, which represents a discount to the traded equivalent, over a period of time (but not to zero)

- trying to ensure that all trades, on or off market, are reported to a central point and price and volume information are disseminated (developed markets have achieved some success in the case of bond trade, which takes place on an inter dealer market, in encouraging dealers to report trades)

In the case of open ended CIFs, custodians, CIF directors or the Securities Regulator may require valuations of unquoted securities to be independently verified. With closed ended and with most open ended funds of the corporate type, the directors collectively take responsibility for such valuations and, even if the rules do not require this, they may often choose to take independent advice.

Where less liquid assets form part of a CIF portfolio, its reports to investors should make this clear and also state clearly the basis that has been used in the valuation of such assets. But it may also be noted that the margin of error in valuations of unquoted investments is large.

5.4   Applying the principles of valuation

5.4.1   Summary of methods of valuing different types of asset

Summary of valuation methods

TYPE OF ASSET	VALUATION METHOD
Cash and short term deposits	At face value
Bonds traded on a recognised market	At the day's closing market price, or the market price available immediately prior to the valuation point
Equities traded regularly on an recognised market	At the day's closing market price, or the market price available immediately prior to the valuation point
Derivatives traded on a recognised market	At the day's closing market price, or the market price available immediately prior to the valuation point
Equities traded irregularly or traded on an unofficial market	Cost (price paid by the CIF) OR the most recent traded price, provided this was a genuine price resulting from several unconnected deals and not simply one trade or several trades by connected parties OR quotes from brokers. Possible write down provision
Short term paper (bills or CDs)	Straight line to redemption, unless there are violent fluctuations in interest rates

TYPE OF ASSET	VALUATION METHOD
Bonds, not traded	*Comparative basis: taking the price of a comparable traded bond, and discounting for less liquidity; OR a methodology designed to attribute a discounted present value to future income receipts and redemption proceeds*
Equities, not traded	*Cost OR estimated value. Estimation methods are (1) Using a fixed multiple of earnings (the P/E ratio) and discounting; (2) comparing with a traded share and applying a discount; (3) the company's net asset value (e.g. in the case of property companies)*
Property (real estate)	*Cost OR independently estimated market value*

5.4.2 Valuation calculation

The concept of a valuation is simple. It is the aggregate of the market values of all the holdings plus cash on deposit less any net current assets or liabilities and any longer term liabilities; accruals are made for income received from investments and for expenses. The resulting figure is then divided by the number of units in issue to reduce this to a net asset value per share/unit.

Example of a CIF Net Asset Value calculation

INVESTMENT	PRICING BASIS	PRICE	VALUE	% OF PORTFOLIO
Equities				
1,500 ABC Industries	Market price	25.5	38,250	3.78
850 DFE Finance	Market price	43	36,550	3.61
2,350 GH Capital	Market price	12.5	29,375	2.91
1,750 JK Engineering	Market price	19	33,250	3.29
2,450 LM Holdings (unquoted)	Earnings multiple	9	22,050	2.18
1,200 NM Engineering (unquoted)	Comparison with ABC Industries	17	20,400	2.02
Bonds				
5,000 Government bonds	Market price	95	475,000	47.03
500 NM Engineering bonds	Discounted present value	85	42,500	4.21
International Equities	Market prices		225,000	22.28
Total investments			932,375	
Cash deposits	Face value		85,000	8.41
Net current assets (liabilities)	Face value		-22,000	
Accrued income	Face value		24,700	
Accrued expenses	Face value		-11,900	
Total			1,010,075	100
Net Asset Value	550,000 shares in issue		1.84	

5

Among the points arising from this are:

- different valuation bases have been used with different types of asset. The CIF Manager will need to agree the basis of valuation of each type of security with the custodian or the directors of the CIF

- investments denominated in foreign currencies are translated at the exchange rate ruling on the valuation date

- amounts defined as current liabilities include amounts the fund is due to pay for purchases of assets which have been contracted for but not yet paid and for redemptions of shares or units accepted but not yet paid

- amounts defined as current assets include amounts the fund is due to receive for sales of assets contracted for but not yet completed and for sales of shares or units made but for which payment has not yet been received

- income is that received by the fund and accrued since the last distribution made by the fund. The definition of income received will vary depending on the degree of certainty that can be placed on the date that the payment is expected to be received, and on the bank payment system. In many countries, whose systems are not reliable, income will not be booked until it is actually in the fund's bank account

- expenses are those accrued at an appropriate fraction of the contracted annual rate since the last payment from the fund to the CIF Manager

The normal procedure in valuing a CIF is for the CIF Manager, or a third party specialist who is contracted to carry out administrative and accounting functions, to obtain a current set of prices or a valuation of listed securities from a specialist service provider or from electronic feeds directly from exchanges. It will add to this its own valuations (independently verified if necessary) of unlisted securities, and the current balance of cash and the income account and accrued expenses. The CIF will maintain an income account for all dividends and interest and the amount accrued in this account is included in the valuation. The annual charge payable to the CIF Manager is normally deducted from the fund on a monthly basis; any amount accrued since the last payment is deducted from the assets and any liabilities deducted also.

5.4.3   Valuation errors and problems

Incorrect share or unit pricing is one of the most common problems in management of CIFs and one of the most potentially damaging to the interests of shareholders or unitholders. Its importance means that any Securities Regulator will give verification and supervision of valuation and pricing a high priority within its supervisory duties.

There are many ways in which a valuation and calculation of a share/unit price can go wrong. Most of these are due to human error. Some of them are:

● using the wrong price for assets, this may either be due to deliberate manipulation, or, more commonly to incorrect transcription or data entry. Governments issue dozens of different bonds with different lives and interest rates – a 5% bond redeemable in 2005 will have a very different value from an 8% bond redeemable in 2005; companies issue many classes of share – preferred, voting, non-voting – all have different prices

● mathematical errors in multiplication or addition

● failing to include a recently purchased security or continuing to include a security which has been sold

● incorrect cash balance

● incorrect accruals of income and/or expenses

● using the wrong number of shares/units in issue as the divisor to establish NAV per share/unit

As will be seen later, even small inaccuracies in price can have seriously damaging outcomes for share/unit holders, and can be very costly for the management company, when they are detected and it is compelled to put them right. This may involve reconstructing a price history over several months and compensating any incoming, outgoing or ongoing investors, who have suffered damage, loss, or opportunity cost.

5.5 Relevance to exchanges, mergers and takeovers and conversions

Correct NAVs are also crucial to protecting investors' interests in situations other than buying, selling or holding units or shares.

5.5.1 Share exchange

Investors may be invited to subscribe for CIF shares/units not in cash but by offering securities in exchange, though some regulators only permit cash subscription for funds. The CIF Manager may choose to transfer the exchanged securities into the CIF portfolio (assuming the asset is an eligible investment) or sell them and subscribe the resulting proceeds for the investor in the normal way. Where securities are accepted into the CIF, an accurate valuation is vital. This is easy with liquid securities but problems could arise if exchange of illiquid securities into the fund is permitted.

5.5.2 Mergers and takeovers

Accurate calculations of NAV are also vital preceding any merger or takeover between CIFs. Though takeovers are not usual in open ended CIFs, they do occur with closed ended corporate CIFs. If the shares or units in the CIF trade at a large discount to NAV, this creates an incentive for outsiders to make a bid at somewhat less than NAV. Arbitrageurs may purchase stakes in closed ended CIFs trading at a large discounts to their NAVs and attempt to encourage takeover bids or other restructuring moves that reduce the level of the discount. They may even try to force conversion of a closed ended fund to an open ended fund, to enable them to redeem their holding at net asset value; or to liquidate the entire fund, in which case they will also receive NAV.

A merger, in international terms, generally involves the exchange of shares or units in one merging fund for shares or units in a second merging fund; clearly shareholders in these funds will not vote for such a merger unless they feel that the proposed rate of exchange offers them a fair deal. A merger may also be effected by means of the creation of a CIF over the top of the two entities to be merged, which will issue its shares/units to the share/unit holders of each of the two funds in proportion to their size. Accurate NAVs assist shareholders to evaluate such proposals.

Illustration of a merger of two closed ended CIFs

Opening Position

CIF A has a NAV of 200 per share and 100,000 shares in issue
= total net assets of 20,000,000

CIF B has a NAV of 100 per share and 400,000 shares in issue
= total net assets of 40,000,000

Takeover Terms

CIF A wishes to take over CIF B and issues one of its own shares for each two shares of CIF B

Result

CIF A will, after the issue of shares to the shareholders of CIF B have a total number of shares in issue of 300,000 = total net assets of 60,000,000

The new net asset value per share will be $\dfrac{60,000,000}{300,000} = 200$ per share

5.5.3   Conversions

CIFs may be established as one type of fund and later seek to change their status. This may apply where legislation has created specific types of fund (such as privatisation or restructuring funds) which later wish to become normal open ended investment companies or could result from a change from closed ended to open ended status. If the conversion is effected by means of a share exchange into another fund, any inaccuracy in the NAV calculations for either fund could create substantial dilution for one group of investors.

5.6   Consistency and clarity

Whichever type of valuation and pricing system is chosen from the wide variety of options the two principles that all Securities Regulators will insist on being applied are consistency and clarity.

Consistency means that the chosen valuation and pricing method must be applied in the same way at every valuation and pricing point, and that there is no possibility of varying it to suit the interests of the CIF Manager or a particular group of holders, while clarity means that the method should be fully disclosed to potential purchasers. Changes in the valuation or pricing methodology must be notified to holders, who may have the opportunity to vote in certain jurisdictions or the time to redeem or sell if they do not like the proposals.

How pricing and charges work

The previous Chapter demonstrated how a share/unit value can be constructed from a portfolio of shares held by a CIF and gave examples of how errors in the calculation could arise. This section deals with:

- the consequences of pricing errors for investors

- how pricing attempts to maintain perfect equity between incoming, outgoing and ongoing investors

- ways of preventing management companies from profiting at the expense of investors through exploiting their superior knowledge or manipulating prices

- the different types of fund charges which can apply and their implications

6.1   Differences between closed ended and open ended CIF pricing

6.1.1   Closed ended funds shares are priced by the market

In the case of closed ended CIFs, following the closing of the initial issue, investors can only purchase and sell shares through a secondary market where the price is set by the balance of supply and demand. The CIF publishes its NAV at regular intervals and this is only one piece of information among many others that investors take into account in deciding whether to buy or sell. The calculation of the NAV in this case is based on the middle market price of the CIF's quoted investments and the directors' or managers' estimated prices for the remaining investments.

The directors of the closed ended CIF and the CIF Manager have no responsibility for the price at which the CIFs shares trade, other than in providing information to investors.

6.1.2   Open ended funds are priced at NAV for purchase and redemption

With open ended funds the issue of pricing is far more important and also far more complex. Here the CIF Manager creates the price at which investors buy and sell. The process of converting a valuation into a price raises important issues of equity or fairness to different classes of investor.

6.1.2.1   Incorrect pricing gives rise to inequity

The following chart shows the effect of selling shares/units to new investors too cheaply – below NAV.

Dilution

	Net assets	Shares/units in issue	Purchase number of shares/ units	Purchase price of new shares/ units	Amount invested	NAV per share/unit
Opening position	1,000,000	100,000				10
New investor buys			100,000	5	500,000	
Closing position	1,500,000	200,000				7.5

The NAV of each share is now 7.5. One of the original investors who owned 1,000 shares worth 10,000 now finds them worth 7,500 and has lost 2,500. One of the new investors who paid 1,000 for 200 shares now finds they are worth 1,500.

The opposite effect would be produced if the fund sold new shares to incoming investors at a price higher than its NAV. Existing investors would benefit and incoming investors would lose. The following chart illustrates this effect:

Concentration

	Net assets	Shares/units in issue	Purchase number of shares/ units	Purchase price of new shares/ units	Amount invested	NAV per share/unit
Opening position	1,000,000	100,000				10
New investor buys			100,000	15	1,500,000	
Closing position	2,500,000	200,000				12.5

The existing investors have enhanced the value of their shares/units at the expense of the new investor.

The words used to describe the phenomena are dilution – in the case of the existing shareholders in the first Table, who have had their interests diluted – and concentration – in the case of the existing shareholders in the second Table who have had their interests concentrated.

It can easily be calculated that the same set of phenomena will result from redeeming at too high or too low a price and that there will be winners and losers in these cases too.

The examples shown above show extreme cases of over or under valuation for illustrative purposes. In reality errors are much smaller than these, but the effect is exactly the same, and can be magnified if the error continues to be present over a long period.

The relative ratios of profit and loss for investors will depend on the volume of transactions at the false price in relation to the existing assets and the extent of the discrepancy between the true NAV and the false price.

6.1.2.2 The nature of the securities markets can also give rise to inequity

Adherence to a carefully constructed set of valuation principles can enable gross errors and abuses to be avoided. But the very nature of market trading practices also creates scope for inequity.

The reason is that securities almost never trade at a single price. In most markets, there is a bid-ask spread. A security is offered for sale at a higher (ask) price than will be offered to an investor wishing to sell it (bid price). The difference between the two prices is called the "spread" and represents the profit of the market maker or dealer.

The size of the spread between bid and ask prices will depend on the nature of the security, the volume of trading and the practices in the market where the security is traded. An example is shown in the next Table. This assumes a 2% spread in the price of shares. In developed markets, price spreads in widely traded securities can be as low as 0.5%. But even in developed markets, the price spreads in less liquid securities can be as high as 10%. The example also takes no account of any transaction taxes, which would further widen the spread.

The spread between bid and ask prices

The following example illustrates the possible effect of bid/ask spreads on the price of a share or unit. If the fund is buying shares in ZZ Enterprises it will need to pay the Ask price (101) and will also have to pay commission to the broker through whom the transaction is done. If selling shares in ZZ Enterprises, the fund will only receive the Bid price (99) and will have to pay commission on the sale to the broker. It should be noted that, in markets in which there are transaction taxes these must also be included in the calculation.

Example of trade in shares in ZZ Enterprises

All-in cost of purchase of ZZ shares	102
Add commission payable on purchase	1
Ask price of ZZ shares	101
Middle market price of ZZ shares	100
Bid price of ZZ shares	99
Deduct commission payable on sale	1
All in receipt on sale of ZZ shares	98

Spread between all-in purchase and sale, 98-102, as % of middle price = 4%

The existence of this price spread in the securities in which a CIF invests raises the question: when valuing the CIF portfolio, what should be taken as the market value of each holding, the bid price, the ask price or some other price based on these?

6.2   Different bases of pricing for open ended CIFs

The different pricing systems in use by open ended CIFs around the world are based on different answers to this question.

6.2.1   Middle market single pricing

The simplest solution is to ignore the spread and the transaction costs involved in buying and selling assets and to take the middle market price as the basis for valuation in all cases. In the case of the example shown in the table, where the price spread is 98-102, the security thus would be valued at 100. Then, the CIF itself will have just one price at which investors buy and sell. Charges may be added to or deducted from this price.

This system was developed in the USA in the 1970s and is used by US mutual funds. It is now in common use in the UK as well. It is simple and easy for the public to understand. It works well in markets where securities are freely traded in large volumes, where transaction costs are modest and the CIFs themselves are large. In these circumstances, the system is unlikely to produce significant inequity between different classes of investor. Securities Regulators who have adopted this approach have accepted that the system cannot be mathematically perfect, but take the view that over a long period of time and across thousands of transactions both in portfolio securities and in shares or units of the CIF, the process will be self balancing.

However, in markets where spreads are wide, where transaction costs are high or where a substantial part of CIF portfolios are held in non-traded assets, this system is very likely to produce a significant degree of disadvantage for some investors most of the time.

6.2.2 Middle market single pricing with notional commission

It is possible to adjust for the negative effects of the price spread in a middle market single price system. This can be done by the CIF adding a notional commission to each purchase and deducting it from each sale. These commissions which reflect the costs the CIF itself would incur in buying or selling are paid into the CIF.

This system was created by the French and is used by SICAVs. Its only drawback is that investors are unlikely to understand why they have to pay the commission and may be irritated by this. Even though the literature may explain it clearly, many investors are likely to assume that the commission is being retained by the CIF Manager.

6.2.3 Middle market single pricing with dilution levy

The adjustment to a middle market single price does not have to be a universal automatic payment by investors, unlike the system in use in France. An alternative is to give the custodian the authority to impose a dilution levy on purchases or sales of a CIF when conditions are such that a class of investors would suffer if the levy was not imposed. When imposed, the levy – which is an amount to cover transaction costs incurred in dealing in underlying assets of the fund and is levied either upon issue or redemption of a CIF share – is paid into the CIF to compensate existing investors for those transaction costs. It is required to be levied fairly across all investors and may not be levied twice; that is, both on subscription and on redemption of any one CIF share.

This is the system adopted by the UK's open ended investment companies. It is realistic, in that in most circumstances there is no need for the levy. It is flexible, in that the custodian has guidelines specifying the circumstances when a levy should be applied. The drawback is that investors do not know whether or when the levy will be applied. In practice, this may not matter since it is only in the most extreme circumstances that the levy would be more than a very small percentage.

6.2.4 Swinging and semi-swinging single pricing

A theoretical possibility would be to have a single price but for the valuation to be based on the ask basis when the CIF had a surplus of sales over redemptions and on the bid basis when it had a surplus of redemptions over sales. Such a system would be termed "swinging" single pricing. However, the pattern of sales and redemptions can often be erratic, so with this system the CIF price could swing frequently from one basis to the other. The effect could be to add price volatility of some 6-10% to the CIF price, and this would certainly deter investors. This system has not been adopted by any CIF industry.

Some offshore funds have been established with a variation of this system where the price moves partway towards the ask basis when the fund is expanding and partway to the bid basis when the fund is contracting, a system known as semi-swinging single pricing.

6.2.5 Dual pricing

The alternative to having a middle market price and adjustments is to have a dual price system. Here the CIF essentially reflects the nature of stock market dealings in its pricing. It has two prices for its shares or units, a bid price and an ask (also known as "offer") price. The bid price which is received by a redeeming holder is based on the bid prices of securities in the portfolio and notional brokerage commission is deducted from this. The ask price, which is the price paid to buy units or shares, is based on the ask prices of securities in the portfolio and notional brokerage commission is added to this.

Since the CIF price spread will depend on the actual spreads in the shares in the CIF portfolio, spreads will vary between CIFs depending on the nature of their portfolios. The price spread of a CIF investing in the shares of small-capitalisation, little-traded companies will be much higher than the spread of a CIF investing only in the largest blue chips.

Though dual pricing is a good theoretical solution to the pricing problem, it does result in wide share/unit price spreads. It is also hard to explain to the public. Though it was the system used for some 50 years by the UK's unit trust industry, it is being replaced in the UK by a single pricing system.

6.3   Historic and forward pricing

6.3.1   Historic pricing

A separate issue concerning pricing is whether dealing in open ended CIFs is on a historic or forward basis. With the historic system, the fund values and publishes a price; this price remains valid for investors to deal at until the next price is calculated, known as the pricing point. When a CIF values daily, the valuation will normally be undertaken at the close of the market, the price will be published the following morning and that day's dealings will all be done at that published price.

6.3.2   Forward pricing

Using the forward pricing system, the CIF accepts deals from investors during the day but does not fulfil the deals until the next pricing point. It then processes all those deals at that price. Only orders received prior to the valuation are fulfilled at the price resulting from that valuation. Any order received even a moment after the pricing point is carried forward to be executed at the next pricing point.

Historic pricing – orders filled at last pricing point

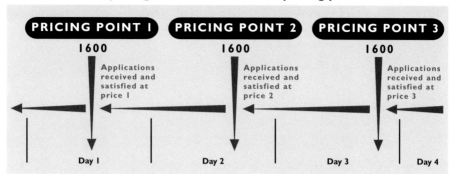

Forward Pricing – orders filled at next pricing point

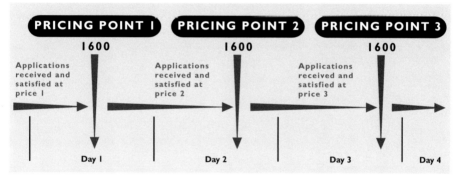

6.3.3   Drawbacks of historic pricing

Though the historic pricing system is far easier for investors to understand, it has very considerable drawbacks which is why most countries have adopted forward pricing. Essentially the historic pricing system allows investors – particularly insiders – to profit from known events. If the market rises sharply, investors can still buy at yesterday's price, knowing that when the fund is valued the price will rise and they can sell for a profit. Or if the market falls sharply, investors can still sell at the higher price derived from a valuation based on yesterday's market prices. If the regulations permit CIF Managers to buy shares in their own funds, dealing as principals (see below), they have an unhealthy incentive to profit in this way. The profits of incoming and outgoing investors of the fund are of course at the expense of ongoing investors whose profits are being diluted.

Where valuations are more widely spaced – weekly or even monthly – the scope for profiting at the expense of existing investors, if a historic pricing system is in use, is far greater.

Though it might seem difficult to ask investors to deal at an unknown price, in reality most investors do not intend to buy a fixed number of shares or units but intend to invest a fixed sum of money. It is also a fact that units or shares in CIFs are primarily designed for long term savers and investors and not for short term speculators; the fact that the forward, unknown price may be marginally higher than expected, which is to their disadvantage, or lower than expected, which is to their advantage, will become immaterial in the context of the return that they hope to make over a five or ten year period. So long as they understand this and know they will receive rapid notification of the price, and can verify this against the published price, investors are likely to be content.

6.4 Effect of acting as principal

The distinction between acting as a "principal" and as an "agent" is an important one to understand. Acting as a principal means that the manager, or any other person, actually becomes the owner of the shares or units by buying them from one investor and then reselling them to another. The manager can also require the custodian or trustee to create new shares/units and buy those shares/units from the custodian or trustee for his own account and require the custodian or trustee to buy back shares/units from him for liquidation.

As a result the CIF Manager is in complete control of the situation as a "dealer" being able to trade with investors and with the custodian.

Acting as an agent, the manager, or any other person, simply facilitates the transaction, but never actually owns the shares or units. The same distinction is made between principal and agent in the case of broker/dealers. A dealer (or market maker) will act as a principal, in that the shares he buys back are for his own account and the shares that he offers for sale are actually owned by him; he hopes to make a capital gain from the transactions that he does. A broker acting as an agent will facilitate the transaction by arranging the purchase or sale of securities and will charge a commission for doing so.

If the CIF Manager is permitted to own shares or units in a fund managed by him, and is permitted to buy units directly from investors and resell them to other investors or is permitted to require the custodian or trustee to create shares/units for sale to him or to buy back and liquidate shares/units owned by him it must be made clear to the investor, that the manager is acting as a principal either in buying shares or units from the investors or selling them to him. In this way the investor may be made aware of the potential conflict.

If the CIF Manager is permitted to act as principal in a historic pricing system, the Manager can "create" large numbers of shares/units on days when the market rises, knowing the price will rise the following day and it will then be able to sell those shares/units at a profit. But in doing so it will have diluted the profits of existing investors in the fund. In certain circumstances the CIF Manager may also be able to sell short if it knows that it can create or buy back the shares/units at a lower price on the next or subsequent days.

Most jurisdictions, notably the US, forbid the manager from acting as a principal under any circumstances. Some jurisdictions permit the manager to act as a principal only in certain conditions, for example where the manager is required to act as the redeemer of last resort in cases where assets cannot be sold quickly enough to meet requests for redemption.

Fund manager, buying and selling as a principal

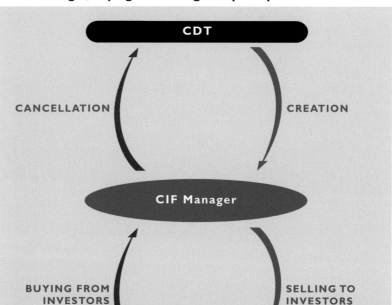

6.5 Charges and how they work

The charges made or fees charged to CIFs for various management and administrative services fall into a number of different categories. These are:

- initial charges (front end loads, sales charges) on the sale of shares/units

- redemption charges when an investor redeems shares/units

- the rounding up of share/unit prices to a convenient figure for dealing

- management charges on a fixed basis

- management charges based on a percentage of assets

- management charges based on performance

- payments to the custodian or trustee

- payments to a registrar

- payments to the auditor

- payments of taxes and duties

- payments of regulatory fees or expenses

- commissions to brokers for effecting transactions

Not all these charges are made to all CIFs in the same way. Different regimes and CIFs which are constructed in different legal forms will use different permutations of these charges and fees. The Securities Regulator may also forbid certain types of charge to be made.

Many regulatory systems define permissible charges and may exclude certain types of charge such as performance fees. They may also set limits to charges. This can be done either by setting a limit for specific charges, or by imposing a limit for the total charges levied over some period of time. Charges are required to be consistent and to be levied at stated regular intervals. They are not permitted to vary from those given in CIF prospectuses and other offering or contractual documents – for instance, by being levied in some months and not in others to massage performance – and usually may not be increased without holders' assent.

In general, in young markets with unsophisticated investors and lack of competition, a system of control of charges is preferable. In a more mature industry where there is extensive competition and clear disclosure, there is less reason to impose controls.

Competition with other financial services also has an impact; for instance, it is hard to levy any initial charges on money market type funds, since banks and other deposit takers do not levy such charges on deposits: such charges would make the funds uncompetitive.

6.5.1   Initial charges

Typically in a young market/industry, CIF Managers will seek to maintain initial charges (also called front end loads or sales loads) on the sale of shares/units. Their aim will be to cover all their marketing expenses out of these initial charges, preferably also making a profit. In this early stage of development initial charges are likely to be in the 5-8% of NAV range. CIF Managers may pay part of these charges to sales agents or distributors. Normally the initial charge is added to the NAV of the fund and shown separately. In some systems, the initial charge may be incorporated in the price of shares/units, thus creating a kind of bid/offer spread.

As the market/industry develops and more CIF Managers are established, competition gradually grows and lower initial charges are used as a competitive tool. The result is an overall fall in the level of initial charges which settle at a lower level of 2-6%. Pressure on initial charges has resulted in an increasing trend towards CIFs operating on a 'no-load' basis, in which case there is no initial charge at all and managers hope to achieve profits by attracting substantial volumes of funds on which they can earn annual management fees for a long period. In some cases this can be compensated for by higher annual charges or even, in the US, by a special additional marketing charge, known by the number of the section of the legislation which permits it as a 12(b)-1 charge.

Many managers, if their CIFs are subject to an initial charge, will operate a system of discounts for volume. This may take the form of a tapering charge, where only smaller investments attract the full charge and larger investments are subject to a reducing level of charge which will sometimes reach zero for very large investments. Managers may sometimes aggregate volumes over a defined period and reduce charges based on a number of transactions during that period.

There is sometimes controversy over the way initial charges are levied.

6.5.1.1 'Sweetheart' deals

Wishing to attract a new and possibly large investor, managers may make a special reduction in initial charge or pay an extra commission just for that investor in order to attract him to the fund, but may not offer the same deal to others. This is patently unfair and many jurisdictions, notably the US, outlaw the practice by insisting that the table of volume reductions is published and unchangeable.

6.5.1.2 Conflict between commission and charges

Clearly an investor is better off paying a low or no initial charge. But, given that shares/units of CIFs are often distributed through brokers, financial advisers or other professional advisers, a no-load or low load fund is unattractive to the adviser if there is no commission payment to remunerate him for his work and advice. There may be a tendency, therefore for advisers to select a CIF with an initial charge sufficient to pay him his commission even though there exists a comparable CIF with lower or no initial charges.

This is solved, by managers of CIFs with low or no initial charge by the payment of a renewal or "trail" commission or fee. By this means the adviser, while receiving no immediate commission, will receive an annual trail fee so long as the investor remains in the fund. This is regarded as both good for the CIF Manager, since there is an incentive for the adviser to keep the investor invested in the fund, and for the adviser who can thus build up a regular annual income rather than being solely dependent on clients making new investments or on "switching" existing clients from one fund to another in order to generate commissions for himself.

It may also be possible for a CIF Manager to pay to an adviser a commission on a CIF which is essentially "no-load" at a rate determined by agreement between the adviser's client and the adviser.

6.5.1.3   Payment of Trail Commissions

There are essentially two approaches to the payment of these.

The manager will be prepared to reduce his margins by paying the fee out of his own annual management fee. This may have the effect of putting upward pressure on annual management charges as the manager tries to restore his margins.

The US approach is known as 12(b)-1, after the section of the Investment Companies Act which has been interpreted as permitting this type of levy. This entails the manager making an up front payment of commission on a no-load CIF, which comes out of his own pocket and which he will have to finance. He is repaid over time by means of a special additional 12(b)-1 charge on the fund. In order to protect his "investment" a tapering redemption charge is levied which will disappear over five years or so (see 6.5.2.2).

Both systems create administrative complexity, since individual investments will need to be precisely tracked in order to determine the level of charge or to whom the payment is to be made. In the case of 12(b)-1, it has been ruled that the persistency of the charge should be matched to the duration of the investment, since otherwise, it was pointed out, the CIF Manager could continue to receive the payment long after his initial financing of commission had been amply repaid.

6.5.2   Redemption charges

6.5.2.1   Redemption charge or back end load

If a CIF Manager levies a low initial charge and the investor sells within a short time of purchase, the initial charge may be less than the costs of processing the purchase and sale transactions, in which case the Manager will make a loss. The same will apply if there is no initial charge ("no load") and the Manager does not receive the annual charge and/or the 12(b)-1 charge for a long enough period to compensate him. For this reason some CIF Managers impose a straightforward redemption charge, usually expressed as a percentage of share/unit NAV, which is designed to disincentivise such early redemption.

6.5.2.2   Tapering back end loads

A flat redemption fee can be off-putting to investors, however, and deter them from investing at all. An alternative is a gradually reducing back end load, whereby the redemption charge will be highest in the first year and then reduce in each following year until, after some number of years, no redemption charge is levied. This is often referred to as a "tapering back end load" in the USA, where it is most common. In the case of "no-load" funds, this can be regarded by a manager as a way of protecting the "investment" he has made in attracting new investors.

It can be presented to holders that this type of redemption charge rewards the long-term investor and deters short-term traders and that it is therefore preferable to have a system which includes redemption charges if the effect is to reduce or even eliminate initial charges. However, investors always object to charges that are not clearly stated at the outset, so clear disclosure of such charges is important. Also, many investors coming to sell their shares/units after a year or two will have forgotten the existence of a redemption charge even if this was clearly disclosed at outset, so that this can be the cause of complaints by investors.

6.5.3   Rounding

When share/unit prices in open ended CIFs are calculated, the precise NAV may run to many decimal places. The correct price might, for example, be 55.83579. In most systems, the NAV is rounded to arrive at a convenient dealing price, for example to 55.84. Where the CIF Manager acts as principal in dealing in shares/units, the Manager will retain such rounding adjustments and careful framing of the rules will be required to prevent abuses. For example, if the rules permit rounding to a tenth of the currency unit, the rounding of a unit from 555.366 to 555.37 creates a rounding adjustment of .004. But if the units were subdivided tenfold, the rounding of 55.5366 to 55.54 would create a rounding adjustment of .004 multiplied by ten, or .04, on units with the same value as the original higher priced unit. Under such a system managers will have an incentive to keep share/unit prices low, which they can easily achieve by subdividing shares/units.

It is preferable for any permitted rounding adjustments to be retained by the custodian or trustee and paid into the fund.

6.5.4 Fixed management charges

In some systems, CIFs may levy an annual charge of a fixed amount which is determined in relation to the costs of operation. There are two problems with fees of this type: they do not align the interests of the CIF Manager with the interests of investors, and they create an incentive for the CIF Manager to minimise costs which may means skimping on the services that investors want and expect.

Another – and unusual – variant on this found within some CIFs and limited partnerships is the allocation of a proportion of the assets in the fund to the management company in lieu of the annual management fee; presumably on the basis that this gives them an incentive to make the fund perform well.

6.5.5 Management charges based on a percentage of assets

The most common system is for the CIF Manager to levy an annual fee based on the value of assets under management. This aligns the interest of the Manager with investors, since both benefit from a rise in the value of the assets, and if the value falls the management fee is proportionately reduced.

Normally, the charge is taken on a monthly basis of an amount which is the aggregate of the daily accruals made between payment dates. This is regarded as fairer to investors, since it spreads the cost over a whole year. The alternative of making the charge once a year based on the net asset value at the year end could create an advantage for an investor who redeemed immediately before that date and thus was able to escape paying the fee. In the case of money market CIFs, which are used by investors as a substitute for a bank deposit, and who thus enter and exit frequently, the accrual principle is particularly important.

The manager too benefits from a more regular and less volatile cash flow. If he were to take the charge only once a year the amount he received would be hostage to the net asset value of the fund on a fixed date. While he would be happy if the market was up on that date, he would be less comfortable if the date fell immediately after a sharp fall.

Annual fees vary widely. In some systems, the CIF Manager pays for all expenses, including the custodian or trustee and auditor, out of the annual fee, and in these cases the annual fee will be higher than where the custodian or trustee's and auditor's fees are paid directly by the fund.

In general, annual fees also vary with the type of asset. The lowest annual fees are payable on money market funds, higher fees are payable on bond funds, still higher fees on equity funds and the highest fees are levied on more adventurous funds such as emerging market or hedge funds. Typical fees (for developed markets) might be:

Money market   0.2-0.5%
Bond and fixed income   0.5-1.5%
Equity (domestic)   0.75-2.0%
Equity (international)   1.00-3.00%

In less developed markets, annual charges of 3-5% are not unknown.

Annual charges may be deducted from the income received by the CIF from its investments in the form of interest and dividends, which has the effect of reducing the amount of distribution or dividend paid on to share/unit holders (see section 7.3) or out of the capital of the fund or from both in the event that there is insufficient income to cover the charge. Here again the principle of consistency is applied. The prospectus must state clearly which practice is to be followed and managers cannot change that to suit their particular purposes. Managers must take the permitted fees at regular intervals and should not be permitted to leave the amount due in the fund in order to boost performance in the short term, only to take out a larger accrual later.

Typically, some managers who offer high income CIFs may prefer to take the charges out of capital in order to boost the apparent yield on the CIF, but it should be made clear to share/unit holders that their capital is thus being eroded. There may also be a tax dimension to the decision of how to account for annual management charges, for instance whether the tax regime permits deduction of the costs of management from the gross income received or not.

Usually, a vote of shareholders/unitholders is required before the annual fee can be increased. However, some systems permit the establishment of open ended or interval funds where the prospectus states that CIF Manager may increase the fee up to a certain stated level upon giving a term of notice to investors, in order to enable those who object to redeem their shares or units before the new charges take effect.

6.5.6   Performance fees

Some regulatory systems, the US for example, do not allow the charging of fees related to the performance of the fund. The argument for this restriction is that performance fees encourage managers to take high risks in pursuit of the profits that will generate high fees for them. In practice, the majority of funds that do levy performance fees are based in lightly-regulated offshore centres. The majority of these CIFs are hedge funds or other funds investing in higher risk assets; such CIFs are often formed as limited partnerships with a fixed life.

The norm with performance fees is to set a benchmark and for the performance fee to be levied on returns achieved in excess of the benchmark. For example, a fund might set its benchmark as an annual return of 15%, with a performance fee of 15% of annual returns in excess of this figure; alternatively, performance against a specific index or out performance of a specific index by a specified percentage may be used.

Usually performance fees are charged only on cumulative gains. This means that if a fund's price rose from 100 to 150, a performance fee would be charged, but if the price then fell to 120 and then rose to 150 again, no fee would be payable. A further performance fee would only be payable when the price exceeded 150, since, if it were charged earlier, managers would be receiving the fee twice over without giving any corresponding value to the holders.

Many funds which charge performance fees also charge an annual percentage fee or a flat fee.

6.5.7   Expenses

Often certain expenses of a CIF are chargeable directly to the fund, and are not covered by annual management fees paid to management companies. These, as mentioned above, could be fees and expenses of the custodian or trustee and auditor; but could also include legal costs, regulatory costs, shareholder registration costs, commission and any transaction duties payable on portfolio transactions, appraisal or valuation costs and investor communications generally.

It is normal for regulation to determine which charges must be borne out of the stated annual management fee and which can be charged separately and directly to the fund.

It is easy to obfuscate presentation of information on such costs – for instance, an "annual management fee of 1.5%" on Fund A sounds a lot better than "total management charges of 1.8% on Fund B". However, if told that the annual management fee for Fund A excludes a series of expenses which constitute a further 0.5% of NAV, making a total of 2% whereas all costs are included in the 1.8% on Fund B, investors might make a different decision.

How issue and redemption of shares/units is done

7

The sale and redemption of shares/units to and from investors lies at the end of the process of valuation and pricing.

Open ended CIFs, whether in trust, contractual or corporate form, are subject to specific regulations governing the issue and redemption of shares, units or participations. In the case of corporate CIFs, some elements of company law may have to be disapplied to enable constant issue and redemption of shares. The form of these regulations varies but there are common features that have been arrived at by trial and error over the eighty or so years that such CIFs have operated.

7.1 Open and closed ended CIFs have different needs

The demands of dealing with issue and redemption for open and closed ended CIFs are quite different. The former have to issue and redeem daily – or at a minimum once every other week – whereas the latter will only issue for a limited period, and rarely redeem at all. There may also be technical differences between issuing and redeeming shares in a corporate type CIF, since a public offering of shares is usually covered by securities laws; issuing and redeeming units in a trust type CIF, which may or may not be defined as securities by domestic laws; and issuing and redeeming participations in contractual CIFs, which are usually but not always defined as securities.

The public offering for sale – whether of a fund share, unit, or participation – is always subject to the terms of an offering document which is usually called a prospectus, which has to be registered with the Securities Regulator, which generally also regulates the minimum

content of the document. Amendments to the prospectus are
generally also required to be registered with the Regulator and
notification of such amendments may have to be published in mass
media before taking effect. Securities Regulators may also require
that other documents – such as the fund rules – are made available to
potential investors on their request; and that forms for application for
subscription or redemption contain specified information.

7.1.1 Issue of shares in corporate closed ended CIFs

Since the procedure for issuing shares in a closed ended CIF of a
corporate type is usually very similar to that for issuing securities in
joint stock companies generally, it is not dealt with in detail here.

The mechanics of founding companies vary from country to country.
Often a group of individuals or companies are required to act as
"founders" of the company, which will register as a company with the
intention of becoming a fund through subsequent licensing by the
Securities Regulator or listing with a Stock Exchange, or both. The
"founders" may simply put up enough capital to create a company, or
may have to pay up a minimum sum set by the Securities Regulator
or Stock Exchange.

The next stage is to raise further capital through a public offering of
fund shares, under the terms of the prospectus which has to meet the
requirements of the Securities Regulator. In other countries, it is not
necessary to go through the "founding" phase, so the fund begins with
the initial public offer.

7.1.1.1 The prospectus and initial public offer

The content of the prospectus broadly obeys the same rules that
apply to the prospectuses of all publicly offered companies under the
relevant securities legislation. The normal content of a prospectus can
be found in Chapter 10.

Although it is possible for any company to advertise a prospectus for
the issue of shares in it and receive applications and subscription
moneys, a closed ended fund will normally appoint both a bank (to

receive cash subscribed for shares) and a broker or bank (sometimes termed the sponsor of the issue) to handle the promotion of the share offer. Usually, such intermediaries will be remunerated by a commission on the sums raised. The regulatory system will restrict the ability to act as intermediary in such share offers to a limited set of regulated companies.

In developed financial markets, the prospectus usually also contains an application form and all applications are regarded as being made "on the basis of" the prospectus and all the information it contains. Applications, together with cheques, bankers drafts or other valid means of payment, will be sent by subscribers to the bankers acting for the sponsors of the issue by the final date announced in the prospectus. The bankers will pay these sums into a special account, which may not be released for investment until the offer period is finished or, in some jurisdictions, until the CIF has reached a certain statutory minimum size.

As soon as practicable after this closing date, the sponsors will announce the number of shares and the total value that have been applied for. Provided the amount raised is above the minimum stipulated, the bankers will transfer the money from the special account to the account of the company which will then issue confirmation letters to subscribers that their applications have been accepted, create a shareholders register and notify shareholders in certificated or non-certificated form.

Normally, the directors or sponsors will have pre-applied for a share listing with a stock exchange so that trading in the shares may commence within a few days of the allocation of shares to subscribers.

7.1.1.2   Further issues of shares

Under most legal systems, limited companies may make new issues of shares only if authorised to do so by their shareholders. This is because in many circumstances the interests of existing shareholders are likely to be damaged by additional share issues, particularly if the

shares trade at a discount to NAV and the new shares are not offered
to existing shareholders in proportion to their existing holdings by
way of rights to which they have an absolute right to subscribe
(preemption rights), but to a set of new shareholders.

There are some situations in which it may be advantageous for
existing shareholders in a closed ended CIF if new shares are issued.

- if the shares in the CIF consistently trade in the market at a
  premium to their Net Asset Value (see section 3.2.6), this is of
  advantage to any existing shareholder who wishes to sell. But it is
  not advantageous for existing shareholders who wish to buy more
  shares. If many existing shareholders wish to do this – perhaps by
  regular subscription – then the directors of the CIF may seek
  authority to make small regular issues of new shares to satisfy the
  demands of such shareholders. Such issues will prevent any
  further rise in the premium to NAV at which the shares trade and
  may help to reduce it. Usually, closed ended CIFs are banned from
  issuing new shares at less than their current NAV, and this acts as
  an automatic mechanism preventing the dilution of existing
  shareholders' interests

- if the shares in one CIF trade at above their Net Asset Value while
  shares in a second CIF trade at below their NAV, it would be
  worthwhile for the first CIF to acquire the second, assuming it
  could secure agreement to a deal at below the second CIF's NAV.
  The merger would be achieved by an exchange of new shares in
  the 'premium' fund for those of the 'discount' fund which valued
  the discounted fund shares at less than NAV. The difference
  between the acquisition price of the shares and the NAV of the
  acquired CIF would add to the NAV of the acquiring CIF

Such situations are rare and the majority of closed ended company
CIFs make only one issue of shares, when they are originally formed.
Normally, there is no termination date for a closed ended CIF, but if a
fund is constituted with several different share classes, each of which
has different rights within a common pool of assets, then a

redemption date when the assets are distributed to shareholders will be essential. This is the form of UK 'split capital' investment trusts and US 'dual purpose' funds. Where a redemption date is announced in a fund's prospectus, it will stand unless it is subsequently altered by a majority vote of shareholders.

7.1.1.3   Buy backs

In some legal systems, limited companies may apply for permission to purchase back their own shares from investors. Where this is the case, closed ended funds in the form of limited companies may also apply for such permission. In the case of closed ended CIFs, this would only be proposed if the shares were trading at below their NAV. Usually, buybacks are not in the interests of the CIF Manager (which will have significant representation among the directors) because they reduce the pool of assets on which the Manager earns fees. So such buybacks are usually proposed only when a CIF's shares stand at a large discount to NAV and the CIF is under threat from external proposals for restructuring. In this event the Manager may fear the loss of the management contract that would result from a restructuring sufficiently to propose that the company repurchase some of its shares from investors. Such a move will usually result in a reduction of the discount to NAV at which the shares trade in the market.

While some countries' regulations require that a company buying back its shares may only do so for cancellation, others permit the shares to be held "in treasury" for subsequent resale. This approach is less disadvantageous to fund managers, so is increasing in popularity.

7.1.1.4   Issue of units or participations in other closed ended CIFs

Legal systems sometimes permit the creation of closed ended contractual or trust funds, though these are not common. They issue a limited number of participations or units in a single offer, as with closed ended investment companies, but are not necessarily listed on Stock Exchanges. They often have a fixed term of existence. Some fixed term funds have a fixed portfolio also. If they invest in bonds this enables them to offer guaranteed income, which can be popular with investors. This is the form taken by American 'unit investment trusts'.

These CIFs do not involve prior creation of a company, being formed either by trust or by contract and being licensed or authorised by approval of the Securities Regulator.

7.1.2 Open ended funds

Open ended funds, whether in trust, contractual or limited company form, are subject to specific regulations governing the issue and redemption of shares, units or participations. In the case of corporate funds, some elements of company law may have to be disapplied to enable constant issue and redemption of shares. The form of these regulations varies but there are common features that have been arrived at by trial and error over the seventy or so years that such funds have operated.

7.1.2.1 *The prospectus*

Prospectuses offering open ended funds will, broadly, contain the same information as closed end funds, but will have additional information as required by regulation. This is identified in Chapter 10.

7.1.2.2 *The process of subscription and issues of shares/units*

There are a number of significant factors connected with the issue of share/units in an open ended CIF. Among these are some crucial ones which will be discussed in greater detail later. There are also several variants as to the date at which the transaction is valid and when payment is to be made and the way in which the cash payment is handled and by whom. There is also, in a few countries the ability of the investor to "cool off" – that is to decide not to proceed with the transaction for up to a limited time.

The normal sequence of events in an individual's investment in an open ended CIF in a developed markets (subject to the variations discussed later) runs as follows.

Flow chart of issue procedure

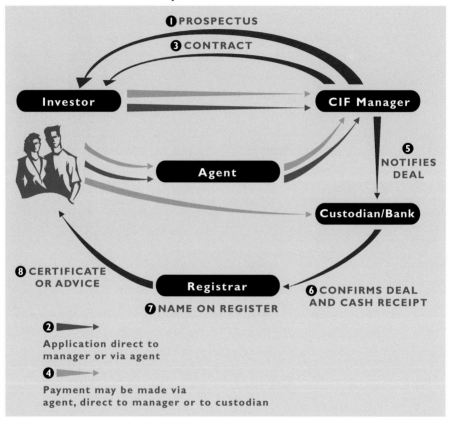

The steps can be explained in greater detail as follows

● the investor completes an application form (Step 2) and sends it to the CIF Manager or to his agent with or without payment (Step 4) in the form of a cheque, voucher or bank transfer. At this stage many managers require that the investor completes a declaration to the effect that he has received, read and understood the prospectus and its terms. The application will include not only the

investor's personal address but may also include instructions
regarding dividends (whether they are to be paid to the investor or
reinvested) and a dividend mandate section, where the investor
may choose to mandate the payment of dividends direct to a bank
account. It is worth noting that even in technologically advanced
countries, physical delivery of a signed application and payment by
post or to an office is needed to open an account though
electronic or phone dealing may be possible subsequently

- the dealing department of the CIF will prepare and issue a
contract note confirming the deal (Step 3); this is sent to the
investor with a request for payment if this has not already been
received. The contract note specifies the date of the deal; the date
of the contract note; the name of the fund; the number and price
of shares or units sold to the investor; any sales charges added to
the price of shares or units; the total amount paid or payable; the
account or client reference number

- the CIF Manager notifies the custodian or trustee of the deal
(Step 5) The investor's payment is recorded and the payment is
passed to the bank or the custodian or trustee (if to the bank, the
bank advises the custodian or trustee of the receipt). The
custodian or trustee confirms receipt of this payment to the CIF
Manager and also to the registrar (Step 6) and authorises the issue
of shares or units. Setting up the system so that the registrar
needs to have confirmation of purchases by investors both from
the CIF Manager and from the custodian or trustee is another
safeguard against fraud

- the registrar enters the investor's details on the CIFs register (Step
7) and issues a certificate of ownership to the investor where a
certificate is required or requested (Step 8). In most systems, it is
the entry on the CIFs register that is definitive proof of ownership;
the certificate is merely evidence of this. In some countries, a
"excerpt from the register" is issued as confirmation. Alterations
to the register must therefore also be subject to strictly controlled
procedures

7

● in developing markets, banks may not have the resources, systems or expertise to act as custodians or trustees and in some instances funds have performed this function themselves, even where there is a legal requirement for an independent depositary. In some systems there is no requirement for an independent registrar, and this function is also undertaken by the CIF Manager. Alternatively, the law may define registration as part of the custodian or trustee's role

Securities Regulators may set time limits within which certain functions must be completed, and maximum period for entry onto the register following receipt of a valid application and the issue of certificates is often specified. Experience shows that even what seems an undemanding target – say six weeks from the date of the deal – can become impossible to meet in practice if a huge flood of purchases overwhelms the capacity of the systems being used or the capacity of authorised security printers. Realistic estimation of an administration system's capacity is therefore essential for the CIF Manager.

7.1.2.3   Redemption procedures

Redemption procedures for open ended CIFs will depend on whether the CIF Manager or the custodian or trustee is acting as principal or agent. Where the custodian or trustee acts as principal and the CIF Manager as agent, the simplest procedure is for the CIF certificates to carry a form of renunciation. By signing this, the investor assigns ownership to the custodian or trustee. The investor sends the renounced certificate to the CIF Manager, who enters the deal on the system, passes the certificate to the registrar for confirmation that the deal is in order and then to the custodian or trustee (who will require confirmation from the registrar) to authorise the release of the cash redemption which the CIF Manager then transfers to the investor. In the case of non-certificated shares/units no certificate exists to be returned, and only the investor's authorisation needs to be received either in written or telephoned or electronic form if the investor has a security PIN number or agreed code word.

If the CIF Manager acts as principal, then ownership of the shares/units passes to the CIF Manager. The manager will still need to check the validity of the redemption with the registrar before making payment but will not need authorisation from the custodian or trustee to make such payment. The manager will pay from its own resources since it will then sell the shares/units to another investor.

Securities Regulators usually set a time limit for the settlement of redemptions. A normal requirement in a daily-valued fund would be for the dispatch of funds to the investor within seven to fourteen days of receipt of a valid redemption.

Practical steps which managers can take to reduce problems with fraudulent redemptions, where no established security procedure exists, include checking that the redeeming investors are who they say they are by contacting the addresses or phone numbers on the register to check that is the holder who is applying for the redemption.

7.1.2.4 Common problems in the issue and redemption process

In newer markets regulators and managers are likely to encounter a number of practical problems in the process of issue and redemption. These mainly concern the timeliness and security of the transaction.

7.1.2.4.a Timing of a transaction

There is sometimes doubt as to the date on which a sale or redemption transaction is actually effected. There can also be delays at the level of a sales agent between the time he receives the order and the time he transmits it to the manager.

The common practice is that a transaction is validated on the date on which the transaction is accepted and the contract or confirmation issued by the manager, in some cases whether or not payment has been received at that time. Alternatively, CIF Managers may empower their accredited agents to accept transactions and issue contracts on their behalf, in which case the effective date will be that on which the agent issues the contract or confirmation.

7

It is important to understand that the new investor will enjoy full ownership rights from the date of the contract, including rights to capital growth, dividends or distributions, special offers, rights issues, mergers and takeovers and any other rights attaching to the ownership of those particular shares/units; this is equivalent to the practice in securities markets generally.

Some jurisdictions allow payment to be made by the new purchaser of shares/units at a later date than that on which the contract is made; others will not permit a contract to be issued until payment has been received. In the event of payment at a date later than the contract date, the NAV calculation of the fund will need to show the amounts due for later payment as debtors as a balancing item, since the shares/units are regarded as having been technically issued at the date of the contract. Once payment is received the amount of the payment will be shown as cash and removed from debtors by a contra entry.

If payment is permitted at a later date, and the investor is in effect buying on credit, non receipt of payment within a period defined in the prospectus will invalidate the deal and it will be cancelled. In no circumstances should managers allow a purchase to be reversed by a redemption until payment has been received for the purchase; otherwise an investor could speculate without risk, simply by redeeming only if the market rose and refusing payment if it fell.

Delays at the level of the sales agent are dealt with as a problem between the agent and his customer, since the manager cannot take any action if he has received no instructions.

7.1.2.4.b Handling payments

The main set of problems in the issue and redemption processes, not unsurprisingly, concerns the payments made by and to the investors.

The flow chart, which describes an issue of shares/units, illustrates three ways a payment for a purchase can be made – to the agent, to the manager and to the custodian or trustee. Of these, clearly the most reliable will be directly to the custodian or trustee, which, as a major bank or other financial institution with a reputation to preserve, could be judged as unlikely to steal cash in transit. But this is sometimes inconvenient in countries in which the banking system is undeveloped and money transmission is hard or expensive. It is therefore customary to allow the payment to be made to the manager, who should then pass it on to the custodian or trustee promptly.

Then there is also the question of redemptions and who should be responsible for paying the investor. While clearly only the custodian or trustee is authorised to draw cash directly from the CIF's bank account, it may be convenient for the custodian or trustee to pass redemption money to the manager for onward transmission to the redeeming investor.

The custom of permitting the manager to deal directly with the investor in receiving and making payments has given rise to a system whereby the manager can keep money received from and due to investors in a specially designated bank account controlled by him. In this way he can calculate daily the net amount due to or from the custodian or trustee depending on whether there is a net surplus of sales or a net surplus of redemptions, when the daily dealings are closed.

All that is then required is for the manager to give documentary evidence of the deals done and to request the custodian or trustee either to authorise a net payment for a surplus of redemptions or to pay to the custodian or trustee any amount of surplus of sales over redemptions. The account is thus balanced to zero at the end of each trading day and movements into and out of the CIF account are controlled and authorised by the custodian or trustee without the need for the custodian or trustee to receive and make individual payments for each transaction.

The greatest risk in cash handling lies at the level of the agent. Sales agents are frequently either incompetent or dishonest and the frequency of loss at this level always causes concern. A 1999 analysis of payments by the UK Investors Compensation Schemes shows the preponderance of settled claims as having been where there has been the involvement of an agent.

There are only really only two ways of dealing with the problem of agents and cash. One is simply not to permit them to handle cash, but for payments only to be made by cheque or bank transfer directly to the fund or fund management company or custodian or trustee and to inform investors never to give cash to agents or make cheques or bank transfers payable to them. The other is to require such agents to be licensed, and to require them to follow the rules for handling of client money set for other similarly licensed financial advisers, stockbrokers, etc. This requires client money to be placed in separate accounts from that of the adviser or agent concerned and may require a custodian to hold such money on clients' behalf.

7.1.2.4.c "Cooling off"

Some jurisdictions permit an investor to cancel a transaction within a certain period of time, if he feels, on reflection, that he has made the wrong decision or if he considers himself to have been the victim of high pressure selling. This is known as a 'cooling off' period. This is not designed as a one way option against the CIF. Forbidding an unpaid sale to be reversed by a redemption if there is a profit, is based on the same principle. The rules usually require full payment for the purchase to have been made and for the investor who cancels to carry the market risk, only being compensated for the cost of the initial charge if any. Such periods are usually between 7 and 14 days.

7.2   The process of registration

Registration can be described as the duty of maintaining the records of existing share/unit holders. There is little difference between the activity of registering the holders of CIFs and other joint stock companies (for a closed ended corporate CIF it is exactly the same); although as a general rule, registers of open ended funds will change more than registers of closed ended funds.

Registers of share/unit holders are essentially lists of names, addresses and the numbers of shares/units held by each registered holder. It is necessary for this to be maintained and kept up to date for a variety of reasons:

- to validate ownership claims – inclusion on a register is the ultimate proof of ownership, unless bearer certificates are issued, in which case physical possession of the bearer (unnamed) certificate is the proof of ownership

- to enable communications to be sent to share/unit holders – reports, notices of meetings and any other information

- to pay dividends or distributions

- to be able to calculate the total number of shares/units in issue, regularly, is crucial for open ended CIFs to attain a correct value per share or unit

Registers are also highly valued by managers as mailing lists for selling their new products or services. This, and the introduction of new technology, has changed the nature of share/unit holder registers in developed markets.

7.2.1   Responsibility for keeping the register of CIF holders

While different jurisdictions may have particular regulations and requirements for keeping a register of share/unit holders, there are two important considerations:

- who is responsible for the maintenance of the register of share/unit holders

- to whom may the actual day to day work be delegated

It is important to distinguish between the organisation which is responsible and the one which does the work. The general principle of delegation within most CIF legislative frameworks is that, while most operational aspects of managing a CIF may be delegated, the organization which is designated by legislation and regulation as responsible for that particular task will remain responsible in law for the proper fulfilment of it, even if it is delegated by contract to another person.

There are several possible variants on the delegation theme, as there are for most administrative functions connected with the management of a CIF:

- the management company is responsible but may delegate to the custodian, if the custodian offers this service, or to a third party which is licensed to carry on this type of business, or, if not required to be licensed, is regarded as competent

- the trustee or custodian is responsible but may delegate back to the management company or to a third party which is licensed to carry on this type of business, if not required to be licensed, is regarded as competent

- registration can only be carried out by an organisation specifically designated to carry on registration business or, increasingly commonly, to a centralised depositary

- in the case of a corporate form of CIF, the directors are responsible for the register of shareholders and for its delegation, usually to a specialist registrar

7.2.2 Registered and certificated systems

It used to be common to issue share/unit certificates, and most registrars, even those which have moved to a non-certificated or dematerialised system, will still issue certificates on request (sometimes only at an additional charge) if they are particularly required. Share certificates are sequentially numbered and contain the name of the holder and the number of shares/units held, the name of the fund and the date of issue; those representing shares/units in an open ended CIF sometimes have a form on the back to enable a holder to renounce his ownership in the event of his redemption.

Certificated systems are cumbersome, requiring the issue of additional certificates if further purchases were made or the reissue of a fresh certificate for a smaller number of shares/units if a partial redemption was made, as a substitute for the certificate which had been returned to complete the redemption. Name changes, mergers, splits or consolidations all require the issue of further or new certificates. Finally share/unit holders would frequently lose or mislay their certificates and thus not be able to complete redemptions without great delay.

There are, however, some advantages to a certificated system, particularly in newer markets. A certificate, although it is not the final proof of ownership (as is a bearer share), physically exists, looks significant and can thus indicate a sense of value to the unsophisticated investor, who is unaccustomed to the concept of dematerialised ownership. Moreover, dematerialised systems need very sophisticated and reliable IT systems; a certificated system does not need such high tech solutions and carries with it its own built in control mechanism.

As the issue of each certificate is recorded and a certificate physically created and issued, and – in the case of open ended funds – destroyed after redemption, duplication of entries or incorrect entries may be less likely, and thus reconciliation of the register total of shares/units in issue with the total of shares/units in issue as per the certificate records may be more reliable and can be carried out manually, albeit with some effort. It may also legitimately be asked whether it is economic for new markets to place a high IT cost on managers, when simpler, albeit more primitive, systems will serve just as well until a critical size is reached.

It is quite common in the case of a certificated system for an indemnity to be required from the investor before a lost certificate can be replaced. This protects the registrar from the possibility that, at some time in the future, the original certificate will be found and a double redemption occur on both the original and on the new certificate.

7.2.3   Dematerialised systems

More modern registration systems, which rely almost entirely on electronic resources, bring many advantages. There is no need to issue certificates as such; share/unit holders will simply receive a "statement of account" which shows the record of their holding. Such a statement can carry a great deal more information than a certificate, such as a history of transactions, with numbers, dates and prices, and payment or reinvestment of dividends, and an up to date value of the total holding at current market prices. There will thus be no need to issue balancing certificates for partial redemptions, or new certificates in the event of name changes, mergers etc. A dematerialised system, in effect, permits the use of an open ended CIF almost like a bank account. In fact, money market CIFs are virtually bank accounts, the development of which would have been impossible in a fully certificated environment.

Dematerialised systems also permit much more effective use of the register as a marketing tool. It is now common to keep registers by individual client names on a single relational database, rather than CIF by CIF (refer Chapter 10). Formerly it used to be difficult to deduplicate a share/unit holder's interest if he held shares/units in more than one fund; as a result, for example, a holder of six different CIFs within the same management group would receive six general promotional mailings. This was wasteful for the management company and irritating for the client. By creating "client facing" systems, it is now possible to send an individual a unified statement of all his interests within one management group, and to keep track of his activity. This, in theory, leads to more targeted and effective marketing.

Dematerialised systems also bring greater convenience to the active investor. Once an account is established, for which even in the most sophisticated markets, the US for example, a physically signed piece of paper is required, an investor may buy and redeem, switch to a different fund or change standing instructions by telephone or on the Internet, using appropriate PIN numbers or security codes.

Payments for redemptions can be dealt with, either by sending out a cheque, a solution which allows for the possibility of fraud or theft, or by electronic transfer to a specifically designated bank account, for which transaction the investor accepts liability in the event that he changes his banking arrangements without notifying the CIF Manager.

7.2.4 Legal aspects of registration and transfer of securities

Ownership rights of holders of securities and transfer of ownership will be subject to a wide variety of different legislative requirements, depending on the country and the type of legal system that it has. Whatever the legal requirements are, there are certain technical and practical matters which any registrar will need to address:

- changes of name of registered holders, by marriage or legal action

- deaths and probate

- changes of address

- shares/units pledged as security by their holders

- share/unit holders who are lost

- lost certificates if certificated

Since it is not the intention of this manual to be a specialist guide to securities ownership and transfer procedures, these are noted for completeness.

7.3 Handling dividends, distributions, accumulation and reinvestment

For simplicity this section refers to both dividends issued by corporate CIFs to holders, and distributions by trust and contractual funds to holders as 'dividends'. The principles of accounting for capital and income are dealt with in detail in Chapter 13 and their taxation is addressed in Chapter 12. This section discusses the options for making payments of dividends, whatever their composition or source.

7.3.1 Frequency of payment

The frequency with which dividends are paid will be determined by the type of CIF which is paying them. CIFs whose advertised purpose is to pay a high income, often try to pay dividends more frequently than those whose primary aim is capital growth. Some high income CIFs pay dividends monthly to coincide with a typical investor's expenditure cycle, while others pay quarterly or less frequently. The frequency of payment may also be determined by the efficiency and cost of making frequent small payments; in countries without a highly developed banking system such payments are expensive or impossible to make.

7.3.2 Accumulation or distribution

At the other end of the spectrum from CIFs which pay frequent dividends are those which do not pay out dividends at all, but rather reinvest all income. This is reflected in an increasing share/unit price as the income is compounded over time. There are frequently tax reasons for this, since some countries seek to encourage saving through CIFs in securities markets by granting tax privileges to them only if income is not paid out, or by taxing dividends if they are paid out but not if they are reinvested. In such cases investors who need to take an income may do so by redeeming shares/units on a regular basis; some CIF Managers offer automatic facilities for this.

Under certain tax regimes, the US for example, open ended funds are required by law to distribute all their income as a dividend to shareholders as an anti-avoidance provision; the same principle applies to closed ended CIFs in the UK.

In the case of some open ended CIFs under certain types of taxation regime, it may be effective for the CIFs to distribute dividends in the form of additional shares (scrip dividend).

7.3.4   Dividend reinvestment

Where dividends are paid out, particularly if they are paid out gross (untaxed) and only taxed in the hands of individual investors at their appropriate rate (in the US for example) CIF Managers offer a facility to reinvest dividends by the purchase of more shares/units. This facility is particularly useful and relevant if the shares/units of the CIF are held in a tax free environment like a pension plan or other tax privileged savings plan. The effect of this is to increase steadily the number of shares/units held over time as dividends are reinvested at each dividend date in more shares/units.

7.3.5   Mandating dividends

Not all investors wish to receive their dividend directly by cheque. Most find it convenient for dividends to be paid directly into a designated bank account and only to receive notification at the time of payment. CIF Managers also prefer to pay dividends this way, since it is much cheaper to transfer money in bulk than to generate and send out individual cheques. This will apply only in countries with developed banking systems.

7.3.6   Bearer shares

The exception to the general rules about payment of dividends will be bearer shares, which carry coupons which need to be cut and presented to a paying agent for payment. Most banks will offer the facility of keeping a client's bearer shares and undertaking dividend collection on their behalf. Bearer shares of CIFs are becoming less and less common. If they exist, their existence is only technical, and the bearer shares are immobilised in the vault of a bank, and what is in effect a register of owners kept in dematerialised form.

7.3.7   Entitlement to dividends and payment

Most CIFs operate a system similar to that used in securities markets generally. Ownership rights start at the date on which the contract is made, and a new purchaser is thus entitled to receive any dividends declared after that date. Immediately after the declaration of the dividend the shares/units will be priced ex dividend (xd), that is to say that any new purchasers of shares/units on or after the date that the shares/unit are quoted "xd" will not be entitled to receive the recently declared dividend but will be entitled to the next one. The payment date, on which cheques will be sent out or bank transfers made, will be some days or weeks later than the xd date.

When shares/units are quoted xd, the share/unit price will decrease by the amount of the dividend per share/unit which has been declared to reflect the fact that a new purchaser will not receive it.

The management of investments

This Chapter deals with investment management issues as they affect CIFs. Investment management is the process of investing the money collected from investors in line with the strategic objective which has been stated in the prospectus and of selecting individual investments which fit that strategy

The Chapter does not set out to explain investment management methods in detail. These include:

- economic analysis to establish the general political and economic background against which markets operate

- the established ways of analysing companies and the securities that they issue and government bonds

- mathematical techniques for the control of risk (sometimes called modern portfolio theory) and of determining ideal portfolio construction

These subjects are, of course, vital and lie at the heart of what investors expect a CIF management to do for them. Inevitably, since most asset management companies manage portfolios other than CIFs, and very few manage only CIFs, some reference is made to other types of portfolio management. The subjects of investment analysis and portfolio management are too extensive to be dealt with in this book, whose main purpose is to explain broadly the concepts of management of a CIF business. There is, in any case, an extensive academic and practical literature on the subject, which can give anyone interested a far more detailed account of the subject than could be given in one chapter of this book.

What this chapter does, therefore, is to give an account of (numbers refer to sections of this chapter):

8.1 the implications of different investment styles

8.2 the organisation and management of the investment department and its relationship with other departments such as marketing and administration

8.3 the specific investment management needs and constraints which are dictated by CIFs which have different structures and objectives

8.4 the way in which the investment process is defined, managed and controlled

8.5 the possibility of conflicts of interest and abuses and ways of identifying and eliminating them

8.6 settlement and investment accounting

8.1 Different investment styles

What are termed "investment styles" are ways of describing different approaches to the process of selecting and managing investments. All have the same ultimate objective – to maximise returns in a way that is consistent with minimising the risk of failure to achieve a targeted return – but the methods which the advocates of each approach or style use to try to achieve that objective can be quite different.

Advocates of the different styles are, like any group which owes allegiance to a belief which is deeply held but cannot be proved, often adamant that their method is superior to all others.

The two major systems which now stand in opposition to each other are generically called "active" and "passive". Of these the active approach is the oldest established (or old fashioned according to advocates of the passive style), while the passive is a more recent introduction, being based on more quantitative techniques (or new fangled as the traditionalists would have it). However, as will be shown later, the two systems are not completely incompatible and can be used in conjunction with one another in various useful ways.

8.1.1 Active management

Active management describes a style which attempts to use various kinds of economic data – GDP growth, inflation, government finances, interest rates, currencies and corporate profits – to determine the likely future, general trend of different classes of asset within securities markets (used hereafter to cover markets in government, municipal and corporate bonds and equities of different types). The conclusion of this kind of analysis, sometimes called "top down", will be to enable an investment manager to position the portfolio he manages according to the future price action of different classes of asset indicated by the forecasts. The most clear-cut decision (but not in any way the simplest) is whether the portfolio is to be invested in securities markets or not at all, given that the alternative to investment in securities is to hold the money on deposit at a credit institution where it will earn interest but where the capital (unless the credit institution becomes insolvent) will remain intact and unchanged.

8.1.1.1 *Asset allocation*

In fact the process of "asset allocation", whereby decisions are taken broadly to divide the portfolio between different asset classes, is more complex than that, given that few managers would wish to commit themselves to such a black and white decision as "all in" or "all out", since the penalty for making the wrong bet would be considerable. Thus active managers, who have the choice between bonds, cash or equities, will try to construct their portfolios in such a way as to maximise returns and minimise risk, by including a constantly shifting mix of several different asset classes.

However not all active managers have the choice of running a "balanced" portfolio, which contains bonds, cash and equities, given that structure of portfolios of CIFs is determined by the objective set in the prospectus, which is the basis on which investors have invested.

8

Some of these stated objectives may require investment in equities only, either domestic or foreign, others in bonds, and still others in short term money market instruments. Many CIFs have the specific objective of investment abroad, either in any market outside the domestic one, in which the CIF is sold, or in particular regions – Europe or Asia for instance – or in specific individual countries. Other portfolios have to meet guarantees, to pay pensions at a certain date or to make payments on the death of a person who has a contract of life assurance, and are therefore constrained by the particular needs imposed by the guarantees.

8.1.1.2   Security or stock selection

The second part of active management, once a general allocation of available money between different broad asset classes has been made, is the process of choosing which specific bonds or which particular shares to buy.

In the case of bonds, the type of issuer and the credit rating of that issuer will to a large extent determine the bonds which will be bought. The asset allocation process, taking account of the promises made in that part of the prospectus which sets investment objectives, will already have determined whether only bonds of the highest quality may be included or whether lower quality bonds may be included. There exists in developed markets a comprehensive system of ratings calculated by such organisations as Standard & Poors and Moody's which enable relative risk of bonds to be assessed based on the credit ratings of their issuers. This enables the total universe of thousands of different bonds to be categorised fairly tidily, for the purpose of selecting the most suitable in order to meet the portfolio objective. Other factors, such as the size and liquidity of the issue and its availability at the time of the purchase, will also play their part. Having said that, the selection process will ultimately depend on an element of subjectivity: the personal preferences of the investment manager, based on his experience, knowledge and skill.

In the case of equities, the method of categorising a much less homogeneous and more variable universe is less clear. The selection of which shares to buy will depend to a much greater extent on the skill of the investment manager, based on his experience, the analysis of current and future profitability and his judgement as to others' opinions and expectations of future value. It is largely in this area where quantitative techniques, often broadly described as "modern portfolio theory", have made the greatest inroads.

8.1.2   Passive management and quantitative techniques

Modern portfolio theory differentiates between systemic and specific risk. Systemic risk is that which describes the uncertainty inherent in large and uncontrollable political and economic events, changes in exchange rates, interest rates and movements of markets measured by broad indices.

Specific risk relates to the risk inherent in the likely volatility of the price of a specific asset against other assets or against some sort of average of all assets of the same class.

To say that systemic risk is uncontrollable is not to imply that its impact on a given portfolio cannot be minimised or even eliminated. This is achieved by the use of derivatives, which can be used to "insure" a portfolio against unforeseen movements of currencies, interest rates and equity indices. The techniques for portfolio insurance can be usefully employed (and are) by active managers, who wish to guard or hedge against systemic risk, but who wish to deal with specific risk, inherent in price movements of individual shares, using classical analysis coupled with their skill and judgement

It is here that the two techniques come into conflict. Modern portfolio theorists argue that specific risk is quickly reduced towards zero as a portfolio becomes more and more diversified, and that, at the point where a portfolio exactly replicates an index (such as the American S&P 500 or the British FTSE 100, both of which aim to portray the overall movements of a market, using the prices of 500 and 100 shares respectively) it has achieved the maximum desirable

8

degree of diversification and will, obviously, then perform exactly in line with that index, leaving that portfolio exposed only to systemic risk. The theorists go on to argue that, since, in developed markets, all available information about companies is in the public domain, it will be impossible to beat the index by identifying anomalous or irregular valuations of individual shares.

Therefore the least risky position is to create what is called an "index fund" whose portfolio precisely replicates the index. This can either be achieved by buying shares in each company in proportion to its weighting in the index, or it can be achieved synthetically by the use of index futures. In either case the precise methodology is subject to a number of esoteric disagreements, but the net outcome is generally understood to be a portfolio which will perform in line with the chosen index.

Index funds have encountered several problems in practice:

● it is uneconomic to run small indexed funds; a fund which tracked the S&P 500 would need to have 500 holdings of varying sizes, and readjusting those holdings to fit the changing profile of the index components would require buying or selling tiny amounts of shares if the fund was small, thus incurring disproportionately high transaction costs

● it may sometimes be impossible to replicate the index in a way which complies with regulatory restrictions on CIF portfolios; this is particularly acute in emerging markets, in which a major company may represent 25% of the index or more, but it is not unknown in major markets in an era of mega mergers, where some companies may represent more than 10% of certain indices

● the process of indexation drives markets in directions which are not entirely rational; in the case of indices (most) which are weighted for the size of the market capitalisation of individual companies and where a smaller percentage of the capitalisation represents the "float" (available to buy, where a large holder, perhaps a government may, own 50%+) index funds are forced to behave as if all the shares were freely marketable, with the result that prices of those shares are artificially inflated

● indices of certain countries, whose major listed companies are multinational, do not represent the economy of that country, and thus an attempt to use an index to synthesise exposure to that economy may be false – the UK is a good example of this, since many of the constituents of the FTSE 100 are, in effect, foreign companies domiciled or listed in the UK, or UK companies the majority of whose business is abroad

An index fund, which has eliminated specific risk, can also be hedged in the same way as an actively managed fund against the impact of systemic risk.

8.1.3   Technical or chart analysis

It is necessary to mention one other investment style which differs from both the others described above. This is generally known as "technical" or "chart" analysis. Its advocates believe that, by constructing a price history of a share, bond, index, currency or commodity and showing this in a variety of graphic ways, it is possible to make predictions about likely future price movements based on historical patterns of price behaviour. Its most fervent advocates maintain that they do not even need to know what the item or asset, whose price history is represented by the chart, is, in order to be able to draw conclusions about the likely future course of the price.

As with other forms of investment style, it is possible to use charts alone as a tool for portfolio management, but it is not necessary to do so, since charts can be most useful in conjunction with more active management or fundamental analysis. Many managers make extensive use of them in this way. Many believe that charts are most useful as a tool for looking at the shares of smaller companies, whose shares are less liquid and the market in them, as a result, more imperfect; charts may well reflect better unusual movements in share prices driven by people with special knowledge. A series of charts which track the declared dealings of directors of listed companies seems to bear out this view.

This Chapter does not attempt here to describe all the many different ways of creating and reading charts, but a typical chart which illustrates one of the methodologies is shown below.

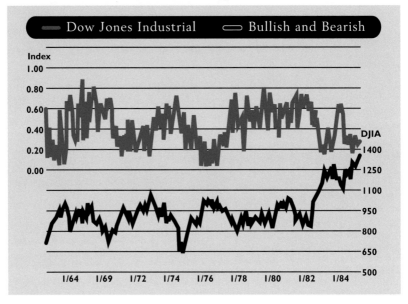

Not all the investment styles or methodologies can be used for managing any kind of investment portfolio. For example, it would be difficult to synthesise an indexed fund of smaller companies using derivatives, since the appropriate instruments do not exist, just as it is hard to hedge the currencies of certain emerging markets for the same reason. The next chart gives an idea of how feasible it would be to apply a variety of active, passive or technical solutions to various types of portfolio – this is illustrative only and based on our view:

How the different techniques can be applied

	Active			Systemic risk control	Purely passive	
	Top down	Bottom up	Technical		Synthetic	Indexed
Equity						
Domestic						
Blue chip	✪	✪✪✪	✪✪	✪✪✪	✪✪✪	✪✪✪
Smaller companies		✪✪✪		✪		✪
Sector	✪✪✪	✪		✪	✪✪	
International						
General	✪✪✪	✪✪✪	✪✪	✪✪✪	✪✪✪	✪✪✪
Single country – blue chip		✪✪✪	✪✪	✪✪✪	✪✪✪	✪✪✪
Single country – smaller companies		✪✪✪		✪		
Sector	✪✪✪	✪✪		✪	✪	
Emerging markets						
General	✪✪✪	✪✪✪	✪✪	✪✪		
Single country		✪✪✪				

✪✪✪ Possible and commonly in use   ✪ Perhaps
✪✪ Possibly   No Star Practically difficult or impossible

8.2 Organisation and management of the investment department

There is no standard way an investment department should be organised, structured and managed. There may be many variants depending on the regulatory environment, the type, scope and size of the funds managed, and the particular style or investment approach that the management company has chosen to follow.

Despite this, any investment department will have certain commonly recognisable components or sections. The differences from firm to firm will depend on how the components are assembled and controlled, the reporting relationships and sometimes whether certain components are included at all.

8.2.1 Different parts of an investment department

Some of the most commonly recognised elements in the structure of an investment department are given below. Most of these elements will be unnecessary if the firm's investment style is "passive" or "indexed". In these cases, different specialist skills will need to be applied (see later).

Organisation of an investment department

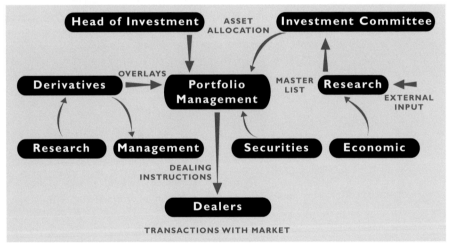

8.2.1.1 Economic analysis

All financial markets operate within the broad context of national and, increasingly, international economies. Economic growth, currencies, interest rate policy, money supply, inflation and taxation all have a greater or lesser influence on government budgets, corporate profits, dividends and interest rates, the trend of financial markets generally and on individual bond and share prices.

The task of an economics department will be to analyse and interpret the mass of statistics which are available and to draw conclusions about likely future impact of changing economic circumstances on world markets generally, on the markets of individual countries, on different classes of asset and on particular sectors within those classes.

This kind of analysis, often called "top down", can help investment managers, who are responsible for the management of individual portfolios, to determine broad asset allocation. The phrase "asset allocation" is used to describe the decision process from which the overall structure of any portfolio will be determined. At its simplest it can describe the decision to be invested in securities or not. More sophisticated versions can help to give guidance as to:

● proportions of the portfolio to be divided between bonds, equities and cash

● in the case of an international portfolio the proportions allocated for investment in different countries and the proportions allocated to bonds, equities and cash in each country

● in the case of certain types of portfolio the allocation of investments between different equity sectors or bond categories

The asset allocation may be decided by an investment committee and made compulsory for all individual managers to follow or used only as a guideline. International investment (outside the base currency of the client) is subject to the risk of currency fluctuations as well as those of the markets themselves; thus a view from the economics department on the relative future movements of currencies against one another will also be factored in, and, if necessary hedged out (neutralised) using derivatives.

8.2.1.2 Research

Research into individual companies or sectors or into the credit ratings of bonds issued by governments or corporations is usually carried on separately from the economic research described in the section above. The output of the research department will be a list of stocks or bonds whose characteristics meet the firm's criteria or style and which can be rated, according to their relative current value and estimated future prospects, as "buys", "holds" or "sells".

The research department may draw on a wide range of sources for its work; these include:

- company reports and other announcements or information to shareholders

- material produced and published by broker/dealers, who have their own research departments

- material from independent research firms, which is sold to subscribers

- visits to individual companies and discussions with their senior management

- a wide range of electronic databases which provide historic comparative data on profits, earnings, dividends and prices of equities and of yields of fixed income securities and the ratings of their issuers

Larger firms may subdivide their research effort into regions (Europe, Asia, etc), into individual countries or into sectors (in an increasingly global market place these sectors – electronics and IT, telecoms, pharmaceuticals etc, may be international in their scope, comparing companies across the globe).

Smaller firms will often rely to a greater extent on outside research either from brokers or independent specialists, or combine research and portfolio management responsibilities in the same people.

The list of stocks or bonds which are recommended for purchase, sale or holding may be compiled into what is sometimes termed a "master list" which individual portfolio managers are either obliged or recommended to follow.

This kind of analysis is often called "bottom up".

8.2.1.3 Portfolio management

Portfolio managers are the individuals designated to be decision makers in the management of specific portfolios. Individuals may often manage more than one portfolio, of which some may be those of CIFs and others of pension or insurance funds or even private individuals, or parts of larger portfolios, particularly those which invest in a wide range of different types of asset and across the world. In the case of large portfolios, for example, one person may be responsible for domestic equities and others for equities of other regions, while a different person may be responsible for the fixed income portion.

The widespread use of technology – which can concentrate many sources of information and data onto a single screen on the desk of a portfolio manager, enabling him to view several different portfolios for which he is responsible in real time, even if portfolio activity is being carried out in different time zones, and to run several separate portfolios as if they were one, by allocating purchases and sales proportionately to each according to its size – enables increasing economies of scale to be achieved.

It is at the point of portfolio management and decision making that all the techniques of managing a portfolio converge – top down, bottom up and hedging, as illustrated below.

Top down/bottom up

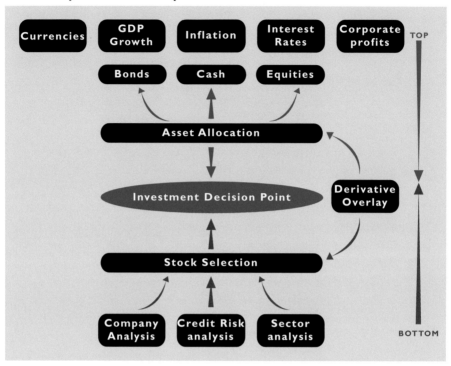

Portfolio managers need to have regard to several aspects of the management of the portfolios under their management, apart from simply selecting the best securities to buy and sell. They will need to have regard to:

- the portfolio objectives as laid down in the prospectus or management agreement, and any special instructions or exclusions (for example certain clients wish to exclude investment in tobacco in the case of funds managed for medical charities or in armaments in the case of funds managed for organisations which are pacifists, such as Quakers, or, in the case of funds targeted at clients who are Muslims, alcohol and other types of activity which that religion forbids)

- alignment of the portfolio with internal asset allocation instructions or guidelines and with master lists of securities

- compliance with investment limitations laid down by laws and regulations
  - which do not permit more than a defined percentage of the portfolio to be invested in the securities of any one issuer or more than a defined percentage of the securities issued by any issuer to be held
  - which exclude investment in unlisted securities absolutely, or limit holdings to a certain percentage of the portfolio
  - which exclude or limit investment in the shares or units of CIFs

- ensuring that the fund does not invest more than the cash it has available, which applies particularly to open ended CIFs

- ensuring that transactions are done with approved brokers, and that "soft" commission arrangements are honoured (this may not be necessary if all dealing is carried out through central dealers)

- ensuring proper communication and liaison with that part of the "back office" which is responsible for portfolio administration and valuation administration

In addition to the day to day responsibilities for management, administration and compliance listed above, a portfolio manager will also be expected to write reports on the management of the portfolio of CIFs as often as the law or particular contractual arrangements requires these should be presented to clients. In the case of other institutional clients, such as pension funds, the portfolio manager may also be required to attend a meeting with trustees or other clients to answer questions or justify decisions.

Portfolio managers' time is also in demand from marketing and sales departments, particularly when units or shares of CIFs are sold through professional intermediaries, such as financial planners or direct sales forces. Such professional sales outlets welcome the opportunity of meeting the fund manager in person and having the opportunity to ask questions about his views on the current portfolio or the outlook for the market.

8.2.1.4 Derivative research and management

During the late 80s and 90s, the use of derivatives in portfolio management has expanded enormously. Derivatives, both futures and traded options, have a large part to play in hedging risk or, in the case of particular funds, leveraging exposure to a certain sector, asset or currency. Thus the highly numerate and computer literate specialists, who are expert in these fields, have gained in influence within many asset management companies. The field of derivatives is complex and ever changing, and it is not within the scope of this chapter to give a full account of all the possible uses of them in portfolio management. But it may be worth defining the two main ways in which they can be used in the context of CIFs, first noting that legislation and regulation in most countries forbids publicly distributed CIFs (unless they are in a special category of leveraged funds) from using derivatives for purposes other than reducing or containing risk. However privately distributed "hedge" funds will almost certainly use derivatives in a much more aggressive way.

The accepted uses for risk reduction are in the fields of:

- portfolio protection

- anticipatory hedging

- cash flow management

- asset allocation

- portfolio insurance

- income enhancement

In practical terms their uses are thus:

● to reduce or eliminate systemic risk by limiting the fund's overall exposure to unexpected currency, interest rate or market fluctuations

● to reduce the fund's exposure to unexpected falls in price of securities which the fund holds by the use of options

● to increase the fund's income by writing options against long term positions

● to protect against the risk of a high cash position in the event of an unexpected market rise

● to synthesise the action of a market, either to achieve an indexed position or to fulfil guarantees in the case of limited life guarantee funds

● to synthesise a temporary change in asset allocation, without buying or selling actual underlying securities

The derivatives department usually acts independently in the case of management of fully synthetic funds (ie funds which do not invest in securities but use only derivatives to replicate the performance of individual securities or indices) or in the case of guarantee funds which are able to provide guarantees of returns or of minimum returns for specific future periods using portfolios of cash, bonds and derivatives.

Often it will also provide an overlay to an existing managed portfolio of securities in a way designed to limit or reduce risk. In this case the decision to hedge will frequently be one of the decisions taken by an investment committee.

In the case of hedge funds, derivatives will be extensively used to concentrate, diversify and manage risk in a whole range of instruments from currencies and commodities to equities and precious metals. Hedge funds are growing in popularity since achieving significantly differentiated performance is becoming harder, as indexing, actual or closet, becomes more and more popular. Many wealthier investors are thus seeking out-performance of the norms with a small part of their wealth, and are prepared to take the sometimes real risk of losing their whole investment.

8.2.1.5 Dealing

The process of actually transacting business in securities for CIFs or other types of portfolio managed for clients of asset management businesses is usually a task allocated to specialists often known as dealers or traders. These people are at the front line between the asset management company and the market. Their skills are not expected to be in analysis or security selection but in the procedures of buying and selling in the market, and they can thus add value to the whole investment process by:

- ensuring that deals are done at the best prices

- negotiating the purchase or sale of larger blocks in the market without excessively disturbing the market equilibrium

- selecting the broker or other means of transacting most appropriate to the nature of the transaction

- ensuring that the lowest transaction costs are paid

Now that there are an increasing number of ways of transacting business other than on the traditional "Stock Exchange", and since commissions are now negotiable in almost all markets (fixed commissions disappeared in the US in the mid-1970s and in the UK in the late 1980s), where previously dealers were to a great extent reliant on brokers, the life of a dealer has become more complicated. Many electronic trading systems now permit asset management companies to circumvent the broker and deal directly with a market maker or each other.

The life of dealers has also become more complex since they often have an important role in compliance. Ensuring that individual employees of an asset management company do not, in their personal dealings, transgress either the rules for personal dealing laid down by the regulator or any internal norms for individual dealings, has become an important function of central dealers, given that most internal rules require personal dealings to be channelled through central dealers.

8.3   Needs and constraints imposed by different types of fund and different styles

In organising and managing an investment department, there are considerations which derive from the type of funds likely to be managed, the spread of different types of assets which will be included and the investment style which the organisation adopts.

For example, asset management companies which intend to offer only passive, indexed products will not need to build the expensive and elaborate economic research and investment analytical facilities which active managers may require. They may also not need to employ classically defined portfolio managers, since the process of replicating an index lends itself to being run on a computer programme. They may even decide to contract out the actual investment process to an outside specialist, as may be done in the case of active managers too (refer section 14.5.3.3.a).

In the case of active managers or those managers which offer different styles of management including passive, some of the most important decisions are those identified below.

8.3.1   Controlled or free

Given the asset allocation process and the process of creating a master list described in described in section 8.2.1.2 above the management of an asset management company has the choice:

● either requiring that all portfolio managers follow the asset allocation process and the specific guidelines laid down by the investment committee and that they change their portfolio weightings as the asset allocation changes from time to time and that they should choose only those securities which have been through the screening process in the research department and which are thus on the master list

- or allowing individual portfolio managers freedom to make their own asset allocations and to select their own securities based on any method they care to use

The advantage of the former is that the performance of the funds managed will tend to be relatively predictable and there will be no violent or unexpected deviations from a central set of returns. Its disadvantage is that the process will be very similar to that adopted by competitors and that the conclusions reached will tend towards a consensual average; this can become what is known as "closet indexing". As a result the returns of all funds of a similar type will tend to cluster round the mean, and there will be no way for the marketing department to differentiate the firm from most others in the market place.

Allowing individual portfolio managers to have their freedom is much riskier from a corporate point of view. It may give spectacular results if the individual is able through his own flair to create significant out-performance of competitors; this in turn will attract new investors and funds managed may grow rapidly as the name of the "star" is publicised. Peter Lynch who managed the Fidelity Magellan Fund for many years is an example of this style of management, while, in a different way, so is Warren Buffet of Berkshire Hathaway. But this style also has risks. Lynchs and Buffets are rare and, in seeking to emulate them, individual portfolio managers are just as likely to make a mess of their portfolios with attendant bad publicity for the firm as the fund falls to the bottom of the performance league.

Of course no decisions in investment management are either black or white. The degree of freedom given to or control exercised over portfolio managers will be shaded somewhere between total freedom and absolute control. Nonetheless the considerations discussed above will govern where in the spectrum they will be permitted to operate. In general large asset management businesses will tend towards the control end of the scale while small entrepreneurial firms will adopt a freer style in the hope that outstanding results will bring them to the attention of the market.

8.3.2   Different clients and different approaches

Most large asset managers will have and offer the capability of managing portfolios for a wide range of different types of client, including CIFs, pension funds, insurance companies, private clients, corporate treasurers, charities and even governments; the clients may be based in countries all over the world.

Only the very largest asset managers would be able to manage any kind of fund for any type of client in any part of the world. Medium sized managers will need to decide on their core speciality. This very often divides between:

8.3.2.1   *The retail market*

This is the market which is the main subject of this book, for which collective investment funds are generally the most suitable and commonly used vehicle. As explained elsewhere, CIFs can be sold to individuals under a number of different guises, apart from direct purchase – these include pension and insurance schemes and as components in various tax favoured vehicles, designed to stimulate savings. The investment management objectives and methods applied to the management of collective investment schemes have their own peculiarities, notably, as shown in the next section, in respect of cash inflows and outflows.

Also taxation considerations in different countries may govern such matters as:

● the value of generating and paying high dividends from equity or bond funds

- the problem of short and long term capital gains and the need to try to balance gains and losses in any given period

CIFs are usually managed in an active way, and their managers strive for top performance in the league tables which are published regularly in the media. Success, which results in a fund being top or in the "top ten" of a table of its competitors over 3, 6 or 12 months, can have a dramatically positive impact on sales, however irrational it may be to judge a fund's results over short time periods. However CIFs which are actively managed are coming under increasing pressure from passively managed index funds, which are cheaper to manage, thus being able to pass this on in lower charges to investors, and are also in many periods out-performing actively managed funds, to the embarrassment of the latter's managers.

Thus the qualities required of those who act as investment managers of CIFs and the disciplines imposed on them are somewhat different from those which are required by managers of institutional funds.

Administration of retail-oriented CIFs is also much more expensive and complex than that of institutional portfolios.

8.3.2.2 The institutional market

The market for institutional asset management is different to the extent that, whereas managing CIFs for retail investors involves collecting and pooling thousands of small subscriptions, managing money for large institutions such as pension or insurance funds will involve a much more complex process of marketing, presenting and persuasion of professional managers or trustees, who are often advised by specialised firms of actuarial or investment consultants. If successful, the sums involved in a single client portfolio can be much larger, many tens or even hundreds of millions of dollars, and thus economies of scale in management and administration can be achieved.

Investment returns and performance against competition is assessed in much more detail and much more rigorously by institutional clients than retail clients. However the periods over which the judgement will be made are longer, and the expectations of the investment managers can be more realistic. Whereas retail investors expect high dividends and high capital gains all the time, those responsible for institutions accept that markets fluctuate and thus expect only relative out performance of a benchmark (an index for instance) or the competitors (better than the median for example). The investment approach required to deliver what the clients expect is rather more systematic than that for CIFs; superstars are not generally welcomed in this part of the investment department, whereas, in the retail side, they can be good for sales, if not only is their performance notable but also the individuals are articulate and presentable and prepared to be quoted in the media.

While institutional money may arrive in large tranches, it may also depart in equally large amounts; periods of poor or substandard performance by asset managers who specialise in the management of institutional funds can result in a haemorrhage of business, since institutions and trustees, and the specialists who advise them, are quicker to spot and act to solve a perceived problem than the less informed retail investor. Retail business, therefore, is often regarded as more stable than institutional, since a retail asset managers may be able to survive two to three years of bad results without being too damaged, whereas an asset manager whose business is predominantly institutional could not.

Managing funds for foreign investors requires additional skills. Not only is the base currency in which they expect returns to be calculated perhaps different from that in which the investment manager habitually works, but also he will have to take account of accounting, taxation, linguistic and cultural factors.

8.3.3   Dividing portfolio responsibility

It may be beyond the capacity of a single individual to manage portfolios which are large and complex and which cover several different asset classes in several different countries. In these cases an investment department may decide to divide the responsibility for

8

the portfolio between several different specialists, while leaving overall control in the hands of one portfolio manager. While this makes practical sense, it can give rise to problems of co-ordination unless it is carefully controlled. Among the common problems are:

- problems of co-ordination between different parts of the world (if regional investment teams are to be based in the region in which they are to invest); despite modern communications technology, time zones and human inertia can give rise to long distance misunderstandings

- conflict between individual specialists when, as a result of changing asset allocation, one person's portion is increased and another's reduced; specialists, particularly country specialists tend to believe that their asset class, country or region is "the best" and become blind to its failings – a classic case of this was seen in the case of the Japanese bubble in the 1980s; this conflict will tend to slow the pace at which asset allocation is changed, leaving a portfolio overexposed to a declining region or asset class

- short term cash problems, as one segment of the portfolio is increasing as another is decreasing its investment proportion; since sales and purchases cannot necessarily move perfectly in unison, investment in excess of funds available may result for a short period of time

The capacity to cover a particular asset class or region does not necessarily have to be maintained within the investment department of a single asset management company. It is quite usual for asset managers to contract out certain specialist tasks to other asset managers. This might aggravate the problems outlined in the previous section, since an outside supplier will fight hard to keep his "slice", and co-ordination may prove problematic.

Quite often, in the case that a relatively modest sized investment is to be made, use is made of a specialist CIF, in which the fund becomes an investor. Indeed for funds which specialise in smaller or emerging markets, institutional investors which are using their investment in such a fund as a component within a larger international portfolio, are an important source of business.

8.3.4   Cash flow and liquidity constraints

One of the characteristics of CIFs, particularly of the predominant open ended variety, is the way in which money flows in and out as a result of periods of strong sales or high redemptions. This may impose an unusual range of constraints on the investment manager, who will, in addition to the many other elements he must keep an eye on, have to keep himself informed about actual and potential sales and redemption trends, which may significantly influence the amount of cash he has to invest (or not to invest). While regular inflows are a feature of pension funds and insurance funds, outflows (apart from a withdrawal of a whole portfolio from management) are not.

Strong positive cash inflow is not usually a problem if the fund's objectives are to invest in leading stocks or liquid and tradable bond issues in major markets. Such markets offer ample capacity to absorb substantial amounts of money. But there have been occasions on which funds which may have become very popular have had to close to new subscriptions, if the investment manager believes that he may be swamped by the new money to the detriment of performance for existing investors. This is one of the occasions when the natural desire of any management company, which offers CIFs for sale to expand funds under management as quickly as possible, is tempered by investment prudence. In the case of CIFs which specialise in investment in small companies or emerging markets, in which liquidity is a constraint, temporary closure of a fund for new subscriptions may be a more common occurrence.

A much more common problem faced by managers of CIFs is that of redemptions, if these are large and continuous and not matched by new sales. The result is a fund suffering a continuous drain on its cash reserves, and the investment manager will have to start selling investments in order to allow the fund to pay out departing investors. This may prove problematic in markets which are illiquid. Not only may it become increasingly hard to raise cash but difficult to make sales at reasonable prices; the effect of this may be to dilute ongoing holders (see section 6.1.2).

What every fund manager and regulator dreads is a "run" on a fund. Just as a sudden surge of depositors wishing to withdraw their money from a bank can quickly result in the insolvency of the bank, so a surge of investors who wish to redeem, can cause tremendous problems for an open ended fund. Most regulatory regimes allow for a moratorium to be declared by a fund which finds itself unexpectedly in this position.

One of the ways of coping with the problems of illiquidity is through the issue of funds which can be described as semi-closed or, as they have been described, "clopen", which, despite being technically open ended, may limit issue and redemption for liquidity reasons. Such funds are generally confined to professional investors, since most regulators do not permit them to be offered to the general public.

Generally, however, investment managers of open ended funds will need to invest in bonds and shares which are liquid and capable of regular valuation. This will, in normal times, protect the fund against the need for extreme measures to be taken. Nonetheless a wise investment manager will keep a weather eye on cash flows.

8.4   Managing, monitoring and controlling the investment process

It must be clear from the foregoing that the management of investments can be a complex business, potentially involving:

- many different people inside and possibly outside the organisation

- a constantly shifting background of currencies, interest rates, taxes and politics

- a wide variety of techniques applied to literally thousands of potential investments

- demanding clients, who expect the results that they believe they are paying for

- a service which gives easily measurable and comparable results in a highly competitive market place

- very large sums of other people's money

- a rigorous legal and regulatory environment

The senior personnel of an investment management business, who are specifically responsible for portfolio management, will devote a lot of their attention to ensuring that the process runs smoothly. The penalties for failure can be considerable, since consistently poor results will result in a loss of clients and probably jobs too; major regulatory failures can result not only in loss of jobs but possible debarment from working in the business.

There are two key areas which require attention.

8.4.1   Compliance

This does not just imply compliance with legal and regulatory requirements – these are important – but also with client contracts and prospectuses. There are few outcomes that are more likely to result in an angry client than a discovery that his instructions have not been obeyed (particularly if performance is poor; if it is excellent forgiveness is more likely), and few outcomes that will bring down regulatory wrath more than failure to fulfil the terms of a prospectus.

Therefore much attention is devoted to ensuring that each client is getting what he has contracted for and what he expects. This may be done by regularly revisiting original contracts and examining the portfolio in the light of them. It is also good practice to ensure that each portfolio manager is in possession of a clear brief for each portfolio under his management, including special instructions and prohibitions.

Legal and regulatory compliance will be applied by the compliance officer or department, which will add to the purely investment based compliance a whole set of other rules relating to dealings and conflicts (see section 8.5).

8.4.2 Quality control

It is increasingly common for large asset managers to have a clearly defined investment philosophy or style and detailed descriptions of how it is to be implemented covering such matters as:

- adherence to asset allocation instructions, the permitted deviation from the norm at any time, and the time within which deviant portfolios must be brought into line

- use of the securities master list and the proportion of the portfolio that may be at the portfolio manager's own choice outside it

- extent and limitations on the use of derivatives

In order to ensure that all is going as it should, there will be a process of regular review of all portfolios with particular attention to those which seem to be behaving oddly. There will also be the need for the portfolio manager to write regular reports to the investors of a CIF or to other institutional clients, in which he will have to explain what he has done in the period under review, why he has done it and why the portfolio is invested the way it is at the reporting date; the latter is a very tough and good discipline on investment managers, who are usually some of the most highly paid employees in any asset management firm and who tend sometimes to behave like prima donnas.

8.5 Conflicts of interest and abuses

The last section of this chapter covers a highly sensitive area, since there is ample scope for abuse in investment management. Much legislation and regulation are aimed at curbing such abuses, in the interest of protection of investors' interests in CIFs. Asset management companies need to be alert to the damage to their reputations and the regulatory problems which may be caused by failure to ensure internal compliance. In order to make doubly sure, some asset management companies even bar managers from undertaking any personal transactions in securities, requiring them to commit their own money either to CIFs or to a discretionary account under someone else's management. This is unpopular with individual investment managers but can be justified in two ways:

- it keeps them from the temptation of profiting personally at the expense of the fund

- it keeps their attention fixed on managing the fund and prevents them wasting time worrying about their personal dealing positions

Despite the attention given to the type of abuse that can damage shareholder and unitholder value by legislators, regulators and management companies, there are still regular cases of malpractice. This is because such abuses are hard to detect and there is an almost infinite variety of ways knowledgeable professionals can use their position and skill to abuse the rights of holders of the funds which they manage.

8.5.1 Front running

One of the simplest ways for an investment manager to profit personally from his position is 'front running', where the manager purchases a security for himself immediately before the fund does. The fund's large purchase can often push up the market price of the security, enabling the manager to sell his holding at an immediate profit. Or the manager may simply pass on the information about an impending deal to a trusted associate and share the profits. Where house rules bar the practice of front running, managers may resort to the use of associates or offshore accounts to escape the rules. A comprehensive telephone recording and monitoring system can act as a deterrent, but mobile phones can easily be used to circumvent these.

8.5.2 Insider dealing

As substantial investors in securities, CIFs or other types of fund will be treated as institutional investors and may possess price-sensitive information before it is publicly disclosed. This too provides managers with the opportunity to trade personally on advantageous terms. Such 'insider dealing' is a criminal offence in most developed markets, but is hard to detect and hard to prove in court. Requirements for personnel of management companies to deal only through the companies' dealing desks are designed to help to identify occurrence of such dealing.

8.5.3 Warehousing

There are also situations in which fund managers can have financial incentives to exploit the investors in their funds. These are more likely to arise when the fund manager is a part of a financial conglomerate which has subsidiaries engaged in corporate activity in the stock market. For example, the conglomerate may be engaged in seeking to mount a takeover for a particular company. Rather than use its own cash to purchase shares, it may instruct the fund managers to purchase shares in the target company for all its funds. In this way a substantial stake, committed to the potential bidder, can be accumulated at no cost or risk to the conglomerate. Even where market and takeover rules require the disclosure of share stakes by associates or people acting in concert, each fund's stake may be held below the threshold above which disclosure is required. This practice, known as 'warehousing', may be beneficial for investors if the bid occurs, but if it does not, the shares may have to be sold at a loss or held as a poorly performing investment.

8.5.4 Rat trading

Unless rules specifically forbid this, it is possible for a fund manager to purchase a large block of shares on behalf of both himself and a number of funds under its management, and to allocate the shares to the respective parties some time after the deal. This enables it to allocate the shares showing profits to its own account, a practice known as "rat trading". Where rules bar the undertaking of trades on behalf of the fund manager (or its parent or associates) for its own account together with transactions for one or more funds, the ability to 'late-book' or allocate shares to funds some time after the transaction still gives the fund manager to opportunity to 'massage' the performance of funds it wishes to appear successful by allocating to them the larger proportion of shares showing immediate gains.

8.5.5 The dustbin

In some markets issues of new securities are underwritten: a bank or broker dealer accepts an underwriting fee and in return guarantees that all the securities will be taken up at an agreed price. It will then seek buyers for those securities. If it fails to find sufficient buyers, and it looks as if the shares will trade at below the issue price, the bank or broker dealer may instruct its fund manager to subscribe for the shares, transferring any loss from its own books at the expense of the investors. This practice is known as 'tail-end underwriting'.

Similarly, if a bank or broker dealer buys an issue of securities (a 'bought deal') and then attempts to place them, it may seek to use any funds under its control to take up any that are unwanted and avoid incurring a loss on its own account.

Clearly here the management company or its affiliates is avoiding failure at the cost of its funds' investors rather than itself.

8.5.6   New issues

Its position as a large institutional investor will lead the fund manager to being offered attractive investment opportunities. In rising markets, new share issues can often be predicted to produce quick and sometimes substantial profits. The fund manager will be offered participation in such issues and will have the right to allocate them among its funds. It is therefore relatively easy for a fund manager to give an upward boost to the performance of any one fund, especially a relatively small one, by allocating all attractive new issues to it.

All the above actions, designed in one way or another to enable the fund management company or individuals within it to profit at the expense of the investors or pensioners whose money they manage, are illegal in most countries. But they all happen, and there have been highly publicised breaches, which have covered each and every one of the practices listed above, in many cases committed within highly respected asset management business within the last five years.

8.6   Settlement and investment accounting

8.6.1   Importance of the "back office"

While the process of portfolio management and stock selection is the most visible of the parts of an asset management business, since investment managers are the "stars", and their success or failure in producing good investment performances has a measurable impact on investors and on the profitability of the firm generally, the less visible parts of the business also have an important role. One of these is the department responsible for keeping the records of the investments in different CIFs and in other portfolios managed by the firm, and for completing the transactions which have been initiated by the investment managers and transacted by the dealing department.

8.6.1.2   Settling transactions

The placing of the deal by the dealing department is only the beginning of a complex process by which ownership is transferred to, and payment received from, a buyer; or payment made to, and ownership received from, a seller. This involves a number of different parties which are:

- the broker acting for the CIF

- the market – whether physical or electronic – through which a counterparty, the buyer or seller, is contacted

- the counterparty, the broker on the other side of the transaction – in the case of a broker/dealer acting as a principal, this may be the same person as the one acting for the CIF

- the CIF's custodian or trustee, and the bank in whose account the CIFs deposits are held, under the control of the custodian or trustee

- the market's clearing and settlement system, through which transactions are completed

- the registrar or central depositary, which is responsible for maintaining ownership records – the last two may be part of one and the same organisation

This apparently lengthy and complex process has simple objectives – to ensure with a high degree of reliability that sellers deliver ownership to buyers and receive payment, and that buyers receive ownership and make payments to the sellers.

In markets in which there are thousands of transactions every day the scope for muddle and failure is considerable; such failures can be costly to all parties to transactions.

The following chart shows the process by which a typical securities transaction is settled. It must be emphasised that this is very generic and there will be many regional variations. Despite these, the process is tending to become more and more similar in developed countries as the investment business and securities markets become increasingly global.

A transaction and settlement process

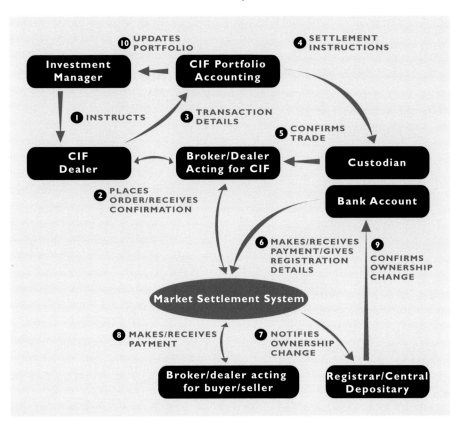

8.6.2 Record keeping and valuation

In addition to its responsibility for settling transactions for the portfolios of CIFs and other clients managed by the asset management firm, the investment accounting department will be responsible for keeping the records of the portfolios (in larger companies the responsibility for settlement of transactions will be a separate section within an overall department responsible for investment record keeping). This is important because it is upon these records that the valuation for the purposes of establishing a net asset value and price (refer Chapter 5) will be based. In this task, it is assisted by the existence of the custodian or trustee, which will itself keep parallel records of the securities that it holds for the CIF; so regular reconciliations between a CIF investment accounting department and the CIFs custodian or trustee will help to ensure that any errors or anomalies are quickly spotted.

Very often, it will be specialists within this department who will be responsible for valuation and pricing, if these functions are kept in-house and not contracted out to a third party. This connects the investment accounting department with the department responsible for dealing in shares/units of the CIF and for issues and redemptions.

The investment accounting department has responsibilities not only to keep accurate and timely records but also acts as a clearing house for information about investments as the following chart shows.

Responsibilities of investment accounting department

The investment accounting department is in the front line when it comes to compliance. In view of the importance that the Securities Regulator places on correct valuation and pricing it will be its responsibility to file regular reports on this to the Securities Regulator and to be available to answer questions in the event of an inspection. It will also be responsible together with the custodian or trustee for monitoring investment limits.

It will also be required to provide information to the auditor at the time of the annual audit of the CIF.

Finally it is responsible for ensuring that the investment manager is provided with a regularly up dated portfolio showing the current investments and for keeping the investment managers informed of any decisions required relating to corporate actions which result from takeovers, mergers, capital increases or any other matters on which a vote is required.

Attracting investors to CIFs

A fund management business must, clearly, have customers – that is, investors in its funds: and, in order to be successful, it must keep them, preferably while also attracting more customers. Constantly having to attract new customers to any business is expensive: while existing customers are usually the cheapest source from which to acquire further new business. If people are already investors in a fund, their contact details are known and they can be contacted through the post, which is usually far more cost effective than having to advertise in print or broadcast media. What is more, if they are already investors, they already know the management company involved, and provided that they have some spare money, may well invest again with the same group if their previous experience has been satisfactory.

There are many books about marketing in general and financial marketing in particular which will give a much more detailed understanding than can be achieved in a single chapter in a book. This Chapter simply focuses on introducing the key aspects of marketing CIFs.

9.1 Who the potential customers are and what affects their choices

The main factors influencing customers in relation to financial products can be described as external, internal and the consumer process, which are illustrated below. It is important to bear these in mind when considering what the company wants potential customers to do, and how it can persuade them to act in the desired fashion: ie, invest in the fund.

Factors affecting financial services choices

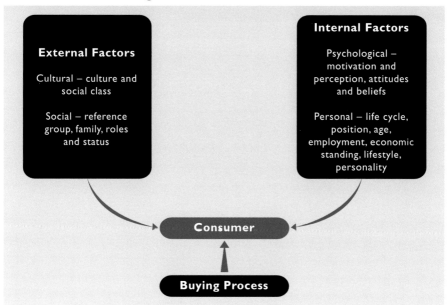

The impact of the chart above on the marketing of funds is that people will tend to make choices which endorse their own image of themselves, which are a result of the factors identified above. If they think of themselves as affluent, open minded and adventurous, they will tend to select funds from organisations which appear to them to be the same. Others may think of themselves as exceptionally intelligent and being one of the few who can identify and appreciate exceptional value; they will tend to seek out products or management companies whose style implies an element of intellect and exclusivity, but not high cost.

People make decisions through a series of processes, which are also relevant: a fund management company must think through how it wishes to be able to influence potential customers at each stage of the process, and what is needed to get them to move towards a decision to purchase shares or units in their particular fund, instead of someone else's.

The buying process

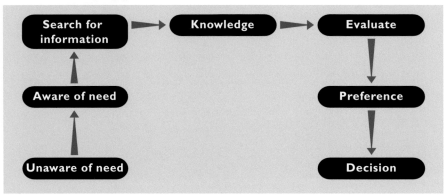

Thus someone becomes aware of a need – let us say, to save for a family wedding in ten or more years' time – and then tries to identify how to meet it. This could be through an insurance policy, for instance, or a CIF, or savings account at a bank. They will then try to find out which will be best, and why; and then to form a preference for the particular provider's product. Finally comes the decision which exact product to buy – usually on the grounds of a particular benefit, such as better performance or lower cost or greatest convenience or safety.

A fund management company needs to help people to reach a decision to buy their products through ensuring that information and guidance is available to them to justify this decision. Personal recommendation ("word of mouth") from previous purchasers is nearly always a strong influence on decision making; thus it is important that fund management companies keep existing customers satisfied. Ensuring that a decision, once taken, can be quickly and simply and easily implemented is also important; if it cannot, the customer may go elsewhere.

9.2 How potential customers can be identified and reached

Within CIF marketing and distribution, a number of different activities are undertaken. These are:

- research: identifying the target customers and their needs

- branding: the creation of awareness of a name that has particular qualities associated with it (a famous example being Coca Cola)

- advertising: placement of paid promotional messages designed to attract customers or promote a particular image

- public relations: management of communication between a company and its various audiences, including the media, to achieve a positive image of the company and its products

- distribution (sales): the various methods of making sales such as employment of salespeople

Two further key parts of marketing activity are communication with investors and product development; these are covered in subsequent Chapters 10 and 11. The chart below shows how marketing, distribution, product development and investor communications come together.

The marketing mix

❶ IDENTIFY CUSTOMERS NEEDS AND WANTS

❷ DEVELOP PRODUCTS TO MEET NEEDS

❸ DECIDE PRICING FOR PRODUCTS

❹ ADVERTISE AND PROMOTE PRODUCTS

❺ SET UP DISTRIBUTION CHANNELS

❻ RESEARCH CUSTOMERS' FUTURE NEEDS

9

- **resources available:** the financing available to the company will affect the ability of the marketing division to pursue different strategies: for instance, sustain the higher fixed costs of employing a salesforce compared with the lower variable cost of paying commissions to advisers on sales made; it may tend to dictate a needed to focus on servicing a small number of larger clients rather than a large number of smaller clients

Essentially, the two extremes of approach to a market which may be defined are a 'leader' strategy, where the company sets out to be consistently and highly visible over the long term, steadily building a business; or an 'opportunist' strategy, whereby a company simply seeks to create products and exploit them effectively, as the opportunity arises. In the first case, the brand will be important; in the second case, the appeal of the particular products will be most important.

9.4   The mechanics of marketing

9.4.1   Management of marketing

Most of the functions of marketing can be undertaken either internally or externally from the management company. The most common structure would be to have an internal department responsible for the function, reporting to the Board, which calls on external service providers as needed.

It is normal for specific targets to be set which marketing is required to achieve in any given year, and for performance to be measured regularly both against these targets and in terms of results achieved against money spent (ie, cost effectiveness). Targets are usually expressed in terms of sales of funds to be achieved within a defined period, and are usually specific to countries or regions, or to different marketing or sales teams (eg institutional sales versus retail sales).

Tracking performance against targets is important, since failure to attain targets has revenue and capacity implications for the management company; if sales are lower than targeted, revenues will be below target; if they are higher than targeted, administration systems and personnel may not be able to cope. As market conditions improve or worsen, targets will need to be adjusted accordingly.

A marketing plan and budget should be created for each financial year, against the targets set, and progress against it should be monitored weekly or at least monthly in terms of:

- **cost** – budgets spent versus budgets allocated, and reasons identified for discrepancies

- **timing** – whether the schedule has been achieved, and if not, why not and the consequences that this will have for the budget

- **target** – whether target sales have been achieved, and if not, why not: this should include tracking sales per distribution channel and/or per sales team against targets and against each other, to assess effectiveness

Usually separate budgets will be agreed for different activities and for particular projects such as the launch of a new fund, with pre-agreed expenditure limits and deadlines for each activity.

Progress should also be assessed in terms of results achieved for money spent. This is done in several ways, including:

- tracking the number of responses to each advertisement or to each mailing campaign (which necessitates having coding and tracking systems in place to check such response), and comparing the results by dividing the cost of each advertisement or campaign by the number of responses received (known as cost per response)

- tracking the amount of money invested as a result of each advertisement or mailing campaign, and dividing the cost of the advertisement by the amount of money it raised, which can be compared for each advertisement to assess effectiveness (known as cost per $ converted or per conversion)

- tracking the amount of money invested as a result of each distribution channel against the cost of servicing that channel to see where best results are occurring and try to assess why

Fund managers in each country will establish their own acceptable cost per 100 or 1,000 of currency units attracted and may, if such data is available, be able to compare their results with other managers, to give a further measure of effectiveness.

Cost control is a vital element of marketing and is important when using external contractors, who should operate under clear reporting and budgetary conditions.

9.4.2 Researching the market

Identifying the market to be targeted by a management company, whether for the company overall, or for a particular fund, is a key task of a marketing department.

9.4.2.1 Institutional or retail

The first question is whether the market to be targeted is 'institutional' or 'retail': that is, whether the company is seeking to attract investments from financial institutions, such as pension, charitable or insurance funds; or from individuals – or both. Most fund management companies have different sections within the marketing or sales divisions to focus on these two groups, since their needs are different.

Differences between institutional and retail clients

	INSTITUTIONAL	RETAIL
Number of such investors	tens or hundreds of thousands internationally	hundreds of millions internationally
Amount invested	generally $100,000 or more per investment	generally $1,000 or more per investment
Level of initial charge acceptable	0 to 2%	0 to 8%
Level of annual charge acceptable	usually 1.25% or less	usually 3% or less
Fund investment objective	have specific investment need which investment objective of fund must meet accurately	have general investment need and risk profile which investment objective of fund must usually meet
Fund portfolio	require detailed information on content and changes	require general information on content and changes
Fund performance analysis and reports	usually monthly or weekly	six monthly
Service	usually require personal service with named liaison person	does not usually expect individual service

As a general rule, the level of information required by an institutional investor, both prior to and after investing, will be much more frequent and detailed than for a retail investor. Special reports are usually prepared for institutional investors, which may be individually generated to meet their specific needs (eg demonstration of compliance with certain portfolio limitations) or for a group of similar investors.

Marketing departments may develop funds which are targeted specifically at institutional investors only, with the possible addition of professional investors or rich individuals (often referred to as high net worth individuals or HNWIs) who may also be permitted by regulation to invest in such funds, since they are judged to be

9

sufficiently expert or to have expert advisers. These funds tend to be located in low tax domiciles (also referred to as 'offshore' domiciles) which permit greater portfolio flexibility and a wider range of legal and operating structures.

9.4.2.2 Obtaining data

Details of potential institutional investors are best derived from professional directories, handbooks or yearbooks or specialist databases. It may be necessary to build up an in-house database, which should be constantly maintained and reviewed for changes in address, personnel, etc.

Data used to identify potential retail target markets is a more complicated area. It can focus on two different aspects: one is essentially demographic and the other attitudinal.

9.4.2.2.a Demographic data

In many countries this information is available from a government statistical office. This characteristically covers:

- age and gender

- income structure

- occupations

- social structure (households)

- asset ownership

- savings from income

- location

- ethnic or religious groups

Such data can be used to assess trends which may have significance for fund managers: for instance, in Europe generally an ageing population is placing increasing strain on state pension systems whose costs are met by current taxpayers (known as "pay as you go" systems). Numbers of workers are reducing as numbers of pensioners increase due to greater longevity. This is likely to lead to greater need for governments to encourage individuals to save for their retirement and to place less reliance on state pensions, which could create more demand for CIFs. The data can also be used to assess likely needs: a relatively recent phenomenon is the development of financial products, whose religious beliefs do not permit investment in – for instance – alcohol production; and who may not receive interest, due to sanctions in religious law against usury.

Traditionally in developed markets the people who have had money available to save or invest have been the older managerial or professional male whose children have left home, so has reduced expenses, and who needs to put money aside for retirement. Another group has developed in recent years: the 25 – 35 year old male or female manager or professional, often living in a two income household, who has money left over to save for pensions or who wants to build up a sum to invest in a home.

The key is to find a group who have money available to save, and then to find out what will be the most cost effective way to reach them:

- where they live (if it is all in the same area, posting literature through doors or local posters might work)

- what programmes they watch or publications they read

- what are their hobbies and interests

- what communication methods they use – phone, Internet, etc

This sort of information helps to target marketing effort: at certain sports for sponsorship, for instance.

If statistical data of this type is not available, informal research done through contacts who represent the chosen target market might be worthwhile.

9.4.2.2.b Attitudinal data

This data is based on research which is usually undertaken by specialist firms, to assist in effective targeting. In the case of the financial sector, attitudes to saving generally, to risk and to decision taking are all important. Different research groups create different labels for groups with different characteristics. In general, these refer to:

- attitude to risk: potential loss of capital as well as opportunity for gain

- sensitivity to price: ie, levels of different types of charges

- ability to take decisions independently, or need for advice

- attitude to saving – passive or active

- savings need – for capital growth or a rising income

- attitudes to use of technology

All these will influence how the fund management company will need to adjust its marketing and sales techniques to meet the target customer's need, in order to make the desired sale. As an example, those who like taking their own financial decisions, and are confident researching for themselves, are price sensitive and like using technology, could be ideal customers for Internet-based services; whereas those who need personal advice and who do not like technology may be best persuaded by a salesman who fills in the necessary applications for them, provided that they are not price sensitive.

9.4.2.3 Monitoring the competition

Most management companies will spend some time researching and monitoring the activities of competitors: both other types of financial products and other CIFs. This is done to ensure that they are aware of potential threats to the attractiveness of their own products, and to enable them to respond effectively to such threats. If a management company has a particular strength – for instance, the lowest cost provider – then it will need to constantly check that this position is not under threat, and identify either what adjustments it is capable of making if a competitor should undercut it, or cases it can make to justify a decision not to move to lower costs. An example might be that it could not then provide some of the services its investors wanted, which the undercutter did not provide and was thus able to charge less.

It is worth noting that little distinguishes the vast majority of CIFs with a similar investment objective from each other; a successful launch of one fund by one firm tends to led to a series of 'me too' funds from competitors. Creating funds or a management company which is distinctive is difficult, though not impossible.

9.4.3   Branding

Branding is essentially the qualities or values which people associate with a particular name, which have an influence on attitudes towards that name. Sometimes a brand is associated with a particular product – let us say, a detergent – and sometimes with a company which offers a range of products. The latter is usually the case in relation to funds – it is the management company (or its parent's) name which is the focus of the brand. The subsidiary company will damage the parent brand if its style contradicts it.

The sorts of values which fund management companies might wish to associate with their names could range from: 'value for money' through to 'exclusive'; from 'conservative' through to 'high risk'; from 'complex scientific approach' to 'gut instinct'.

If a brand name is to be achieved, consistent effort over many years will be needed, with all supporting promotional activity and materials being consistent with the brand image. Mailing very glossy brochures, for instance, is inconsistent with a 'value for money' brand.

9.4.4   Advertising

Advertising is used to inform and to persuade, and to alert people to opportunities. It can be used to develop awareness of a management company's name and qualities, or to promote a specific fund or range of funds.

Influences on the method of advertising selected will be:

- the target market and its characteristics

- budgets available

- the message to be conveyed and its suitability to different media: television is good for creating awareness, but poor at conveying large amounts of detail, which is often required for financial product advertising due to regulation. Putting a lot of detail on screen is costly; unless people record the advertisement, the information is difficult to retain, and response has to be separately through a phone call or other contact. Print media are excellent for conveying detail, though, and are relatively cheap. Choice of media can also affect perceptions of potential customers: some have more confidence in financial groups which advertise on television because – in their view – this is expensive, so it shows they are big and able to finance such expenditure. Advertising the existence of a website is an increasingly popular method of enabling people to access information

There are essentially three types of CIF advertising:

- brand or image advertising, promoting the qualities of the management company

- 'one step' product advertising which includes subscription information so an investor can subscribe immediately

- 'two step' product advertising, which encourages investors to apply for detailed subscription information about the product or products advertised, which they can then use to subscribe if they so decide

One step advertising essentially requires the publication of prospectus type information: it is therefore quite expensive and relatively more rare, unless it is a legal requirement.

Advertising also supports the work of advisers and salesmen: it is much easier to sell a product from a known provider than from someone the potential investor has never heard of; it can also be used to promote Internet dealing facilities.

The results from different advertisements should be constantly monitored, in terms of:

- which advertisements work better than others – that is, if the different advertisements are placed in the same media on the same page on the same day, which gets the highest response and conversion rates

- advertising within which publications or during which programmes works best – that is, which achieve the highest response and conversion rates, at which times or in which positions (for instance, financial pages versus general news pages)

- what timing works best – that is, whether advertising around holidays achieves a higher response or conversion, or not; or over weekends or on weekdays, etc; and different times of day

It is very important to keep file copies of all advertising placed, together with details of its placement and support for any claims or facts given in it. This is both for regulatory reasons, and for self defence – in case customers subsequently complain about inaccurate or misleading advertising.

Investment performance, which is an important component of fund advertising, is covered in Chapter 10.

9.4.4   Public relations

Public relations focuses on the creation and maintenance of
favourable perceptions about a management company and its funds.
This is usually done through informing and persuading opinion
formers, whose views then influence a wider range of people.

Characteristically, opinion formers include:

- journalists and commentators

- subject specialists

- members of parliament and of political parties

- government officials

- community or religious leaders

- consumer organisations

Most management companies will have an internal department
responsible for the public relations function and may hire external
advisers also. Their primary function wil be to ensure effective
communication of messages about the company to the selected opinion
formers, maintaining the visibility and good reputation of the company.
They will also be expected to promote the launch of new funds,
creating a favourable environment for sales of shares or units, possibly
with events such as press conferences or visits to relevant organisations
(a favourite is foreign trips for journalists to visit countries in which
new funds will invest, particularly where breweries are involved).

Public relations departments must also keep up to date information
on all the company's products and key facts about the company,
ready to answer queries; and must respond effectively and promptly
to questions about relevant issues. They, and external agencies, should
facilitate communication; it is also important that somebody who is
technically competent and an able public speaker should act as a

spokesman for the company, and build relationships with relevant opinion formers.

A particularly effective use of public relations is to ensure a favourable mention of a fund on the same page as an advertisement for a fund appears. Where journalists are regarded as expert and unbiased, this effectively endorses the appearance of the fund and carries weight with potential investors. This helps to form the 'preference' highlighted earlier.

A common method of attaining publicity is for managers to comment upon the prospects for markets in which their funds invest; though this can backfire if the market immediately contradicts this view.

Public relations departments are also expected to anticipate and plan for any damage limitation exercises that may be needed if, for instance, a market is suspended so issue and redemption of funds investing in that market is also suspended. Indeed, public relations is all about anticipation of events, positive or negative, and planning to maximise the benefit for the company concerned.

A key factor in public relations is credibility; opinion formers tend to have good antennae for stories and any weaknesses in them; and competitors will always help them to seek such weaknesses out. It is very important that public relations departments and company spokesmen should be authoritative and credible on a continuing basis; backing all publicity with succinct and relevant supporting data is always worthwhile.

9.4.5   Promotion

Promotion can include anything from giving out free branded gifts, to appearing at financial or other exhibitions or sponsoring sporting or artistic events. It is a range of activities designed to keep the management company's name in front of the target audience. Promotion should be consistent with the brand of the promoter and be directed at the company's target market. Sponsoring sporting or other events is popular because institutional customers, advisers and

9

sales teams can be invited to attend the event, as well as putting the company's name in front of the audience at the event. However, the type of event should be carefully considered: sponsoring a horse-riding event is one thing, since it is a competition at which some will succeed and some will fail, with no particular connotations; but sponsoring an individual horse which falls at the first fence in a competition or race has less good connotations for fund management companies, who – in investors' minds – have to finish the race with the best results.

Management companies can also stage "roadshows" of their own, visiting towns and cities where they have clients or potential clients, or financial advisers or sales teams, and making presentations on new or existing products. If institutional investors are to be attracted to a particular fund, it is quite common to stage a formal presentation with detailed information support in major cities where such investors are based, to explain the proposed fund to the target market. Funds wishing to attract international institutions would normally do roadshows in New York, Frankfurt, London, Hong Kong and Tokyo at a minimum.

Alternatively, management companies can contact companies with employees who have savings or pensions needs and arrange to make a presentation to them at their place of work, and set up particular schemes on their behalf.

9.4.6   Investor communications systems

Marketing departments are usually responsible for putting together investor communications materials and for the creation and maintenance of marketing databases of existing and potential customers. Regular, good quality communications are an important part of building customers' confidence in a management company's abilities.

A schedule and budget is usually created to cover those investor communications which are required by regulation to be issued, to ensure that deadlines are not missed. There will usually be a designated person who will be responsible for their correctness and timely issue. Chapter 10 outlines the usual content of such communications.

Good quality databases which can be called up quickly are also vital to maintaining customers' confidence in the competence and efficiency of the management company. Traditionally fund registers were held fund by fund, and an investor with holdings in three funds would have three different register entries; today it is more common to have a customer account per individual, which lists all their transactions in all the management company's funds. These databases should be capable of calling off information on: investors in a certain area (to invite to a roadshow, for instance); investors of a certain age group (those due to retire, for instance, who could be sent details of a new retirement product) or by other common characteristics.

It is advisable that such databases should also record details of how sales came about, to track the type of approach most likely to appeal to that individual (eg direct mail rather than personal call). Management groups who distribute their products through different sales channels will need to be able to identify which customer was reached by which channel, and which adviser or salesperson, in order to correctly track and pay commissions due. Financial advisers, in particular, can be sensitive if management companies send marketing materials direct to their client, in case the client buys direct and the adviser gets no commission; whereas, if the mailing information is sent to the adviser for him to send on to his clients, he can ensure that any purchases resulting from his mailing bring him commission income.

9.4.7   How to get the product to the customer: distribution

Distribution channels are the different routes used by fund management companies to reach potential and existing customers. These channels can be broadly categorised as:

- financial advisers: these are licensed experts who advise clients on how to invest their money and who may recommend the products of a management company amongst a range of other products

9

These advisers may be remunerated by commission on fund sales paid to them by the management company concerned, or by way of a fee paid by the client for their time. The second method is regarded increasingly as desirable since in this case the adviser is clearly acting as the agent of the client; whereas when they are paid commissions, it could be questioned whether their advice is wholly uninfluenced by commission considerations. Such advisers include private client stockbrokers and bankers (further information about commissions is given in section 6.5)

- affinity groups: this is where an organisation of people who have a particular affinity – a charity, club, trade union or church, for instance – agrees to recommend the products of the management company to its members, in return for a commission paid to the organisation that helps it to fund its activities. Such organisations are not usually required to have a licence to operate financial services

- sales forces: salespeople employed by a management company or by a sales network are contracted to sell the products of that management company, usually on a partly commissioned and partly salaried basis. The split between commission and salary is because, if fully commission only, salespeople will sell the wrong product to the wrong people in order to generate money to meet living costs; and if salaried only, they are not hungry enough to go out and make new sales. Such sales teams may sell directly to the public, or may be focused on selling to financial institutions. At a minimum, such personnel should be trained; it is preferable that they should have passed competence tests and their names be held on a register by the Securities Regulator

- direct selling: this occurs when a management company sells its products directly to the investing public, usually using a combination of advertising and promotions with direct mail. A rising trend is the use of management company websites and electronic dealing in funds through the Internet through the management company; this is particularly strong in the US but less common, as yet, in Europe

An additional distribution channel which is well established in the US, but not elsewhere, is the 'discount broker'. These are brokerage services through which investors can buy funds from a range of management companies at no or low charge, rather than at normal brokerage or advisory commissions. Discount broking is generally done free to the client (ie, there is no transaction fee) for no load funds – the broker being remunerated by the management company out of their management fees; or at a small set charge, usually set by reference to the size of the transaction, for other funds. Such services are increasingly offered on line.

Each distribution channel has its advantages and disadvantages for a management company. Some management companies use a variety of channels, while others use only one. Each channel requires its own mix of support services in order for them to be effective. The key considerations in deciding which channels to use are cost and control.

Comparison of distribution channels

	FINANCIAL ADVISERS	AFFINITY GROUPS	SALES FORCES	DIRECT SELLING
cost	variable: only get commission on sale	variable: only get commission on sale	fixed if salaried or partly salaried: variable if partly or wholly commissioned	fixed if internal: variable where additional external services are used
control over channel	none: will only recommend funds if performance is good and commissions are competitive	none except through contract terms: may move to a higher commission payer; may fail to sell	higher if directly employed; lower if externally contracted: may move to higher commission payer	high if internal
support	brand or product advertising fund factsheets general product literature regular performance information regular briefings hospitality website dedicated support team dealing desk	brand or product advertising general product literature briefings or events website dealing desk	brand or product advertising fund factsheets website dedicated support team dealing desk	brand or product advertising general product literature website help desk dealing desk
additional systems	commissions tracking and payment customer account marked as client of adviser	commissions tracking and payment customer account marked as affinity group	commissions tracking and payment customer account marked as salesperson's client	

It is relatively rare for a fund management company to be able to afford to have its own employed sales force; firstly, they lack a wide enough product range to offer the customer, and secondly the costs of supporting even a partially salaried sales force is high. However, a fund management company can be part of a group – such as a life assurance provider, which may have its own sales force or a bank, with a branch network – which may have its own salesforce which can sell funds as part of the group's products (the higher commissions payments usually payable on life assurance products can mean relatively low fund sales, however).

Sales can also be contracted out to external networks – such as banks with branches. While this can enable fund mangers to reach new clients, this sort of arrangement is always potentially vulnerable – where the contract is an exclusive one (ie, that bank sells no other funds than that management company's) the bank may not make the effort to sell the funds; or it may subsequently decide to create its own funds, if it finds the funds are popular; or it may decide to sell another manager's funds instead, since it offers a higher commission. If the arrangement is not an exclusive one, the manager may have little influence over getting the bank to sell its funds, in preference to other managers', unless it pays a higher commission (which reduces its own profits) – but then, the other manager may up its commissions too.

Another factor worth bearing in mind is that networks which sell clothing, or food, or banking, are not necessarily well fitted to selling funds; their personnel will need special training either in sales (since bank clerks tend to be hired for their numeric and not sales skills) or in funds.

Incentivising sales through sales teams or branch networks is often done by creating a special incentivisation structure. This can be based on a club structure, where the higher the sales achieved, the greater the benefits and recognition attained; and/or on a series of levels whereby those who recruit and manage other salespeople get part of their commissions.

9.5   Differences in marketing open ended and closed ended CIFs

As a general rule, the marketing effort relating to selling a closed ended fund relates to a single issue of shares. Thereafter, unless a regular savings plan or pension plan is operated by that fund (refer Chapter 11), it will no longer need to raise money and so will not require substantial ongoing marketing effort. The exception to this arises when a closed ended CIF attracts the attention of a predator who wishes to take it over or liquidate it in order to realise net asset value. Closed ended funds under such threat will often turn to major public relations and advertising campaigns to try to demonstrate to their investors that such bids should be refused – not always successfully.

Open ended CIFs, however – and interval funds, to a lesser extent – can be issued and redeemed at any time and have a need to attract new investors to increase the size of the fund or reduce the impact of redemptions. They also operate regular savings plans and pension plans, which will also require publicity to maintain demand for these services. Apart from the introduction of new funds, which are nearly always introduced with a fanfare of advertising, mailings and public relations effort, to attract a (hopefully) reasonable sum on launch, it is quite difficult for a marketing department to predict which funds will be likely to attract most investment and which it is therefore most worth marketing. Thus marketing effort supporting open ended funds may be relatively random, with the investment department identifying to marketing at regular meetings which funds are performing best and which are therefore most likely to be marketable. This may change from week to week or month to month, so flexibility is needed.

9.6   Regulation of marketing

The degree to which marketing of funds is regulated varies from country to country. The most common principles of such regulation are:

- that the entity which is marketing the funds (ie the fund management company) should be licensed

- that those who sell funds or advise which ones to select should have appropriate competence and be honest

- that the issuer of fund marketing materials (the fund directors or management company) must take responsibility for their completeness, accuracy and content

- that the employer of the sales agents must take responsibility for their conduct

- that the content of sales and marketing materials should be accurate and not misleading

- that investors should receive sufficient information about a fund to make an informed choice

- that the way salespeople represent a fund should not be inaccurate or misleading

- that the status of the person selling or advising on a fund should be clear (ie, they are commissioned salespersons or representatives of the management company only, or are giving financial advice across a range of products)

- that where advice is given as to which fund or funds to invest in, that the advice should be based on knowledge of the customers' financial position and appropriateness of the fund or funds for their needs

- that advertisements must carry a minimum amount of information as to licensed status, etc and should carry risk warnings where specific products are mentioned

- that the basis of fund performance should be made clear and that only fair and relevant comparisons with other funds or investments should be made

9

In addition to fund and securities market regulation, other regulation may also apply to marketing and advertising. This can include competition or antimonopoly law, advertising standards and data protection law.

The ability to distribute funds may also be affected by law and regulations governing the practice of "cold calling" – phoning or turning up in an office or home in person to sell funds without a prior invitation. Some countries have rules that sales of funds made in such circumstances may be subject to cancellation rules; that is, the buyer is entitled to cancel the transaction within a specified number of days and get their money back. In order to prevent abuse of such provisions, it is usually required that the investor take the risk of losing (or gaining) money during the cancellation period – they will only receive back the value of their investment as of the date of cancellation, instead of the value that they invested. They are, however, entitled to be paid back any initial charge made on the sale. Other countries simply do not permit such sales to be made.

Communicating with CIF investors

There are a wide variety of methods of communicating with fund investors, which can be broken down into five different parts:

● those required by regulation

● those associated with selling products or promoting the management company

● those necessary to keep customers informed

● performance information

● dealing with customer enquiries and complaints

Some communications may cover more than one purpose: for instance, regulation requires – usually – that a fund must have a prospectus; but this can also be used as a sales tool; annual reports are required by regulation but can also be an opportunity to keep customers informed or to market other products.

Investors can also obtain a wide variety of other information about funds from broadcast financial programmes, printed articles and books; trade associations of funds also offer generic explanatory literature and statistics.

There are some general principles which should be applied to all customer communications:

● always assume materials are being written for someone who knows nothing about financial matters: never use jargon

- all communications should be clear and simple – if necessary, test them on friends or relations who do not work in the financial sector

- all materials should be consistent with the relevant brand; a style should be set for each communication (eg annual report, newsletter) and followed

- maximum use should be made of graphics, since most people find these easier and quicker to understand that pages of prose

- the contact details of the management company should always be included and easy to find

- printed matter should always be clearly dated

- samples should always be maintained for the files for future reference, as should evidence supporting information given

It is usual to have a person who is responsible for overseeing production of investor communications; that person may also be required to check that they comply with regulatory requirements and sign off to this effect. Legally responsibility for the correctness of some documents – such as a prospectus – and its compliance with regulation will lie with different organisations and individuals, depending upon the legal structure of the fund. Coordination will also be required with the administration department or registrar who deals with despatch of mandatory information to fund investors and careful attention will be needed to meet regulatory deadlines for despatch of such data.

10.1   Communications required by regulation

The precise nature and content of documents required by regulation varies from country to country. Generally they are as outlined opposite.

Typical investor communications required by regulation

COMMUNICATION REQUIRED BY REGULATION	CONTENT	TIMING	RESPONSIBILITY FOR CONTENT
prospectus or mini prospectus or 'key features' document (see section 10.1.1)	● *all information needed to make an informed investment choice* ● *risk warnings* ● *subscription and contact details*	● *required to be offered to investor prior to investing* ● *required to be updated annually for open ended funds; or if material change occurs*	● *corporate fund: directors of the fund* ● *trust fund: management company and trustee* ● *contractual fund: management company or management company with custodian*
annual report (see section 10.1.2)	● *audited accounts* ● *fund performance* ● *details of distributions made* ● *current portfolio and changes in period* ● *outlook for fund* ● *contact details*	● *required to be published in mass media or mailed to investors each year usually within 3 months of financial year end*	● *corporate fund: directors of the fund* ● *trust fund: management company and trustee* ● *contractual fund: management company or management company with custodian*

COMMUNICATION REQUIRED BY REGULATION	CONTENT	TIMING	RESPONSIBILITY FOR CONTENT
semi annual report (see section 10.1.3)	● *briefer version of annual report* ● *accounts are unaudited*	● *required to be published in mass media or mailed to investors each year usually within 3 months of end of first half of financial year*	● *corporate fund: directors of the fund* ● *trust fund: management company and trustee* ● *contractual fund: management company or management company with custodian*
net asset value or price per share or unit (see section 10.1.4)	● *fund contact details plus unit prices or NAV*	● *required to be published daily for open funds, monthly or quarterly or less for interval or open funds*	● *corporate fund: directors of the fund* ● *trust fund: management company and trustee* ● *contractual fund: management company or management company with custodian*

10.1.1   The prospectus

While a prospectus is primarily a legal document, it can also be a marketing document, provided that regulatory requirements are met.

10.1.1.1 Characteristic prospectus content

10.1.1.1.a Closed ended CIF

The main information that is required to be given in a closed ended CIF prospectus is broadly similar to that for any public offer of shares in a company. It includes the following:

- the name and nature of the fund and its investment objective

- the number of shares or units being offered for sale and the offer price

- information on the capital structure if more than one type of share or unit is to be issued and the life of the fund, if limited

- the minimum number of shares or units (of each type, if there is more than one) that will be issued (if there are applications for fewer than this the issue may be aborted) and the maximum (if any)

- the names and addresses of all the directors and of any founders where they are different from the directors, and the members of any Supervisory Board (these directors are chosen either for their expertise, or for their appeal to potential fund investors, or both)

- the names and addresses of the firms acting as lawyers, sponsors, auditors, bankers, custodians, trustees, registrars, appraisers (valuers) and investment managers

- basic information on the contracts between the CIF and the custodians and investment managers and any others to whom it plans to contract out services

- details of the fees, charges and expenses that will be taken from the CIF's income or capital to pay for these services

- a report from the auditors confirming the current state of the CIF's finances (normally nominal)

- disclosure of any interest of any directors in any of the contracts for services of any third parties

- details of the remuneration of any directors of the CIF

- statement of the rights of shareholders to vote and receive information

- circumstances in which the fund may be liquidated

- details of procedure for annual meetings of holders, other meetings of holders and reports to holders

- the directors' or management company's intentions as regards payments of dividends to holders

- a statement of intent to apply for a share listing on a stock exchange, where applicable

- information on the total costs of the share or unit issue which will be taken from the funds subscribed by holders

- regulatory registration, where applicable, with any required disclaimers (ie, regulatory registration does not imply endorsement by the regulator)

- risk warnings associated with the assets in which the fund will invest

- how to buy shares or units

- the general tax liability of the fund and of the investor

- date of prospectus

10.1.1.1.b Open and interval CIFs

Again, there will be a difference in information required for an open or interval fund, due to the obligation to redeem. The key additional information about open or interval funds will be:

- how units, shares or participations are priced and where to obtain this information

- how to subscribe for and redeem holdings in the fund (including partial redemptions where some, but not all, the holding is redeemed, subject to the minimum amount required remaining in the fund) and the charges that will apply

- past performance of the fund, once it is more than a year old, usually since inception or for at least the last five or ten years

Open or interval prospectuses are also usually required to be updated annually, or when any material change is made which affects the term of the offer being made.

10.1.1.1.c Risk disclosure in prospectuses

Risk disclosure is seen as a key element of prospectuses. Many attempts have been made to represent risk numerically, but it is very difficult to adequately convey the range and impact of the risk factors involved.

The US, which has the most advanced requirements for disclosure of risk requires a statement in words as to the types of risk involved. An example of one form of risk disclosure is:

Statement of fund objectives for the Growth Fund

"The Growth Fund"

The Growth Fund is an open ended investment company whose aim is capital growth through investment in listed shares and bonds. The manager will vary the proportions of the fund's assets held in shares and bonds respectively in response to their assessment of prospects. A minimum of 15% of the fund's assets will be held in bonds and deposits at all times. There is no specific target for income distributions but the initial annual yield (net of basic rate personal tax) is expected to be about 5%. The manager intends to hold a widely spread portfolio with holdings in at least 50 different companies.

Risk factors

The Fund will invest the bulk of its assets in shares and bonds whose prices fluctuate. The Net Asset Value of the Fund may be subject to wide fluctuations in the short term. The income distributed by the Fund may vary considerably from one period to the next.

10.1.1.1.d Charge and cost disclosure in prospectuses

Whereas future performance of a fund is never predictable, if the level of charges and costs which a fund will pay is clearly disclosed, the impact of these charges can be ascertained (refer section 10.1.2.10 on page 233) and comparisons made with other funds. This is why regulators require total charges and costs of operating funds to be clearly disclosed, rather than obfuscated by managers, who are generally keen to present charges in the best possible (usually confusing) light. If charges are presented in a clear and comparable way, then investors can assess which fund is likely to offer them better value.

10.1.1.1.e Short form prospectus

Recognising that prospectuses have become very long and investors may be put off reading them, some regulators are permitting use of a short form prospectus, which must contain the following information:

- date of prospectus

- name of fund and contact details of management company, custodian, auditor, etc

- regulatory reference number of fund

- how to get more information on the fund

- investment objective and strategy and past capital and income performance of the fund (the last in a mandatory format over set periods), with risk warnings; also a history of NAV per share since inception or for the last 5 years

- fees and expenses of the fund (entry fees, annual fees and costs and exit fees – again in a mandatory format)

- management, organisation and capital structure of the fund

- pricing, dealing, applicable minima and dividend/distribution policy

- information provided to shareholders

10.1.2   Characteristic content of an annual report

The essence of an annual report is that it should tell the fund investor (exactly as it would tell a shareholder in a company) what has been happening over the previous year – how the money they have invested has been used, and what results it has achieved.

A CIF's annual report should include information on the following:

i   the fund's assets and liabilities at the accounting date

ii   changes in the value of the fund and its investments from the previous accounting date

iii the fund's income and expenditure during the year

iv   income distributions paid to investors in the period

v   details of the portfolio as at the accounting date

vi   information on investment transactions since the previous accounting date

10

vii statement of the fund's objectives

viii a report from the CIF Manager on the performance of the fund since the previous accounting date and some indications of the manager's views of future prospects

ix the NAV of a share or unit as on the first day and the last day of the reporting year

An outline of the content of the report and its significance for investors is given below. While the tables given do not show this, it would be normal to show the comparative figure for the previous year alongside the current year's figures, for comparison purposes.

10.1.2.1 Assets and liabilities

The fund's assets are its investments, cash deposits, accrued income and any money owed to it. Its liabilities are what it owes. The primary liabilities are to the fund investors, but there may also be amounts owing in respect of securities transactions or to service providers such as auditors or custodians.

A simplified example of a fund's balance sheet is shown in the first Table opposite. Open and closed ended funds will normally publish balance sheet data for the preceding as well as the current year of account, so investors are in a position to monitor the company's financial performance in detail. Open ended CIFs should include data on the changes in assets and liabilities over the year and amounts subscribed and withdrawn by investors over the year, as shown in the Statement of Movement of Holders' Funds Table. If this is not done, fund investors cannot identify the impact of increase in portfolio value from increase in assets from new fund investors' contributions.

Growth Fund Balance Sheet as at 31 December 1998

Assets	CU Millions	Assets	CU Millions
Fixed assets		*Shareholders' funds*	
Investments (at market value)	150	Issued share capital	100
		Capital reserves	90
Current assets		*Current liabilities*	
Cash at bank	35	Due to market	45
Due from market	50		
Total assets	235	*Total liabilities*	235

This example shows investments at market value, which is appropriate for open ended funds.

A fundamental question in accounting for closed ended funds is whether the fund's assets should be stated in its accounts at cost or at market value. International accounting conventions permit the valuation of assets on the basis of the lower of cost and market value. However, in the context of CIFs, best practice is to use market value since this gives the most accurate picture to investors of the current value of their investment.

For closed ended funds whose balance sheets do not contain portfolio details, a separate note or Net Asset Value Statement should state the current market value of the fund's portfolio as shown in the next Table.

10.1.2.2 Net Asset Value (NAV) Statement

For investors, a CIF's NAV is the single most important piece of information since it shows how their fund has performed in the period. The investors will want to assess this performance against inflation and other indices. Even where this is not a requirement, the CIF Manager should recognise investors' legitimate interest in this and provide investors with as much data as possible.

NAV statement for the Growth Fund as at 31 December 1998

	CU
Value of investments	205,000,000
Plus Current assets	75,000,000
Less current liabilities	45,000,000
Net current assets	30,000,000
Total net assets	235,000,000
Number of shares in issue at 31/12/98	1,500,000
NAV per share	156.67

The historic performance of NAV can be shown in the form of a table of figures or a chart. An example of useful presentation for the investor is shown below. The investor can compare the growth of the fund's NAV with the consumer price index and the stock market index. This table may also be expressed in a variety of graphic ways, which some investors may find easier to understand.

Performance of the Growth Fund to 31 December 1998

DATE (END OF QUARTER)	GROWTH FUND NET ASSET VALUE	STOCKMARKET INDEX	CONSUMER PRICE INDEX
12/96	100	100	100
3/97	105	104	103
6/97	103	105	105
9/97	110	108	107
12/97	125	120	112
3/98	115	117	117
6/98	135	134	121
9/98	132	125	125
12/98	157	138	130

10.1.2.4 Income and expenditure

This statement tracks money flowing into and out of the fund which is associated with the income received from fund investments and expenses of operation of the fund. It should include only the items relevant to the investment income and expenses of the fund. The subscriptions to – or withdrawals of money from – the fund by shareholders are not income and should not be categorised as such.

In the situation of an open ended CIF where all the expenses of the fund are met from the management fee charged by the CIF Manager, the income and expenditure statement can be extremely simple as shown in the next Table.

In many cases, audit and custody or trustee and regulatory fees will be payable directly by the fund and will, like annual management fees, be deductible from the fund's income in calculating its own tax liability.

While most tax regimes regard management and other expenses as tax deductible in principle, not all do, and even in those regimes which do allow expenses to be deducted, they may only be deducted from income which is received before deduction of tax.

Some types of closed ended investment companies may charge other expenses directly to the fund including some expenses of management. Such charges should be aggregated into one figure in the Statement of Income and Expenditure and analysed into appropriate categories in a note to the statement.

This statement is also important in the case of funds which pay out net income as dividends, because it shows the fund investor how much dividend he can expect to receive and enables him to compare that figure with previous years.

Statement of Income and Expenditure of the Growth Fund for the year to 31 December 1998

INCOME FROM INVESTMENTS	CU MILLIONS
Dividends (net)	19.3
Interest	2.59
Total income	21.89
Less expenses [1]	-2.05
Taxable income	19.84
Tax at 25%	4.96
Less tax deducted at source from dividends at 25%	-4.83
Tax (due) / reclaimable	-0.13
Net income available for distribution	19.71
Dividends declared totalling	19.5
Income carried forward	0.21
Total net income distributions per share [2]	CU 13

[1] 1.5% on weighted average of net assets of CU 205,000,000 plus other expenses itemised in a note

[2] On 1,500,000 shares

10.1.2.4 *Distributions paid to investors*

The statement of income and expenditure table given in the Table above shows this information: refer 'total net income distributions per share' (italicised).

10.1.2.5 *Details of the portfolio as at the accounting date*

The most valuable feature of CIFs for the individual investor is transparency. Clear statements of the assets held by the CIF are essential to give investors a true picture of the fund and to retain their confidence. Regulations will normally require the full portfolio of investments to be published at least in the annual report and many regulatory systems require it to be shown in the half-yearly reports as well.

CIF Managers should establish clear categories of investments and be consistent in their treatment of different investments. The next Table shows some categories commonly used.

An example of categorisation of investments

CASH DEPOSITS	EQUITIES		BONDS	
Domestic or foreign currency	*listed on an official market*	*unlisted*	*listed on an official market*	*unlisted*
	domestic	*foreign*	*domestic*	*foreign*
	categorised by industrial sector		*government convertible*	*corporate unconvertible*

It is a considerable help to the investor if the total amounts in each category are summed as shown in the next Table. Notes should be appended explaining the valuation treatment of unlisted assets, and of listed assets where trading in the shares has been suspended.

Statement of the Portfolio of the Growth Fund as at 31 December 1998

Note: Examples (eg "Example A") indicate how such data is shown under each heading: they do not add up to total given for each type of asset held.

HOLDING	INVESTMENT	MARKET PRICE	VALUE CU 000	% OF FUND
	Equities		*170,150*	*72.4*
	Domestic Equities [1]		*155,730*	*66.3*
10,500	*Example A*	*35*	*3,675*	*1.56*
	International Equities [2]		*14,420*	*6.1*
	USA		*9,200*	*3.9*
2,000	*Example B*	*83*	*1,660*	*0.7*
	UK		*5,220*	*2.2*
35,500	*Example C*	*6.5*	*2,310*	*1*
	Bonds		**53,280**	**22.7**
	Government bonds		*39,275*	*16.7*
10,000	*Example D*	*89*	*8,900*	*3.8*
	Corporate bonds		*14,005*	*5.9*
3,000	*Example E*	*79*	*2,370*	*1*
	Cash deposits [3]		*10,850*	*4.6*
	Accrued Income		*7,200.3*	*0.3*
	Total		*235,000*	*100*

[1] *All listed on an official stock exchange*
[2] *Prices converted at exchange rates ruling on 31/12/98*
[3] *Including CU 4,800,000 in 90-day Treasury Bills due for repayment on 30/1/99*

10.1.2.6 Investment transactions

Regulations vary in their requirements for disclosure of investment transactions. Best practice internationally is for the annual report to contain details of all investment transactions undertaken by the fund in the preceding year, though the interim report may carry only a summary. The dates of the transactions and the prices at which trades took place are normally omitted. All separate purchases of one security may be aggregated; likewise with sales. Where a new holding is acquired as the result of a takeover or merger this is normally stated in a note.

Investment transactions in the Growth Fund undertaken between 31.12.97 and 31.12.98

PURCHASES		SALES	
Security	Value CU 000	Security	Value CU 000
Equities		Equities	
2,500 Example A	1,230	1,250 Example B	1,843
3,900 Example C	2,190	2,950 Example D	1,055
Bonds		Bonds	
10,000 Example E	4,250	4,000 Example F	3,180
Total purchases	55,350	Total sales	48,840

Sophisticated investors – and regulators – can use these figures to calculate the total turnover of the portfolio of the fund vis a vis other funds to see if managers are dealing more or less than their competitors. The calculation is sales/average assets x 100%. In the example above, the Growth Fund's total assets at the year-end were 235 million; at the start of the year they were 185 million, so average assets were 210 million. So the calculation is 48.84/210 X 100 =23.3%.

Some Securities Regulators now require the publication of the names of brokers or other intermediaries with whom transactions exceeding a certain percentage of total transactions were done, and the average rate of commission charged. This is to ensure that investors can see if a certain broker was particularly favoured or if the rates of commission were above-average. This may be quite innocent or it might signify collusion for purposes not necessarily in investors' interests. Securities Regulators too will be interested in this information.

10.1.2.7 Statement of investment objectives

A statement of this kind is shown above, in the first table of this Chapter. The objectives can then be compared with the manager's report, to check on the correct alignment of the two.

10.1.2.8 Manager's report

The manager's report should explain the background to the fund's performance over the year and comment upon the investment results.

Report to shareholders for the Growth Fund

The Growth Fund

Report to shareholders for the period 1st January 1998 to 31st December 1998.

Thanks to positive markets for much of the year, the Fund's Net Asset Value rose from CU 142.5 at the end of 1997 to CU 156.67 at the end of 1998, a rise of 9.9%. This compares with a rise in the Local Stock Exchange Index of 8.5% over the same period, and with an increase in the Consumer Price Index of 5.8%. The longer term record of Net Asset Values is shown in the table on page 2. Income distributions totalling CU 13 per share were made during the year, an increase of 12.1% over the previous year's total.

The fund attracted new subscriptions of CU 32.5 million over the year and we extend a welcome to over 5,000 new shareholders.

Despite unsettled conditions in the financial markets at the start of 1998, short-term interest rates fell from 15% at the end of 1996 to 8% at the end of 1998. The rate of inflation too fell from an annual 13% to under 6%.

These developments would probably have prompted a stronger gain in the prices of shares if the economy had showed more signs of improvement. However, the recession lingered into the last quarter of the year and overall GDP is estimated to have fallen by about 1% in 1998. The greatest difficulties were experienced by companies dependent upon exports. The stabilisation of the exchange rate meant that they found it harder to achieve sales in highly competitive overseas markets. As a result, the fund sold its shareholdings in many engineering and capital goods companies.

The fall in interest rates has resulted in a small upturn in business in the construction sector. There is a shortage of modern commercial buildings and we consider that the sector has scope for considerable progress over the next few years. The fund has therefore added to its existing shareholdings in three construction companies and purchased shares in several others.

After a difficult time in 1997, the financial sector consolidated in 1998, with several large banks taking over weaker rivals. As the economy improves, they should be well placed to increase profitable lending and after avoiding the banking sector completely for the last two years, the fund has now purchased shares in two of the largest banks.

The fund reduced its holding of bonds from nearly 29% of total assets at the end of 1997 to 22.7%. With economic prospects slowly improving, it is likely that more bonds will be sold to increase investment in shares over the next six months. The fund's holding of cash deposits, which was 4.6% at the end of the year, will probably also be reduced. This is likely to mean that the fund will show a smaller increase in income distributions in the current year than it did in 1998.

If, as expected, the economic recovery continues, then company profits are likely to start to improve over the next year and the stock market should respond favourably. As compared with the past two years, prospects are much improved.

Reports to investors have a formal structure but need not be formal in tone or appearance. A simple example is the replacement of figures of the form 12,164,850 in a table of numbers with figures of the form 12,165 in a larger typeface in a column headed '000. This makes the numbers far easier to read. Differentiation of types of data through different typefaces can also improve readability. Rather than have notes in small type within tables or text, they can be placed separately in larger type.

CIF Managers often fill their reports with large quantities of data relating to the economy, interest rates, and so forth. Most of this in itself will mean nothing or very little to most individual investors. What the manager's report should do is to draw out the significance of the data. The report must cover the events of the past, but what investors are more interested in is the future, and though managers will not want to make predictions, they can explain the implications of recent events for markets and their fund.

In good times, when markets are rising and investors are enjoying high returns, good communications may seem to make little difference. But when conditions are poor, when markets and NAV are falling and investors see negative returns, then the confidence established previously by good communications can encourage investors to retain rather than sell their holdings. A small amount spent on good communications can result in the retention by the CIF Manager of revenue streams it would cost substantially more to purchase in the form of new subscriptions by way of marketing expenditure.

10.1.2.9 NAV per share or unit or participation

This figure shows the increase (or decrease) in the value of the share or unit in the reporting period, and enables comparisons with other funds over the same period.

Fund Performance 31 December 1997 – 31 December 1998

FUND	NAV 1.1.98	NAV 21.12.98	INCREASE/ DECREASE
Growth Fund	*142.5*	*156.67*	*+9.94%*

10.1.2.10 Total expense ratio

Many countries required that this figure appears in fund reports. This is the total cost of operating the fund in the previous accounting year, which may be required to be expressed in real terms – for the Growth Fund, expenses of 2.5 million in the year; or as a percentage of the net asset value of the fund (in this case, around 0.87%). It enables investors to compare the actual total costs of operation of their fund, compared to other funds and removes the potential for obfuscation of charges and expenses.

10.1.3 Semi-annual report

This report is essentially an unaudited version of the annual report, with slightly less detail given in it on the portfolio reporting side, covering the first half of the financial reporting year.

10.1.4 Net asset value or price per share or unit

This figure, often required to be accompanied by prices for the fund for the same day, is usually required to be publicised daily for open funds, and whenever issue and redemption is taking place for interval funds. Closed funds also publish net asset values – the timing of such publication varies from annually through to daily, depending on the regulatory requirements and/or the decision of the management of the fund.

The publication may be done on the Internet, or in print media. Publication of a single priced fund will generally look something like the table below.

Daily price disclosure for open ended fund

	INITIAL CHARGE	BUYING/ SELLING PRICE	+/–	YIELD
Growth fund	*3.5%*	*157.9*	*0.35%**	*8.04%*

*on previous day's price

Daily price disclosure for closed ended fund

	PRICE*	+/–	52 WEEK HIGH	LOW	YIELD	NAV	DISCOUNT
Growth fund	31.34	1.5	32.45	22.35	2.1	36.52	14.2%

*closing mid price

10.2 Sales and promotional communications

An enormously wide variety of sales and promotional communications
are used in relation to investment funds. Some – such as advertising –
are covered in Chapter 9. This section identifies a few of the most
common promotional communications.

10.2.1 Newsletters

Where a management company has a range of funds, it may choose to
send out newsletters covering current investment issues and other
information that they think will be of interest to investors. These can
also be used to advertise new products to existing investors.

These particularly tend to be used for communicating with financial
advisers. Increasingly such information is being made available on
closed user groups within fund management company Internet sites.

10.2.2 Yearbooks

This name is slightly misleading in that it implies that it is a status
report or summary on a previous year. In fact, these publications are
essentially mini-prospectuses for each open ended fund in a fund
management company's range, covering performance over the last
year, and including application forms and all information needed by a
potential investor. These publications are particularly useful when the
management company does not wish to advise investors which of
their funds it should select: it can simply give them the yearbook for
them to read and make their choice.

It is quite common to include decision-trees in such publications,
which help investors to identify whether they need income, or
growth, or both, and what level of risk they wish to accept, in order

to find out which funds are most likely to be suited to their needs. An alternative is to show grids which help people identify their preferences.

Relationship between risk and return

TYPE OF ASSET CLASS	PRICE FLUCTUATION	POTENTIAL FOR CURRENT INCOME	POTENTIAL FOR GROWTH
Shares	moderate to high	low	moderate to high
Bonds	low to moderate	high	low
Short term instruments	very low	moderate	very low

Historical performance indicates that investment in shares has been more likely to give higher returns over the longer term compared with other asset classes. Investors who need money at short notice take the risk of having to sell during a downturn.

10.2.3   Web sites

Web sites are increasingly used by management companies not only to display information, but also to provide dealing in the funds offered by that company. This is most developed in the USA; but even here, a new investor cannot simply decide to buy a new fund and deal on the Internet – a physical signature has traditionally been a requirement to open the investor's account with the management company. Once such an account is opened, on line dealing can be done.

Security of transmission remains an issue in many countries, however.

10.2.4   Factsheets

It is quite common practice for fund management companies to write a factsheet on each fund under management which summarises the main information that its sales and administrative personnel, and financial advisers, need to know. These documents are capable of being read at a glance and focus on the key features of the product.

10.3 Necessary investor information

In a dematerialised system, a regular statement of transactions on an account during the relevant period is issued to fund investors (refer Chapter 7). This usually identifies the following information:

- period covered by statement

- name, address and customer reference number of the investor

- name of the fund

- opening number of shares or units held and possibly their value at the opening date

- the number of shares or units purchased or redeemed during the period and the value of each transaction

- dividends paid in the period, or reinvested (identifying if net of tax and appropriate tax rate)

- closing balance adjusted for the value of transactions during the period

In a certificated system, certificates or dividends will have been issued as appropriate (refer Chapter 7).

10.4 CIF performance information

CIFs compete both with other savings and investment media and with each other to attract investors' money. Competition is often based upon demonstrating that one investment has, in the past, produced a better result than another.

Most CIFs therefore compete primarily on performance, and most CIF Managers therefore wish to demonstrate superior performance. The way in which the figures quoted for the performance of a fund are calculated and periods for which they are quoted are usually subject to stringent rules to prevent manipulation or misleading presentation.

10.4.1   Common comparisons

The managers of funds therefore usually set a target to beat. This may be:

- an average of other funds of the same category or sub-category or all other funds

- a stock market or bond index

- the interest rate on deposits

- the rate of inflation

In order to be able to determine whether or not the fund has provided a return to its investors superior to the chosen comparator there must be two givens:

- the statistics which are needed to calculate the comparator must be available and reliable

- the net asset value of the fund must be capable of being calculated reliably

In developing markets the inflation and interest rate comparators can usually be found from government or other published sources and can thus be calculated; but a stock market or bond index may not yet exist. In some cases, too, it may be doubtful whether a net asset value for some types of CIF is calculable with any degree of accuracy. This means that not only is the comparison with other CIFs impossible, but comparison with the available comparators is worthless.

Over time, however, a reliable net asset value will be available for each CIF, and can be judged to be sufficiently representative to make comparisons meaningful.

10.4.2   Comparing like with like

In order for comparisons to be statistically sound the figure for each comparator must be calculated in the same way in every case and over the same period of time, and must be seen to be objective – that is, not capable of being manipulated to someone's advantage.

In the case of the net asset value per share of CIFs and other investment funds, the calculation methodology is usually clearly set out in regulations – the problem of calculating it being not the methodology but the availability of accurate market prices of securities. Therefore all funds should be capable of calculating a net asset value per share on the same basis.

It is worth noting that, once data is available for all funds, it will be possible to construct an index showing the average performance of all funds. It will also be possible to produce tables showing the performance of all funds in descending order of return, with medians and upper and lower quartiles marked. In developed markets, both advisers and individual investors use such tables to assess fund performance.

The rates for deposits and for inflation are freely available. However, since there are a number of possible statistical methods of calculating these (the most obvious being whether to take a simple or a compound rate), it would be best if an index of each could be published by an independent source.

The nature of the comparator will also affect the proper basis of comparison with a fund. If fund offer to bid prices are used for a comparison, these include charges for entering and exiting the fund, as well as other costs paid by the fund in the relevant period. Comparing this figure to an index will not be fair, because an index does not include costs of investment. Offer to offer figures are therefore used for index comparisons. Comparing a fund on an offer to bid basis with returns on a deposit account in the same period will be fair, however, because the interest paid on the account will have been net of charges (though this will not be stated!).

10.4.3 The calculation

Having assembled the data for the time period over which it is desired to make the comparison, the calculation is mathematically simple. It is as follows:

$$\frac{B}{A} \times \frac{100}{1}$$

where B is the net asset value per share on the last day of the period over which it is wished to calculate performance and A the net asset value per share on the first day. This Table shows an example.

Fund Performance over the period 1.1.98 – 30.6.98

FUND	PRICE 1.1.98	PRICE 30.6.98	INCREASE/ DECREASE
Fund A	125	136	+8.8%
Fund B	324	398	+22.8%

But how should the two funds be judged if fund A had paid a dividend of 25.0 per share on 31.3.98 and fund B had not paid a dividend at all? Clearly the result for fund A shown above has been reduced by the value of the dividend paid out; if it had not paid the dividend the outcome would have been different.

In order to be fair to both funds it must be understood that shareholders in funds have two different sources of profit – dividends and capital gains (increase in value of share). Total return (the combination of income and capital gains) is therefore the measure universally used by independent analysts for the purposes of comparing returns and making performance comparisons.

10.4.5 Total return

In order to calculate total return it is assumed that the dividend is reinvested in shares of the fund. The investor therefore ends up owning more shares in Fund A at the end of the period. To find out how many more shares the investor obtains, it is necessary to know the price of the shares of the fund which has paid the dividend on the day after the dividend has been declared. The calculation for Fund A is therefore as in the next Table.

Calculating total return

DATE	NO OF SHARES	PRICE	VALUE	INCREASE/ DECREASE
1.1.98	100	125	12,500	
31.3.98	100	147	14,700	
1.4.98 (ex dividend)	120.49*	122	14,700	
30.6.98	120.49	136	16,387	+31.1%**

* the dividend of 25 on 100 shares is worth 2,500, sufficient to buy a further 20.49 shares

** $\frac{16,837}{12,500} \times \frac{100}{1}$

In this case, the computation shown in the above Table establishes that, contrary to the figures shown in the previous Table, Fund A actually gave a better total return to its shareholders than Fund B after dividends are taken into account.

Of course this calculation does not take into account taxation. In some countries the taxation of income and capital gains is at different rates. This means that the actual net returns to individual investors will depend on their own tax positions. It is therefore useful to individual investors to know not only what the total return was, but also its components in the form of income and gain, so that they may estimate their own net returns. Where figures net of tax are used, then the rate of tax deducted should be identified.

Ideally performance statistics should be calculated by an independent company or agency. CIF Managers are not the ideal people to do this; nor is a securities regulator. A trade association of CIFs, when formed, might be an alternative source.

10.4.6   The use of the performance statistics

To avoid the misleading use of performance statistics, there need to be rules as to the time periods over which performance can be shown; and any projections based on past performance should be forbidden.

Common rules governing performance include:

- a ban on projections into the future based on past results, including a ban on annualising performance data from shorter periods

- a mandatory statement which must appear in conjunction with the quotation of any performance statistics – for example: "past performance is not necessarily an indicator of future performance"

- performance figures should not be given for periods of shorter than one month and should be current

- if figures for short periods are quoted, then a figure for a longer period should also be given. Usually this is for a minimum of 5 years or since the inception of the fund, whichever is the shorter

- quoting performance figures to specific dates – the last day of each quarter, for example, rather than to some arbitrarily chosen date – so that real comparisons can be made

- it must be made clear whether charges are included or excluded both in relation to funds and to investments or indexes with which comparisons are made

- inclusion or exclusion of income from performance data must be clear

- income deemed to be reinvested should be subject to consistent treatment, in particular whether income is deemed to be reinvested gross or net of income tax

- whether all data is quoted gross or net of tax should be made clear

10

The regular publication of tables comparing the performance of all CIFs in newspapers and other media should be encouraged, so that shareholders can see whether their CIF is doing well or badly in comparison with others.

10.5 Queries and complaints

10.5.1 Dealing with queries

All fund management companies have to deal with a range of queries and complaints. As a general rule ordinary queries are dealt with by customer services divisions. These will cover a wide range of issues from whether people can invest for their children and how, to queries about taxation paid and when dividends are payable. These queries can broadly be classed as administrative and can be dealt with separately to more serious complaints. It is good practice, however, to have deadlines within which such queries should be answered; indeed, some companies set a series of standard response deadlines including the maximum number of rings on a telephone within which it should be answered.

One way of dealing with common queries is to prepare a standard list of the most common questions and their answers and print them so they can be sent out to all potential investors. Such lists can also be used by personnel who deal with these queries. It is generally worth logging common queries so that new materials or systems or procedures can include answers to them, or so that clear pointers are given to where to find answers, to avoid such questions in future.

10.5.2 Dealing with complaints

Complaints are a more complex area: procedures and deadlines for handling them are sometimes set out by regulation and sometimes not. Where rules do exist, it is often a regulatory requirement that a complaints ledger must be established and each complaint, and how it was dealt with, must be entered into the ledger. The ledger must be made available to the regulator for inspection upon request. In addition, there may be a requirement that a person who has sufficient seniority to resolve complaints is put in charge, rather than junior personnel who lack the necessary authority to sort problems out.

Regulators usually require that fund management companies identify the body responsible for regulating them on printed materials and letterheads, so that complaints about the management company can be addressed to the relevant organisation. It is usually a principle that a complaint should first be addressed to the organisation concerned; only if that firm fails to respond to the complainant's satisfaction within a reasonable period should the matter then be referred to the appropriate regulator or ombudsman (an ombudsman being an independent adjudicator which ombudsman scheme members pay for, and whose judgement they accept as binding). Regulators or ombudsmen may themselves provide public information advising people what they should expect from a regulated entity such as a fund management company and how to complain if things go wrong.

Complaints should be seen as a form of feedback about the quality of the management company concerned. Large numbers of complaints about administrative errors indicate poor quality management, or lack of focus on the back office, as opposed to front office, side of the business. The time and effort taken to resolve complaints are costly and can be unproductive; though there is some evidence that customers whose complaints are resolved satisfactorily are likely to remain loyal customers.

It is therefore preferable to plan systems and procedures to ensure that the minimum of errors occur, and to monitor complaints trends to see if further action needs to be taken.

While many complaints may be administrative – failure to amend addresses, incorrect details on contracts, etc – some will be more serious, where customers may have suffered a loss as a result of an error or omission. This can easily happen if an error has occurred in fund pricing, and investors have received too little upon redemption or paid too much upon subscription. Where such errors have minor impact – less than a half of one per cent of the price, for instance – it is generally accepted that the cost of correcting the error is too high by comparison with the benefit of correcting it. However, errors of a larger amount than this will give rise to compensation being due to those who have suffered loss or damage.

10

It is sensible for any fund management company to build into its procedures a series of cross-checks to try and avoid such errors arising: in common sense terms, it should never be left to a single individual – who however good, may be off colour one day – to oversee all aspects of valuation and pricing.

Meeting investors' needs

Management companies tend to create new fund products in one of two ways, usually described as 'investment led' or 'marketing led'. 'Investment led' firms tend to create new funds because they wish to invest in a new market, or asset or group of assets; while 'marketing led' firms tend to try and identify a need, and create a product to meet it.

Investors will usually buy funds to meet a perceived need: ranging from a general need – for income, or for growth, or both – to a specific need, to meet a particular future cost, such as school fees or a wedding. Realistically, however, it is more accurate to say that investors are sold CIFs to meet a perceived need; the adage that "insurance is sold, not bought" generally holds true for CIFs, also.

Key issues in developing CIFs are:

- who the potential investors are and what their perceived needs are – or what do they lack

- what the most effective structure is, in order for the fund to be attractive to investors and acceptable to regulators

- whether the fund can be made more attractive by provision of additional services or "wrappers"

- whether there is a sufficient supply of the required type of assets to make the fund work

- the competitiveness of the fund compared with relevant comparators

● how profitable the resulting product will be for the management company and what would be done to enhance this

11.1 Investors and their needs

11.1.1 Retail investors

Potential investors' need in relation to fund products will vary according to three key factors:

● their time horizon – usually defined as short (around 1 – 3 years), medium (around 3 – 7 years) and long (7 years or more) term

● their risk tolerance – that is, at its simplest, their willingness to accept that they could lose money in pursuit of gain

● the role of the fund or funds within their total investments – what other financial provision has been made to meet the investor's current and future needs (eg pensions)

It will also be influenced by their cultural preferences; historically, for instance, continental Europeans have invested in bonds more than shares, while UK investors have invested in shares rather than bonds.

Most investors will wish to have a mix of investments to meet different needs: for instance money market funds for short term needs; with longer term equity funds to build capital for retirement.

While some fund management companies deliberately set out to create a range of funds to meet most investment needs (often referred to as a "family of funds"), others will focus on a particular asset or sector – for instance, funds investing in emerging markets equity, which generally attract investors willing to take a long term, high risk investment strategy. If a family of funds exists, investors can be offered 'portfolios' of different funds in varying mixes, to meet their changing needs over time. An example of this type of approach is given opposite.

CHAPTER II

Possible CIF portfolios

PORTFOLIO TYPE	CONTENT	OBJECTIVE	INVESTOR NEED
Short term	100% short term instruments	minimum risk to money invested in the short term	maintain 100% of capital value and get some income
Capital preservation	30% short term investments, 50% bonds, 20% shares	preserve the value of money invested within conservative portfolio over the medium term	maintain capital value and get some income
Balanced portfolio	10% short term instruments, 40% bonds, 50% shares	give a combination of income and growth over the long term	achieve reasonable income and capital growth
Growth portfolio	5% short term instruments, 25% bonds, 75% shares	achieve higher growth than conservative investments over the long term	achieve growth
Aggressive growth portfolio	85% shares, 15% bonds	give high returns over the long term	achieve high growth

In general, investors seem to be more sensitive to loss of money than concerned with achieving high returns. Recently funds have been developed using derivatives that can reduce or remove the downside risk of investing in shares ('protected' funds); these have proved quite popular, though the cost of derivative coverage reduces the upside gain.

One way to help investors identify which sort of fund would best suit them is to develop a decision tree, or questionnaire, which identifies their needs for them (refer section 10.2). Products can also be developed upon this basis.

11.1.2 Institutional investors

Institutional investors will tend to buy funds to meet a specific investment need. This may arise because they lack the expertise to manage a particular type of portfolio themselves, or because it is not cost effective for them to hire their own management internally. An example of this arose in the UK: in the 1970s, when insurance companies became able to invest abroad they lacked expertise in foreign assets. They invested in both closed ended and open ended funds which invested abroad instead: in effect using external management. As they subsequently acquired general foreign investment expertise, they moved away from investing in general international funds, but continued to invest in emerging markets funds, since buying in their own managers had not been cost effective.

11.2   Choosing the most effective structure

Many considerations are involved in choosing the most effective structure for a fund, the key ones being:

- tax effectiveness

- portfolio content

- acceptability to investors

11.2.1   Tax effectiveness

As outlined in Chapter 3 and analysed in Chapter 12, different CIF legal structures may have different tax liabilities; as, indeed, may the type of assets they hold; and the investors who buy them.

The structure which will be chosen is the one which minimises the tax liability of the fund and of investors in the fund. This may involve creating the fund in one of the low tax domiciles ('offshore' instead of 'onshore'), provided that such a fund is permitted by regulation to be offered to the target market.

11.2.2   Portfolio content

Some asset classes necessitate the use of certain operating structures. A CIF which proposes to invest largely in illiquid assets should take the interval, or ideally closed ended form so it will not suffer from redemption pressure and have to sell assets too cheaply; at the other end of the spectrum, it would be pointless to have a closed ended fund which invested only in highly liquid money market instruments, since it would make liquid assets illiquid, in effect.

Historically most countries' fund industries started with closed ended funds, since there were insufficient liquid assets available to enable open ended funds to operate. Open ended CIFs developed only as liquidity developed in the underlying assets.

Most fund regulatory regimes set portfolio restrictions which are designed to ensure proper diversification (refer section 5.2): the total amount of a fund which may be invested in any one issuer, for instance. When it is desired that the portfolio should be more concentrated, the low tax domiciles which have more flexible portfolio restrictions may prove a more attractive base in which to create a fund; provided that a fund from the chosen domicile is permitted to be marketed to the target investors.

Where the CIF's proposed portfolio can be held within a number of different structures and suffer no relative tax disadvantage, it will be perceived investor preference that will dictate the structure chosen.

11.2.3 Investor preference

Most retail investors generally prefer to be able to get at their money quickly and to be able to redeem at net asset value; hence the greater success of open ended funds internationally (refer section 3.2). They may also be put off buying closed ended funds by the requirement to buy and sell these funds through a stock exchange, which may intimidate those unfamiliar with such a system.

However, more sophisticated investors may appreciate the opportunity that closed ended funds offer to buy at a discount and to receive income on full NAV and the greater exclusivity perceived to be attached to such funds.

11.3   Use of additional services and "wrappers"

11.3.1   Services

There is a range of services which CIF Managers can offer in relation to their products which may improve their attractiveness to potential investors. Given that in developed markets, many CIFs are very similar, the availability of special services from a CIF Manager may be a product's only distinguishing characteristic other than its brand identity. Examples of these services include:

11.3.1.1 Fund accounts

This is a facility for investors to open an account with a management company, through which investments in funds operated by that management company can be made. There is an increasing trend for such accounts to be able, once opened, to be operated online by the investor.

11.3.1.2 Regular savings plans

These are a facility which enables investors to save a specified amount at regular intervals (usually monthly or quarterly) and invest it in one or more CIFs operated by the same CIF Manager.

Regular saving has several benefits, both for investors and for CIF Managers. Investors find saving smaller amounts regularly less difficult than lump sum investment. It is also a mathematical fact that investing a fixed sum in assets whose price fluctuates lowers the average cost of the shares purchased. If markets rise, and so do fund share prices, investors' money will buy fewer shares; if markets are down, and fund share prices lower, their money buys more shares. This effect is known as "cost averaging". The greater the volatility in the price of the shares, the greater the effect of cost averaging, which by reducing the average acquisition cost of shares also adds to the investors' annual return. Given the difficulty experienced by professionals – let alone amateurs – in getting market timing right, cost averaging can offer considerable benefits. For CIF Managers, whether a regular savings facility is offered for open or closed ended funds, it creates known buyers for fund shares at known dates, which can ease the redemption or share sale position respectively. These plans cannot function, however, without efficient – and low-cost – money transmission facilities.

11.3.1.3 *Withdrawal schemes*

Investors who need a certain level of income a month can be offered an "income top-up" facility whereby, if income from the fund is insufficient for their needs, they sell the necessary number of shares to make up the specified total figure required. Alternatively, they can be offered a general facility for capital withdrawals, subject to retaining a minimum holding in the fund. Considerable care needs to be taken with the "income top up" option, particularly the way it is marketed, because investors often do not understand that this can greatly reduce the capital invested in the fund. Securities Regulators, who are aware of this, study such options carefully.

11.3.1.4 *Income distributions*

The CIF norm is for income to be distributed to investors half-yearly (refer section 7.3). More frequent distributions, such as quarterly or monthly distributions, may be a facility which can be offered for high-income products. This option may be restricted to direct payments to an investor's bank account or other low-cost payment method: if money transmission systems are not up to this, or are expensive, this may not be a viable option.

11.3.1.5 *Automatic reinvestment of distributions*

Many funds offer the facility for income simply to be reinvested into a fund, rather than distributed (refer section 7.3). In some countries such reinvestment is mandatory rather than optional. Investors wishing to receive the equivalent of an income, in a mandatory reinvestment environment, can instead be offered an automatic facility to redeem the number of shares/units that equates to the income that would have been distributed and receive the cash.

11.3.1.6 *Exchanges*

CIF Managers may choose to accept payment in securities or vouchers, as well as cash, for shares or units in their CIFs (refer

11

section 7.3). If the costs of disposal of securities for the individual are high or such disposal is difficult to achieve, this can be an attractive marketing ploy. However, the CIF Manager needs to factor in the extra costs required to deal with exchanges if the securities are not eligible for retention in the fund.

11.3.1.7 Switching

Where CIF Managers operate a range of CIFs, they often offer existing investors in their CIFs privileged terms on switching into another one (that is, redeeming out of one fund and investing into a new one). They may, for instance, reduce or eliminate the normal exit and/or initial charge or apply a set fee which is considerably lower than the normal charge.

Other, more general services, would include freephone lines, Internet access to information and – possibly – dealing; plus provision of taxation information.

11.3.2   "Wrappers"

These "wrappers" generally derive from the way that tax exemptions or alleviations are granted by governments in order to encourage investment or to encourage provision for old age. Experience in different countries shows that the most successful form of tax-incentivised savings scheme is one that has an annual limit on contributions, no time limit on the duration and no penalties for early withdrawal. The wrappers can take one of several forms:

● an annual entitlement of an individual to invest up to a certain amount in a specified range of qualifying assets: here the investor has an account, and holds the chosen eligible assets within that account. UK Personal Equity Plans (PEPs) and now Independent Savings Accounts (ISAs) take this form, as did the French 'Plans d'Epargne Personnel' which kick started the French funds market. The US has pension related wrappers of this sort known as 401(k) plans and Independent Retirement Accounts (IRAs)

- a pension or life assurance scheme, which usually qualify for tax relief of some kind, which in turn acquires shares or units in an underlying fund or funds

- tax reliefs given to specific types of fund (in addition to those normally applied to funds) provided that they meet certain additional defined criteria: this is usually applied to funds investing in certain categories of asset such as venture capital or new companies, to encourage their development (the ability to offset losses against gains is usually very important to the attractiveness of these funds)

Where an account is operated in addition to the underlying fund, this creates additional operational expense which may have the effect of making the product unattractive to investors. There may also be additional requirements – for instance, to provide detailed information on underlying investments to investors – which may also add to costs. British Personal Equity Plans were unattractive for fund managers to operate in the early years due to the complexities and cost of fulfilling original operating requirements and to the comparatively low ceiling on fund investment that was applied. Once the government relaxed these requirements – in particular, more than doubling the amount that could be invested in funds, the plans became cost effective to operate and were marketed much more strongly as a consequence.

11.4   Impact of supply of assets

A critical constraint on developing fund products is the availability of assets in which to invest – this could be restricted by the supply of assets in the relevant market or by fund portfolio restrictions set by regulation.

Emerging markets generally only have a limited supply of assets, many of which will be illiquid; so closed ended funds will dominate. As time goes on, and the market becomes more attractive to investors, liquidity will increase and supply of assets will increase to meet demand and open ended funds become possible. Once liquid markets exist, indexes can be created and derivatives markets start to

11

become possible, and 'protected' funds which use derivatives to
decrease downside risk become possible.

Chapter 8 explores issues relating to asset classes and their
characteristics further.

11.5   Need for profitability

No management company is going to a launch a product that they
believe will be unprofitable, except in the case where they believe
that they must have the product for competitive reasons. Section 6.5
explores the various charges that funds may levy; but this is not the
only factor affecting the profitability of individual funds. The other
factors are:

● average size of holding: administration costs are virtually identical
  for any size of holding. The larger the average holding, the greater
  the profitability. Where it is predictable that average holdings in a
  CIF will be small, the initial product design should seek to
  compensate for this by lowering administration, investment
  management or reporting costs. Consideration should also be given
  to methods of encouraging individuals to increase their holdings,
  possibly by offering special terms; encouraging reinvestment of
  distributions may also be useful

● duration: the costs of attracting new investors (by advertising or
  by paying commissions to agents) will often equal – or may even
  exceed – the initial charge. Profitability then depends on how long
  the investor holds his investment. Consideration should be given
  to schemes which incentivise the investor to hold for longer terms:
  for example, penalties on withdrawal in the early years –
  increasingly used and referred to as a "tapering back end load"
  (refer section 6.5)

● performance: the greater the rate of growth in the CIFs assets, the
  larger the sum taken by the CIF Manager as an annual percentage
  charge. The predominant effect on the growth rate will be the
  movement of the market, but any returns in excess of the market

average, or declines lesser than the market average, can contribute significantly to revenues. Investment managers may be motivated by personal incentives to achieve this

● costs: containing or reducing operating costs through systems improvements can contribute as much to profits as what investors may perceive as a substantial increase in the annual charge. Levels of marketing expenditure should be carefully considered also

In a highly competitive developed market, it is not unusual for a CIF product to be priced and sold on a basis that requires an average holding period of five years for the CIF Manager to show a profit. This is generally the result of erosion of the initial charge through competition. Even where regulations require total expenses disclosure, investors usually are more sensitive to the level of initial than annual charges, so that where price competition develops, it usually focuses first on initial charges. But if a CIF Manager develops an innovatory product that proves popular, it is also possible for the manager to make an initial profit averaging over 1% on sales. The normal range of profitability is between these extremes.

Economies of scale are a major factor in CIF Management. At the same time, the costs of launching new funds are relatively low. A commercial approach that is often seen is for the CIF Manager to make frequent launches of new funds in the hope that a minority of them will prove successful in attracting substantial public subscriptions. Those that do not are, after some time, merged into larger funds with broadly similar objectives. This approach is possible only with open ended funds where procedures for merger are relatively easy and low-cost, which is rarely the case with closed ended funds.

In the US, generally regarded as the trend-setter for CIF developments internationally, annual charges to a fund may be as low as 0.35% and are commonly below 1%. Admittedly this is the rate for CIF Managers which manage billions of dollars in a market worth trillions; but that was not the case when it started. This is worth bearing in mind when considering long-term strategy.

11.6   Typical fund families

For historical reasons, different countries' fund industries have
resulted in a preponderance of different products. For instance, in the
US money market funds were hugely successful in the 1970s (and so
were French money market funds in the 1980s) because government
restricted the level of interest payable on deposits. This meant that
retail investors got a much lower level of interest than that that was
available in wholesale money markets. Money market funds came
along which pooled large amounts of retail investors' money together
and so could access wholesale markets and offer higher interest rates
– and proved highly popular.

By contrast, the UK has hardly any money market funds, largely due
to the competitiveness of retail deposit-taking institutions.

A large proportion of the funds in most countries, however, can be
divided by the primary distinguishing features of funds. These are
those that aim:

● primarily to provide income

● primarily to provide growth

● to provide a mixture of both

Each will have within these categories a range of funds which involve
varying levels of risk; in general, the higher the level of income or
growth to be provided, the greater the risk to the capital involved.

Most countries' fund ranges would fall within the groups outlined
opposite.

Common CIF products and structures

TYPE OF FUND	ASSET BASE	OPERATING STRUCTURE COMMONLY USED	COMMENT
Money market funds	short term money market instruments which can be realised at any time at 100% of sum invested	open ended	must facilitate redemption and pay back 100% of amount deposited; closed end structure would make liquid assets illiquid and prevent maintenance of 100% of capital value
Income or "High Income"	domestic or foreign money market instruments	open ended	must facilitate redemption
	listed or liquid domestic or foreign national or local government bonds	open ended	must facilitate redemption liquidity needed for constant portfolio changes
	listed or liquid domestic or foreign corporate bonds	open ended or closed ended	closed ended form offers no particular advantages for investors in new CIF issue
	unlisted and untraded domestic or foreign corporate or government bonds	open ended or closed ended	closed ended structure preferable when portfolio not traded or listed
	listed or liquid domestic or foreign equities, shares or units in other CIFs	open ended or closed ended	closed ended form offers no particular advantages for investors in new CIF issue
	mixture of listed or liquid bonds and equities, foreign or domestic, shares or units in other CIFs	open ended or closed ended	closed ended form offers no particular advantages for investors in new CIF issue
	real estate	closed ended	real estate is too illiquid to be held in open ended funds

TYPE OF FUND	ASSET BASE	OPERATING STRUCTURE COMMONLY USED	COMMENT
Guaranteed income	government or corporate bonds	closed ended with a fixed life	guarantee cannot work with changing investment base
Growth	listed or liquid government or corporate bonds, domestic or foreign	open ended or closed ended	closed ended form offers no particular advantages for investors in new CIF issue
	listed or liquid equities, domestic or foreign	open ended or closed ended	closed ended form offers no particular advantages for investors in new CIF issue
	mix of listed and liquid bonds and equities, domestic or foreign	open ended or closed ended	closed ended form offers no particular advantages for investors in new CIF issue
	illiquid bonds or equities, domestic or foreign	interval or closed ended	interval needs some liquidity; closed ended may be preferable
	real estate	closed ended	real estate too illiquid for open or interval form
Balanced	mix of liquid or listed bonds and liquid or listed shares, domestic or foreign	open ended or closed ended	closed ended form offers no particular advantages for investors in new CIF issue
Flexible	can shift from money market to securities at any time	open ended	closed ended form offers no particular advantages for investors in new CIF issue

An interesting variant is the "split capital" (UK) or "dual purpose" (USA) closed ended fund, which issues two sorts of shares, capital and income. In its simplest form, the income shares have the right to all the income achieved by the fund, and the capital shares have the right to all the capital growth achieved by the fund. Such funds have to have a fixed life though investors may agree by majority vote to prolong this life. Here a single fund provides both income and growth, but separately to different classes of investor.

Beyond the general definition of "growth" – and to a much lesser extent, of "income" – are a wide range of possibilities for what are often termed "specialisms". These break down, broadly, into the following:

- **geographical:** funds which invest internationally (eg Global Fund), within a region (eg European Fund) or within a country only (eg Germany Fund); or funds which invest in a particular type of market or markets – such as emerging markets

- **sectoral:** funds which invest in a particular sector – usually internationally – eg telecommunications, energy, healthcare; or with a particular focus on larger or smaller companies; or on privatising companies

- **index:** these are funds which seek to replicate a particular stock market index, which is often, but not always, based on a national market (eg the "Footsie" or FTSE 100-share index). These are becoming increasingly popular as developing technology makes them easy and cheap to operate (mostly computerised) so their charges are low; and since most "active" fund managers fail to beat the index

- **ethical:** these are funds which focus their investment, either nationally or internationally, on companies which are considered "ethical" in their operations (the definition of "ethical" varies somewhat); a variant on this theme are "environmental" funds whose businesses in general are environmentally friendly or improve the environment in some way

- **fund of funds:** there are CIFs, both open and closed ended ones, which invest in other CIFs which again are either open or closed ended

- **venture capital or development capital:** funds of this type seek to invest in new businesses, or those whose shares are not yet listed or traded but plan to develop to that level

- **feeder:** this is a fund which exists only to invest into another designated fund, operated in a different domicile

- **derivatives:** these are funds which invest wholly in derivative instruments, sometimes known as futures and options funds or geared futures and options funds

Clearly the ability to operate these funds will depend on the availability of the asset – freedom to invest internationally – for instance, or presence of derivatives and indexes.

11.7   Pursuing a narrow focus

Some fund management companies build a highly successful niche business offering only a narrow range of funds. Examples of this might include managers that specialise only in open ended bond funds or money market funds sold to retail investors; or creating only closed ended funds investing in emerging markets for institutional investors.

Given the difficulty in distinguishing any one management company from another in the hundreds that are present around the world, such niche strategies can provide a useful distinguishing characteristic.

CHAPTER

The taxation of CIFs and their investors

12.1 Taxation is key to CIFs' competitiveness with other investments

Fund taxation is very complex and varies greatly from country to country. This Chapter does not seek to be an exhaustive guide to CIF taxation in any particular country, but rather explores the issues and problems, their implications for CIF Managers, and looks at some different solutions in different countries.

The taxation of CIFs is a key issue for their managers. Taxation affects both the attractiveness of CIFs compared with other investments, and also the systems that may have to be designed and implemented in order for CIFs to operate efficiently and cost effectively and to be capable of providing the necessary tax liability information to their investors. Accounting practice (see Chapter 13) will affect taxation strategy – for instance, if accounting standards do not require the capital and income of a fund to be distinguished, it will be impossible to apply taxation separately to these elements. Taxation and accounting considerations relating to CIFs are often, therefore, inextricably intertwined.

Most people will always try to avoid paying more tax than is absolutely necessary. In developed markets, existing CIF structures are often a direct result of past and current taxation regimes, since their managers have had to design vehicles to minimise tax liability and maximise returns in order to attract investors. Hence the use of the trust or contractual CIF forms which in some countries have been more effective in minimising personal tax liabilities than a corporate form.

Tax incentives have a major impact on the direction of savings flows. For example, tax incentives given by the UK government to invest in certain qualifying assets, through the so called Personal Equity Plans

12

("PEPs") played a major part in expanding the UK open ended fund market nearly six fold from $51 billion in 1986, when the incentives were introduced, to £297 billion at the end of 1998 (source: AUTIF). PEPs have now been succeeded by a similar type of plan called Individual Savings Accounts ("ISAs"). The US, likewise, has seen a massive influx of money into mutual funds, much of it resulting from tax incentives relating to retirement plans invested through CIFs, both through Independent Retirement Accounts ("IRAs") and the so called 401(k) market. In the same period – 1986 to 1998 – the total value of money invested in mutual funds rose more than six times from $716 billion to $5.7 trillion (source: Investment Companies Institute).

The tax incentive does not, therefore, have to be within the CIF itself, provided that the CIF is neutral (see 12.5) from the taxation perspective, or at least not disadvantaged, but may lie within a complementary product or "wrapper" as in the case with a pension or savings plan of the type described in the previous paragraph.

Governments sometimes deliberately seek to use taxation incentives as levers to influence the behaviour of individuals or corporations. While the motivation for introducing such incentives is understandable, the consequences are rarely as straightforward or beneficial as anticipated. In general tax incentives work when they encourage people to do what they want to do but do not work when they try to motivate people to do things they do not want to do. CIF Managers in virtually every market in the world lobby governments hard either to remove tax disadvantages or to achieve favourable treatment.

12.2   Political and social factors in CIF taxation policy

It is worth considering why governments should consider that CIFs merit favourable treatment as a taxable group. Fundamentally, it is because free market economies need to attract individuals' savings to finance their future development. Most people do not have sufficient capital to be able to achieve a good spread of risk in direct investments; do not have the expertise to choose them; and if they did, would find the cost of investing their small amount of money to be disproportionately high in relation to the benefits achieved. CIFs provide a solution to this problem, offering spread of risk, expert management and economies of scale which make them cost-effective. Therefore they are able to raise money for investment in capital markets which otherwise would be spent or kept unproductively under the bed in cash. It is this role in channelling savings that justifies favourable tax treatment, though CIFs are hedged around with operating and tax regulations designed to prevent abuse of this status.

A factor which can substantially affect taxation policy of CIFs – particularly in developing markets – is the tax collection system available to the government concerned. It is clearly much easier to collect tax at the enterprise or CIF level, where there may only be tens or hundreds of thousands of entities (which retain their own accounting personnel and tax advisers), than at the individual level, where there will be millions of people who are not experienced in dealing with tax and accounting issues. Many countries simply do not have the capacity, as yet, to deal with individuals' taxation, which imposes restraints on CIF taxation strategy.

Accounting practice will also have an impact on taxable revenue streams to and from investment funds (see Chapter 13).

Last, but not least, it is worth pointing out that in today's global markets most investors have access to neighbouring countries' CIFs. There are two separate issues here, tax evasion and tax avoidance. Ignoring the evasion aspect, investors are likely to choose funds where the overall impact of taxation is less. A notable feature of Western Europe's markets is the gradual convergence of the tax regimes applying to CIFs which has been driven by investors' ability to opt for lower-taxed funds domiciled outside their own country. Tax legislation that makes domestic CIFs unattractive will in the long run simply drive capital towards other countries' CIFs.

12

12.3 Main taxes affecting CIFs

The main forms of tax payable by CIFs internationally are:

- income tax – payable on any income to the fund whether from interest on deposits or bonds, dividends from equities, or rental from real estate

- capital gains tax – levied on any profit made on the sale of assets held by the fund, other than that received as income

Many countries make inadequate distinctions between capital and income, and tax both dividends and capital gains as "profits". Most developed countries make a distinction between the two.

Where both forms of tax outlined above exist, but are levied at different levels – say 35% on income but only 25% on capital gains – there will be an incentive to "convert" income into capital in order to minimise tax; and if these rates were reversed, to "convert" capital to income. These differences can give rise to a variety of innovatory CIF structures designed to avoid or minimise the overall level of tax paid by an investor. If these CIFs become too attractive and damage taxation revenues substantially – or if the CIF structure is used by entities which are not really savings vehicles – taxation authorities will have to change the rules, thus giving rise to the ever more complex taxation regulations applying to CIFs in most countries.

CIFs may also be liable to a large variety of other taxes – for instance, value based levies relating to securities transactions or value added tax on the fees paid to service providers – but are likely to have the same liability as any other entity transacting business in the securities market. Such taxes are unavoidable but will not usually substantially affect the competitiveness of the CIF form.

Tax liabilities will affect the way CIF transactions are recorded, the form in which accounts are kept and the presentation of income statements and balance sheets, as well as information to be given to investors.

12.4   Potential CIF tax liabilities

Possible elements of CIF taxation

The following Table shows how taxation may theoretically have an impact on the income received by a CIF and paid out to its share/unit holders at different levels and on the capital gains made by it. It must be emphasised that no regimes tax CIFs at all possible levels – that would be intolerable and ensure that CIFs were not bought by anyone.

TAX LEVEL	CAPITAL GAINS	INCOME
1 Issuer (in which CIF invests)	possible	tax withheld on interest or dividend payments
2 CIF	tax as profits, whether or not distributed	tax as profits, whether or not distributed
3 CIF payment to individual share/unit holder	if distributed as dividends, subject to withholding tax	if distributed as dividends, subject to withholding tax
4 Individual	tax as income or capital gains	tax as income

CIFs may be liable to pay tax on income or gains received from their assets which may already have been taxed in the hands of the company or organisation in which investment is made; on revenue or profits of the fund; and on distribution of income or gains to their investors. In addition, investors themselves may have taxation liabilities on their CIF returns, particularly if their tax rates are higher than any taxes paid by the fund. In theory, therefore there may be four levels of taxation applied on returns received by CIF investors, whereas only two at the most would usually apply to a person holding shares directly in a company instead of through a fund.

A key factor is whether CIFs are permitted to offset their own tax liabilities against tax already paid at source on income or gains that they have received. If they cannot, they are likely to suffer something like the problem shown in the next Table. In this case the CIF investor will have paid 20% more in tax than the direct investor in the investee company X; so the fund would have to produce a dividend which was at least 20% higher than company X in order to attract investment.

Double taxation problems for CIFs: dividend via a CIF

	DIVIDEND AMOUNT	LESS WITHHOLDING TAX	DIVIDEND RECEIVED BY FUND	DIVIDEND RECEIVED BY FUND INVESTOR
Dividend paid by investee company X to fund Y	100	20	80	
Dividend paid by fund Y to investor	80	20		60

Double taxation problems for CIFs: dividend received directly by the investor

	DIVIDEND AMOUNT	LESS WITHHOLDING TAX	DIVIDEND RECEIVED BY INVESTOR
Dividend paid by investee company	100	20	80

In the two cases shown above it is clear that an investor via the fund is worse off, since he is having to pay what is described as withholding tax twice, whereas the direct investor only pays it once.

12.5   CIFs should be at least 'tax neutral' or 'transparent'

The principle which has become generally accepted internationally is that CIFs, whether corporate or contractual, open or closed ended, should be neutral or 'transparent' in tax terms: that is, they should leave the individual investor in the same position taxwise as if he had purchased the underlying assets of the CIF personally. The general idea is that the fund itself suffers no tax, since this would interpose an additional level of taxation between the assets held by the fund and the returns the investor in the fund receives from them, compared to a direct holder of these assets. A term used for this approach in the US, which has a completely neutral approach to tax, is "pass-through". Many European countries, including the UK, adopt a tax neutral stance on income, but, by allowing capital gains to accumulate inside the CIF without suffering tax, introduce an element of tax privilege – essentially by permitting investors to defer their personal tax liability.

However, in countries where CIFs are in the early stages of development, existing tax regimes often fail to take any account of the distinction between a corporate CIF and any other company. This can impose several layers of tax burdens on such CIFs and their investors, notably when there is not distinction between capital gains and income which are both aggregated and taxed as "profit".

The situation may be aggravated by the fact that until a solid framework of law is established and enforced, business owners are often suspected of exploiting all possible means of avoiding the payment of taxes, so tax codes for business are often complex and exacting. Changes to existing legislation are often driven by the perceived need to prevent tax avoidance, often with unintended and unwelcome consequences for CIFs. Legislators and Securities Regulators need to work together to ensure that tax laws do not thus penalise CIF investors.

The aim of transparency or fiscal neutrality is entirely logical if the position of the individual investor is considered. He may purchase securities himself through the medium of the stock exchange, or he may buy shares in a CIF. In both cases he owns securities. Why should his tax treatment differ?

12.5.1   Tax incentives and CIFs

In most countries where CIFs play a significant role in drawing individual investors' capital into equity markets as a source of long-term capital, there is a possible counter-argument: that the CIF investor should enjoy a tax advantage relative to the direct investor in securities as is the case in some European countries. If this argument is accepted, however, then it is more efficient and equitable to create a special class of tax-privileged plans than to give CIFs themselves a tax advantage. This leaves CIFs as 'tax-neutral' while the tax-privileged plans themselves – which are associated with specific individuals, subject to whatever limits the government decides – may permit investment in CIFs. This is the approach used in the US and to some extent the UK, where Independent Retirement Accounts and Section 401(k) pension plans and Individual Savings Accounts respectively may be used by individual investors to hold investments in qualifying CIFs on a tax-exempt basis.

Essentially there are three potential elements of tax incentives for such plans:

- tax-free (or tax-deductible) entry: that is, the contribution is made out of gross income rather than net income of the individual

- exemption from tax for capital gains in and income from the portfolio

- no tax payable at the time the investor withdraws money from the scheme

The most attractive schemes may combine all three.

In the special circumstances of the privatisation funds and specialised restructuring funds used in emerging economies, such funds may need to be given special tax status initially, particularly if their tax burden would otherwise be unduly onerous, but after some period of time their tax treatment should fall into line with that of other forms of CIF.

The pursuit of 'tax-neutrality' for CIFs is not easy even in a developed tax system, principally because of problems over the treatment and definition of capital gains, as discussed below.

12.5.2   Preventing abuses of CIF status

Any special tax treatment for CIFs should be limited to suitably qualifying funds: usually these are required to have regulatory approval and to meet specific tax authority requirements. Regulatory approval seeks to keep undesirables from exploiting investors attracted by "tax free" labels, while tax authorities seek to prevent misuse of "tax free" status by securities traders, trading companies and others.

When dealing with closed ended corporate funds it may be difficult to distinguish a CIF from a normal limited company. Giving special tax treatment to closed ended CIFs could encourage the proprietors of ordinary limited companies to adapt the structure of their own companies to try to secure the more favourable tax treatment: if they succeeded, the State could lose substantial tax revenues. Tight definitions of qualifying companies are therefore required.

An example is the definition of 'investment trust companies' in UK tax legislation. These are closed ended investment companies which benefit from 'tax transparency' in that they are not liable to capital gains tax on realisation of gains provided such gains are reinvested: an advantage that would be highly sought after by other limited companies, which are liable to the tax. However the rules restrict this tax concession to companies which fulfil the following criteria:

● the company must be resident in the UK

● the company's income must be derived wholly or mainly from investment in securities (over 65% of total income) or rental from eligible properties

● no more than 15% of the company's assets may be invested in the securities of any one issuer

● the company may not retain more than 15% of the income it receives from investments

● the company's shares must be listed on the London Stock Exchange

● the company has to submit its annual report to the tax authorities. If these show that the company is not in compliance with the above requirements the tax authorities will withdraw the tax concessions and charge tax as if it were a normal company

The US taxation authorities, amongst others, use a similar approach for their investment companies.

12.6 Policy on taxation of CIF income

In theory the taxation of CIF income should be simple, but in practice it is not, due to the varying sources of income that a fund may have, and the different levels of tax that may, or may not, be payable on them.

12.6.1 The US and Europe have different approaches

There are essentially two ways of approaching the application of tax to fund income. One is that of the USA, which is the "pass-through" system. Whatever income the fund receives is simply passed on to CIF investors with no tax intervention. The investor receives a statement annually from the CIF which identifies dividends distributed to him for the period (which includes short term gains as well, see below). The investor must then declare these dividends on his tax return. It also assumes that most interest on bonds and dividends from shares is paid out gross by the issuer – without withholding tax. Added to this is the requirement to pay out short and long gains. This probably is the most transparent approach to CIF taxation; but it demands a taxation system that can deal with millions of individual tax returns, and a degree of sophistication on the part of the investor who will have to deal with dividend statements which show several different sources of distributed income and gains each of which may attract a different tax rate.

Another approach is exemplified by the UK and most of Europe, which is essentially based on "tax credits", sometimes called the imputation system. This means that UK companies deduct (or withhold) tax at the basic rate of income tax from dividends before distributing them. The CIF which receives such a dividend net of tax passes on this "tax credit" to its investor, who will then only pay more tax if his tax rate is higher than the basic rate of tax.

Example of tax credit

Stage	Tax deducted Yes/No	Rate	Tax credit passed on	Tax credit received	Net	Tax payable
Profit before tax[1]	N – 100					
Profits/corporate tax	Y	30				
Dividend tax relieved against profits tax or vice versa Adjusted profits tax[2] [3]		10				10
Paid by corporation	Y	20	20		80	20
Received by fund				20	80	
Paid by fund	N	0	20		80	0
Received by shareholder	Y/N			20	80	0[4]
Total tax paid by company, fund and shareholder combined						30

[1]Different countries may tax interest on bonds or interest on bank deposits at different rates

[2]If dividends or interest are received from abroad, there may be double tax relief or not

[3]The assumption is that the whole of the profit after tax is paid out as dividend

[4]But if personal rate higher than 20 then shareholder must pay difference between rate and 20. Some countries allow a person whose tax rate is zero to reclaim the amount of the tax credit. These may be individuals or exempted persons, like pension funds

Unfortunately for the "tax credit" system, CIFs are unlikely only to receive income that has borne tax at source. It is possible that tax is not deducted from interest paid to the fund on domestic government bonds or bank deposits, or from any domestic real estate rental income which the fund receives; or that any such tax is payable at a different rate on each. The picture becomes even more complicated when the CIF owns foreign assets, potentially in a range of countries, each with their own, varying, tax regime which may mean that the fund is unable to claim excess tax paid or may need to pay domestic tax on their receipt. Where investment abroad is concerned, the availability of international double tax treaties is therefore an important consideration in establishing the returns that funds may be able to make.

These differences in tax rates on various types of income may require complex accounting adjustments and tax calculations (see below) and will certainly require careful records to be kept. Individuals completing their tax returns frequently expect CIFs to be able to give them detailed information on tax liabilities that they may have; providing such information is one of the services provided by CIF Managers to their investors.

12.6.2   *Complexity of accounting for different sources of income*

Whatever the general framework of tax legislation, CIFs will have certain defined liabilities to tax on their income and capital gains. In different jurisdictions, CIFs may receive gross income and income taxed at different rates at source. A variety of methods are therefore needed to account for the fund's taxation liabilities.

For example, take the case of a CIF in a jurisdiction that has a relatively transparent system. The CIF receives dividends and interest payments from domestic listed securities net of income tax at a rate that corresponds to the basic rate of income tax for individual investors. The fund has a liability to the basic rate of tax on this income but this liability is met by the tax credits passed to it by the issuers of the securities it owns. Such income therefore flows through the fund with no actual tax being deducted or paid (see lower Table on page 266).

But this is not the end of the story. The fund also keeps some money on deposit with banks where it earns interest which is paid without any deduction of tax. It also invests in some foreign shares; here dividends are received net of the relevant countries' withholding taxes, which may be higher or lower than the domestic rate. It also holds some eurobonds whose interest is paid gross.

Assuming the legislation defines the fund's tax liability as the basic rate of tax, and taking this rate of tax as 20%, the fund's tax liability would be calculated along the lines of the Table on page 271.

It is assumed (as is usually the case) that the management expenses of the fund are a valid deduction from its gross income in computing its tax liability. Where sufficient gross income (from sources such as bank deposits and eurobonds) is generated to cover the management expenses, then the procedure is straightforward. However, the fund may not generate sufficient gross income. Suppose, in the example given in the next Table, the management expenses were 30,000 instead of 14,000. In this case the tax deducted at source would amount to more than the fund's actual tax liability. Then the question is whether the fund is entitled to reclaim the tax deducted at source from dividends on domestic shares and from interest on domestic bonds. In some regimes such reclaims are permitted while in others they are not. If such reclaims are difficult and protracted, then CIF Managers will tend to generate sufficient gross income to cover management expenses in order to avoid making such reclaims.

A CIF's income tax liability

SOURCE OF INCOME	INCOME RECEIVED	TAX DEDUCTED AT SOURCE	GROSSED UP INCOME	TAX COMPUTATION
Domestic shares	8,000	2,000	10,000	
Domestic bonds	8,000	2,000	10,000	
Overseas shares	7,500	2,500[1]	10,000	
Eurobonds	10,000	NIL	10,000	
Bank interest	10,000	NIL	10,000	
Total gross income			50,000	
Less: management expenses			14,000	
Taxable income				36,000
Tax due (at 20%)				7,200
Less: Tax deducted at source				6,500
Add: tax reclaimable [1]				500
Tax payable				1,200
Net income				34,800

[1]Under an appropriate double taxation treaty, the fund may reclaim the difference between its own tax rate and any higher rate deducted at source

12.6.3   Differential income tax rates may be problematic

If the tax regime sets the rate of tax on CIFs' income at a higher level than applies to individuals, this may not matter if a) the differential is fairly small and b) individual investors would incur substantial transaction costs and/or high risks if they invested in securities directly. This is likely to be the position in emerging economies. In more mature markets, any differential will tend to encourage investors to sidestep CIFs and invest directly in securities.

If the tax regime sets the tax rate for CIF income at a lower level than would apply on direct purchases of securities, then it creates an incentive for investors to channel all securities purchases through CIFs. This may be desirable in the initial stages of development of a CIF industry where a government is keen to develop a culture of savings. However in the long run it is also likely to have undesirable side effects. One is that affluent investors will almost certainly try to establish CIFs under their own control and run them as private portfolios in order to benefit from the lower tax rate.

If tax is payable on income paid through funds, but not on bank deposits or government bonds, for instance, funds are unlikely be able to compete effectively with these lower-risk investments since diversification and professional management are unlikely to be strong selling points for CIFs which invest in relatively risk free assets.

12.7 Policy on taxation of CIF capital gains

The main reason developed economies have capital gains taxes is to deter investors from evading tax by converting income into capital gains; even in these countries, however, capital gains are often permitted tax-free provided they do not exceed a specified annual figure. Conversions of income into capital will only start to occur in conditions where a considerable degree of financial sophistication has developed and where a significant number of people would benefit from them. An example would be Germany, which does not levy capital gains tax at all on assets held for more than six months, thus providing an apparent opportunity to convert taxable income into tax-free capital gains. However, Germany has a number of anti-conversion rules – including a requirement that gains made when bonds are bought at a discount must be taxed as income.

12.7.1 Complexities of capital gains tax

Taxes on capital gains can cause even more complexities for CIFs and their investors than taxes on income. The main reason is that in many jurisdictions, capital gains in the hands of individuals are taxed at a lower rate than income, or not taxed at all, or exemptions are given for small gains in any given year. This creates an incentive for individuals (and CIFs) to convert income into capital gains, and anti-avoidance provisions may become necessary to counteract this. The fact that under most regimes CIFs could not pay these gains out to investors as income would

not matter, since investors who wished to convert the gains locked into
the fund into cash could simply sell sufficient shares to obtain the cash
equivalent of the gain. In today's capital markets such income-to-capital
conversion strategies are relatively easy to devise.

The principle of fiscal transparency suggests that the CIF itself should
pay no capital gains tax on its realised profits but that individual
investors should be liable to capital gains tax when they sell their CIF
holdings. But consider the situation of the direct investor to start
with: if he owns a portfolio of securities and manages them actively,
he will realise gains and incur capital gains tax on his profits from
time to time. If the investor is permitted to hold CIF shares
indefinitely without incurring any capital gains tax, while the CIF
itself incurs no tax on its internal realised gains, and the individual
only becomes liable to gains tax when he sells his CIF shares, this
does in fact represent a concession for the CIF investor as compared
with the direct investor in securities. The extent of the concession is
unquantifiable because it depends on the behaviour of the individual
investor in securities. For example, if he trades actively he will incur
tax sooner than if he adopts a 'buy and hold' strategy.

The US approach is to require CIFs to distribute all gains in the year
in which they arise, and tax the investor on these at his appropriate
rate which may vary with the amount of the gain and the investor's
income. However, as discussed above this is a complex way of
handling the problem in countries whose tax collection system and
investors' sophistication are not of the highest order.

However, the alternative regime, which is that the CIF is subject to
tax on its realised capital gains, while the investor is also subject to
gains tax when he sells, and the investor receives no relief or credit
for capital gains tax already paid, then this does represent a form of
double taxation which penalises the CIF investor as compared with
the direct investor.

12.7.2   The different approaches to the taxation of gains

To date, no country has found an entirely equitable, simple and cost-effective approach to capital gains tax, primarily due to the "conversion" problem. There are three main approaches to the issue and one hybrid solution.

12.7.2.1 The European approach

Many – but not all – European jurisdictions grant CIFs exemption from capital gains tax on their realised investment gains. Usually this exemption is subject to the restriction that the gains are not paid out to investors but are retained within the fund and reinvested. The individual investor is subject to capital gains tax on the profit when he sells his CIF shares. Basically this taxation policy represents taxation revenue deferred rather than foregone.

12.7.2.2 The US approach

The US – under the "pass-through" system – makes both short-term (under 18 months) and long-term capital gains (over 18 months) subject to tax in the hands of the fund investor and not the fund. In order to deal with the "conversion" problem, short-term gains are taxed at the investor's income tax rates which are higher than long-term capital gains rates. All gains, therefore, are distributed gross of tax, as are dividends and interest.

12.7.2.3 Complete exemption approach

In less developed economies, governments may prefer simply to exempt individuals' capital gains from taxation altogether. This is unlikely to result in any substantial loss of tax revenue: even in developed economies, capital gains taxes on individuals raise insignificant amounts of revenue as compared with income taxes.

12.7.2.4 Use of a tax credit

A compromise solution is possible, whereby the CIF bears capital gains tax at a lower rate than individual investors (say half the normal rate) and passes on a credit of this amount to an investor when he sells. But perhaps the individual investor is for some reason not personally liable to the tax (which will depend of course on the specific gains tax regime). Then he will have to make a tax reclaim. Moreover, suppose that the regime taxes capital gains as additional income, and that there are several progressive income tax rates. Then there are issues about how the tax credit given by the CIF will be applied against the individual's tax liability. And there are also difficulties regarding losses carried forward from previous years (if the regime permits this) and their offset against CIF gains. So such a compromise solution certainly adds to the complexity of the tax system.

The effect of the different systems

	US APPROACH [2]	EUROPEAN APPROACH [3]	CREDIT APPROACH
Capital gain	100	100	100
Fund tax	0	0	30
Retained	0	100	70
Distributed	100	0	0
Shareholder receives	100	0	0
Shareholder pays	[4]	0	0 but receives credit for tax already paid by fund
Shareholder sells shares in fund pays tax	Y	Y	Y
Tax payable	[5]	[6]	[7]

[2] Known as "pass through"

[3] The general principles only are shown here; details vary

[4] Shareholder pays special rates which are differentiated between short gains (under 18 months) and long gains

[5] Capital gains tax payable in principle, but previous tax paid on distributed gains deducted

[6] Paid at the appropriate rate of capital gains tax applied to individuals. UK adds gains to income so tax payable at highest marginal rate; Germany no capital gains tax on individuals

[7] Paid at appropriate rate, but after deducting tax credits received

12.7.3 Effect of the chosen taxation base of CIFs' capital gains

Where CIFs are subject to capital gains tax, the variations in the taxation of capital gains may be rather wider than those in the taxation of income.

12.7.3.1 Deemed cost of acquisition

Whatever the rate of tax, there is also the issue of what the CIF's original cost of acquisition of the asset is taken to be, bearing in mind that several purchases of the same security may have been made over several days or indeed several years. It is also likely that, in the case of a security held for many years, there may have been sales as well as purchases and other events which may have affected "cost" – such as rights and scrip issues, mergers and reconstructions. There are three options for the basis for capital gains taxation: Last In First Out (LIFO), First In First Out (FIFO) and Average Cost (AC). All three are illustrated in the next Table.

Under international accounting conventions, all three methods are equally valid. Legislation may not lay down which basis CIFs must use but leave it to CIF Managers to decide. In general the Average Cost method is the simplest and least prone to distortions in use by CIFs.

The FIFO method, which assumes that the price of the first securities bought is the taxable base for gains or losses on the first sale of the same securities, will obviously result in large tax liabilities in conditions of high inflation unless some form of indexation of costs is permitted. If so, the government will publish an index which may be used to uplift the nominal cost of assets to a higher cost which is used as the basis for computing liability to capital gains tax. Even when such indexation is permitted, the rules for its application may still result in some taxation of 'paper' or nominal gains. This can result in erosion of a fund's assets, and even where the effect is small, it represents an arbitrary imposition. Depending on how taxation is accounted for, it may also disadvantage ongoing investors in a fund at the expense of outgoing investors.

12

The LIFO method, which assumes that the price of the last securities bought is the taxable base for the first securities sold is less vulnerable to inflation within a normal range but as a system is better suited to single infrequent asset transactions. Where a CIF buys shares at differing prices over a period of time and sells the shares in equal tranches over an extended period, the application of LIFO will produce arbitrarily variable tax liabilities on each sale.

In contrast, the AC method effectively averages the tax rate across all purchases and sales. As a system it is therefore least likely to produce relative disadvantage for incoming, outgoing or ongoing investors in a CIF.

Different methods of computing capital gains tax

NUMBER OF SHARES BOUGHT (+) OR SOLD (–)	SHARE PRICE	RESULTANT HOLDING OF SHARES	AVERAGE COST COST	GAIN	LAST IN FIRST OUT GAIN/LOSS	FIRST IN FIRST OUT GAIN/LOSS
+100	100	100	100	–	–	–
-50	125	50	75	–	1,250 (50X25)	1,250 (50X25)
+100	80	150	78.33	–	–	–
-100	100	50	35	–	2,000 (100X20)	1,000 (50X NIL) +(50X20)
-50	100	NIL		3,250 {50X(100-35)}	NIL	1,000 (50X20)
Total taxable profit				3,250	3,250	3,250

12.7.3.2 Offsetting gains and losses

Another issue in relation to funds' capital gains tax liabilities (and indeed those of fund investors) is the ability to "net out" losses against gains. This means that, where assets have been sold at a loss during the current tax year (or sometimes aggregated over previous tax years), these losses can be deducted from gains realised in the same year, thus reducing the capital gains tax liability. The ability to offset losses against gains, within specified parameters, is given in most developed market CIF taxation regimes.

12.7.3.3 Problems of cost free acquisition

A common problem with privatisation funds, where privatisation entitlements, usually received free of cost, have been exchanged for shares in the fund, concerns the taxable base value of the entitlement both in the hands of the investor and in the hands of the fund. It can be argued that the cost base for capital gains tax purposes is zero, which can give rise to enormous tax liabilities both for the fund and for the investor. A similar problem can arise in the case of gifts from one person to another or when a company making an initial public offering of its shares decides to allow employees to have the benefit of a number of "free" shares.

There is no logical solution to these problems, which are, as in the case of so many anomalies in fund taxation, only solved for reasons of political, economic or social policy.

12.7.3.4 Indexation for inflation

It is common to permit indexation of capital gains against inflation in both developed and developing markets, either within the fund (if capital gains tax applies) or in the hands of the investor. This will, clearly, reduce the liability to capital gains tax.

Accounting principles for CIFs

13.1 There are special accounting standards and principles for CIFs

Developed financial markets have created special accounting standards for CIFs, referred to as "Statements of Recommended practice" (SORPs) or "Generally Accepted Accounting Principles" (GAAPs). Also within the long list of standards published by both the Federal Accounting Standards Board ("FASB") in the US and the International Accounting Standards Committee ("IASC"), based in London, there are quite a number which relate to accounting for securities and derivatives, which have to be followed in the presentation of accounts to share/unit holders.

A special approach to CIF accounting is needed for both open and closed ended funds because, even though many funds are constituted as companies, they do not behave in the same way as trading companies. A CIF is more like a box containing certificates representing ownership of assets, with a group of people (the fund Board; the custodian and the CIF Management company) who control access to the box and what is inside it. Unlike other companies, the CIF usually has no full-time employees, no office or factory, and no plant and equipment.

This Chapter deals with the technical accounting principles and dilemmas relating to the way the statutory financial accounts of funds are constructed and presented. There are other aspects of the operation and administration of CIFs which would normally be covered under the general description "accounting". In this book these may be found in the following places.

- the whole question of valuation and pricing, an important aspect of financial presentation of the results of CIFs, is dealt with in detail in Chapter 5

- the format of reports to share/unit holders is in Chapter 10

- reports to the Securities Regulator may have to be presented in yet another format

13.1.1 To whom the accounts are of interest

Accounts of CIFs are of interest to:

- actual and potential investors who are concerned with the investments held by the fund, their capital value, the income from them, and the costs of achieving this performance

- the Securities Regulator, who is concerned with ensuring that the fund is being managed in accordance with the Law and Regulations

- the taxation authorities who will regard the accounts as the basis for assessing the liability of the fund or its investors to tax

- creditors and potential creditors of closed ended funds which have the power to borrow

Both company and fund accounting rules are designed to prevent manipulation of these figures, on which investors base their financial decisions, and on the basis of which the licence to operate as a CIF given by the Securities Regulator is granted and continued, and on which tax is assessed.

13.2 Key principles of CIF accounting

Key principles of CIF accounting are:

- income and capital of the fund must be accounted for separately: this means that –

- accounts must clearly show the total return achieved on the CIF's investments, both in capital and income terms, separately identified (open ended funds must account separately for the movements in holders' money associated with purchase and redemption of holdings)

- taxes due to be paid on income and on capital either by the fund or the holder must be clearly and separately identifiable

- the operating expenses of the fund and of fees to contracted service providers to the fund must be clearly identifiable and attributed to capital or to income, or to both

- the derivation of distributions to investors must be clearly identifiable as being from income or from capital or both

- the basis on which the investments within the portfolio are valued must be clear and must be consistent unless good reason for change can be demonstrated

- the basis on which accounting is done – usually historical cost convention – should be clear and should be consistent throughout the accounts (this may be mandatorily set by the tax authorities or the Securities Regulator)

- whether investments are accounted for at trade date or at settlement date should be clear (regulators may set specific rules on this) and consistent; reason for any change should be recorded

- the accounts should clearly and consistently apply the accruals concept; where it is not applied, reasons should be clearly recorded

- the custodian should keep in respect of each CIF parallel accounts to the CIF Manager, and these accounts should be reconciled at stated intervals

13.2.1   Open ended and closed ended funds have different accounting needs

Despite the fact that closed ended funds are generally constituted as joint stock companies with a fixed capital and open ended funds (whether in the corporate, contractual or trust form) have variable capital, there are elements which are common to the accounts of both types. Both open and closed ended funds are usually required to include in their accounts (annual and semi-annual report contents in general are covered in Chapter 10):

- a balance sheet, or in the case of an open ended fund, a statement of net asset value, which is in effect a balance sheet, showing assets and liabilities

- a profit and loss account (operating statement), showing the amount and source of income received, the fees and charges for management and services, the amount of tax payable, and the amount of the net income to be paid as dividend

- a portfolio statement, showing the securities and cash held at the date of compilation and highlighting the main portfolio changes during the period under review

- notes to the accounts, detailing their basis

- the net asset value of the share or unit at the beginning and end of the accounting period

- the figures for net asset value per share or unit and the amount of the dividend or distribution from the previous year, given for comparison

- the custodian or trustee's statement and signature as well as the auditor's report and signature

- a statement of total returns – that is, the CIF's investment performance – which shows the gains or losses on investments and income from them, clearly identifying tax and management fees and fund operating expenses deducted either from income, or capital, or both; also making clear the amount of that return which is to be distributed to CIF investors

- for investors in open ended funds, the net increase/decrease in funds resulting from the sale and redemption of shares/units is added to the figure derived from the calculation described as "returns to holders". For open ended funds this is called is the "Statement of net increase/decrease in holders' funds"

Closed ended corporate funds will also have to include any other requirements of joint stock company law, securities law, the civil or commercial codes, and corporate taxation from which they lack an exemption.

13.2.2 Standardising CIF accounting

CIFs are usually required to produce an annual audited report and a six monthly unaudited report, both of which will be sent to Securities Regulators (who may require more frequent reporting as well) and to investors. In some countries, the annual report must be made up to the end of a mandatory accounting year (for countries which have a year-end fixed by law – usually 31 December), even if a fund has only been operating for only part of it; in others, the accounting year may start from the date of inception of the fund.

Open ended CIFs which value their shares/units daily are, in effect, producing a balance sheet each time they carry out a valuation and calculation of net asset value (see Chapter 5), with a full statement of assets (investments at market value and current assets) and liabilities (current liabilities and share capital represented by the current number of shares/units in issue).

In several countries, trade associations for CIFs have worked together with professional accounting bodies to produce recommended accounting standards for different types of CIF. Usually, neither existing accounting rules nor the regulations made by Securities Regulators provide precisely detailed rules for the presentation of financial statements by CIFs. This can lead to different CIF Managers presenting information in quite different ways. It is certainly helpful to investors and to regulators if all CIF Managers use the same format, and a trade association of CIFs is best suited to the task of negotiating a standard with regulators and auditors.

In many countries accounts are required to be completed in formats whose complexity and obscurity will signify little to the ordinary person who may be an investor in a CIF. For this reason, Securities Regulators may permit special forms of accounts to be sent to holders which are shorter and clearer than those required to be submitted to Securities Regulators, tax authorities or other government departments. The purpose of these short-form accounts is to show investment return, and the costs of achieving it – they are, therefore, a statement of information underlying the net asset value. Such accounts are required to include a statement of total return, a statement of movement of holders' funds (open ended and interval funds only), a statement of assets and a distribution table, where applicable. The following two sets of accounts are those which typically would be used in presenting information about open ended CIFs.

13

Total return statement contents

	Revenue	Capital	Total
Realised gains/(losses) on investments	–	9,463	
Other gains/(losses) eg currency	–		
Income on investments	2,564	(739)	
Gross return	2,564	8,724	11,288
Less			
Management fee	(947)		
Expenses	(216)		
Interest payable	–		
Net return before taxation	1,401	8,724	10,125
Less			
Taxation	(265)	–	(265)
Total return for the period	1,136	8,724	9,860
Less			
Distributions to holders	1,136	–	(1,136)
Net increase/decrease in holders' funds from investment activities		8,724	8,724

Statement of Movement in Holders' Funds for the period 1.1.98 to 31.12.98

	1998		1997	
	$000	$000	$000	$000
Net assets at start of period		33,106		34,366
Movement due to sales and repurchases				
Amounts received on creation	3,728		2,735	
Less: amounts paid on cancellation	(5,005)		(1,638)	
		(1,277)		1,097
Net increase/(decrease) in holders' funds from investment activities*		8,724		(2,442)
Retained distribution on accumulation units**		97		85
Other items (specify)		–		–
Net assets at end of period		40,650		33,106

* resulting from Statement of Total Return shown above
** dividends retained and added to the value of the unit

Source: IMRO SORP, AITC SORP

The statement of movement in funds shows up some valuable information by combining investment returns with the impact of sales and redemptions on the total value of the fund. Thus in the accounts shown above for the year 1997 illustrate that relatively poor investment results (2,442) were flattered by net sales (1,097) , whereas in the year 1998 a good set of investment results (8,724) were slightly reduced by net redemptions (1,277). Of course the net asset value per share/unit, adjusted for dividends paid, would show the true investment return, but the statement of movement of funds has the advantage that investors can see the impact of sales and redemptions too. Some investors do not wish to invest in a CIF which has grown too large or too small, since they believe that either may have an influence on the way the portfolio is managed and hence the returns to them. Also the statement above would prevent a CIF Manager making vague and potentially misleading statements such as "during the past twelve months the value of fund XX has increased by YY%", omitting to mention that the majority of the increase has been derived from sales and not from investment returns.

13.3 Accounting bases

13.3.1 Accounting for income

In developed markets, CIFs normally use the accruals basis for accounting for income. This means that the income from certain securities, particularly fixed interest securities, is apportioned evenly over the relevant period within which it is due. For example, if a CIF owns a bond that pays interest six-monthly and the CIF values its assets weekly, then the appropriate fraction (7/178) of the next income payment will be added to the Accrued Income account at each weekly valuation.

Dividends on shares are not usually accrued, since they vary in amount, and are not totally predictable. They are usually recognised for accounting purposes at the date on which the shares become ex-dividend (the date after which a new purchaser will not be entitled to receive the dividend just declared) on the understanding that the dividend will be received on a known date in the near future.

This method of accounting for income is, however, unsatisfactory when there is a high risk of default on interest payments, or delays in payment and receipt, or the date of payment of a declared dividend is uncertain. This may well apply in emerging markets both in respect of equity dividends and bond interest. For this reason a mixture of accruals and cash accounting (when dividends or interest are only entered into the accounts upon receipt) for income may be more appropriate in these markets, as shown in the next Table.

Income accounting

TYPE OF ASSET	ACCOUNTING BASIS
Debt securities not subject to abnormal risk of default (eg government bonds)	*Accruals*
Debt securities subject to serious risk of default	*Cash*
Blue chip equities (low risk of failure to pay dividends as stated)	*Accruals*
Other equities	*Cash*

13.3.2   Accounting for expenditure

Expenditure should be accounted for on an accruals basis. This means items are recorded as incurred and not at the time of settlement. Likewise fees for CIF Managers, auditors or custodians should be accounted for on an accruals basis. In the case of an open ended fund, it is clearly inequitable to wait to the end of the year to charge the annual management fee, since investors who sell before the year-end escape paying their share. Likewise it is inequitable to charge the fee at the start of the year since investors selling before the year-end then pay more than their share.

Managers also prefer to receive a regular stream of payments rather than gamble on one payment in a year, which, since it is based on the net asset value of the fund, might be significantly higher or lower than expected because of market conditions on the date of deduction.

Modern practice with open ended funds is for one-twelfth of the annual fee to be charged each month; fees are accrued at daily or weekly valuation points up to the date of each monthly payment.

13.3.3   Accounting for securities transactions

In accounting for securities transactions, normal practice in developed markets is to account for purchases and sales at the date of the trade, not at the date of settlement. The reason is that the CIF is exposed to the capital gain or loss resulting from the trade from the date of the trade and not from the settlement date.

However, where there is a real risk of non-settlement of trades, particularly where there is no effective legal remedy for such a failure, then it may be appropriate to adopt settlement date accounting for securities transactions. The problem with this approach is that, if settlement takes a long time, then the valuations may be significantly distorted during the period between transaction and settlement of a large purchase or sale; its use therefore is only recommended in extreme situations. Regardless of this, the accounts should always show separately those transactions that have been settled and those that have not.

13.4   Potential problems in developing markets

In developing markets, the adaptation of existing accounting frameworks has often produced systems that are quite inadequate and unsuitable for CIFs. Over time, reforms are likely to bring them closer into line with the systems in use in developed markets.

The main problems associated with accounting for CIFs in developing markets are associated with corporate funds, which are usually ill-served by ordinary company accounting rules which do not allow for two features of funds:

● their fixed assets' value will change constantly and sometimes sharply, unlike most ordinary companies' assets which are carried at cost or depreciated cost

● in the case of open ended funds, their issued capital will also change constantly

Contractual funds, since they are not legal entities as such, can usually have a self-standing accounting regime designed specially to accommodate their unique features, so they are generally less of a problem. Corporate type funds, particularly of the closed ended type, however, will have to address a range of issues. Such closed ended corporate style funds have often been used in cases of privatisation or corporate reconstruction, and are often created with inadequate attention having been paid to the format of their accounts, since to the accounting profession they are technically companies and bear more than a superficial resemblance to an ordinary commercial enterprise. As a result their financial reports may have to be squeezed into an accounting format for which their business is ill suited and which will consequently deliver a set of accounts devoid of meaning. Accounting in this way may also give rise to certain taxation problems to the disadvantage of shareholders. In the next sections some of these problems are discussed.

13.4.1 Accounting for varying fixed asset values – the nominal value problem

The required allocation of a nominal value to shares in funds of a closed ended corporate type can give rise to a range of problems. Under many countries' company law, a fund may have problems when the value of its nominal capital needs to be adjusted to take account of increases or decreases in the value of fixed assets (the securities held in the portfolio) on the balance sheet. Shares or units in open ended funds of all types do not usually have a nominal value, since they are continuously issued and redeemed at varying prices, and since open ended funds do not have to show what would be conventionally regarded as a balance sheet.

Examples of problems which may arise in the case of closed ended funds of the corporate type include:

- being required to call shareholder meetings if the company's value falls to less than a certain proportion of nominal value – say 50%

- a company being regarded as insolvent if the value of assets falls to below the nominal value of the shares

- being required to issue new share capital to bring the total nominal value of shares in issue in line with a higher value of fixed assets, which involves time-consuming and expensive shareholder meetings and registration

There are a number of solutions to this:

- not requiring a nominal value to be placed on shares (shares of no par value are permitted in the US for example)

- making any allocated nominal value per share very low

- allocating the nominal value of shares to issued share capital and the difference between the nominal value and the price at which the shares have been issued to a share premium account on the passive side of the balance sheet (which does not solve the second problem above)

13.4.2   How to adjust liabilities (passive side) if the value of fixed assets changes

The last solution, which is commonly used, gives rise to another accounting problem, however:

- when sales of fixed assets shown on the balance sheet at cost are made at a profit, this has to be reflected on the balance sheet since it is not a theoretical profit (as is that thrown up by a current market value higher than cost) but a real one

- when assets are revalued and the increase or decrease is shown by an adjustment to the value of fixed assets

13.4.3   Portraying market value of securities

The most significant accounting policy decision is how and where to show the market values of securities held as investments. There are two choices:

- to require the investments to be revalued at the balance sheet date

- to require that investments are shown at cost on the balance sheet, with market values dealt with in a note

In the case of closed ended funds there may however be reasons why it is difficult or inappropriate to use market values:

- the fund may hold a high proportion of its assets in illiquid investments that are not traded on a stock exchange and whose market value is hard to assess

- the sale of assets at market prices may produce capital gains tax liabilities for the fund (in the case where the fund is not tax-neutral); an adjustment may have to be made in respect of potential tax liabilities

- revaluation of assets to market values (even where no sale takes place) may, in certain tax regimes, produce a capital gains tax liability

Besides that, the disadvantage of showing the market value in the balance sheet is that it will only be accurate once a year. Unlike other typical commercial assets (land, buildings and machinery) the market value of securities will fluctuate daily. It is therefore more meaningful for the market value of assets to be shown on a non-statutory schedule or note attached to the accounts. This gives some scope for directors to give estimates of current values of securities which are not listed or traded with suitable warnings that these are estimates.

These reasons should never apply to open ended funds where regular valuations of assets produce a NAV at which investors buy and sell. Open ended funds should always include their assets, which are required to be of a more liquid character than those held in closed ended funds, in their accounts at market values.

However, even if the market values of the portfolio of securities is shown separately from the balance sheet as suggested above, there will still need to be adjustments to cover the situation when securities are sold at a profit (or loss) from the balance sheet value. This will need to be reflected in the balance sheet since it is a "real" rather than a "theoretical" event.

Thus increases or decreases on the asset (active) side of the balance sheet resulting from sales at prices higher or lower than cost are usually accounted for by setting up "reserves" on the liability (passive) side of the balance sheet. These reserves may include:

- capital reserves – reflecting realised or unrealised profits (less losses)

- revenue (or income) reserves reflecting income received but not paid out by way of dividend

This approach to accounting for realised and unrealised gains is now generally accepted practice in most developed markets, whereby fixed assets are shown on the active side of the balance sheet at current market value, with a corresponding entries on the passive side of the balance sheet for capital reserves, realised and unrealised. These are shown under capital and reserves and are included in "total shareholders' funds", since the gains, realised or unrealised, and the income not paid out belongs to shareholders. If this accounting methodology is adopted, then "total shareholders' funds", less any long term liabilities, divided by the number of shares in issue will produce a figure for net asset value per share.

The statement of total shareholders' funds will show a transfer from one entry to the other when an asset is realised, in the following way.

When a sale is made and a gain (loss) realised, the associated unrealised gain (loss) figure is deducted from the "unrealised capital reserve" and the realised gain (loss) is added to the "realised capital reserve".

Realised and unrealised reserves

	Unrealised Reserve	Realised Reserve
as at 1.1.98	11,120	15,160
Realised gains	(1,120)	1,120
as at 31.12.98	10,000	16,280

Effectively the unrealised gain reserve simply reflects the variation between the market value of assets and cost of assets. But when an investment is sold at a profit or loss, this is a real event and must be permanently reflected in the balance sheet, which is done through the realised gain reserve. Regulations will normally state that neither realised nor unrealised reserves may be distributed to shareholders, except in the case of a liquidation or a formal reduction of capital.

Capital reserves for closed ended funds

	ASSETS	THOUSANDS	LIABILITIES	THOUSANDS
as at 31/12/97	investments at cost	200,000	shareholders funds	150,000
	add unrealised gains	100,000	realised gain reserve	50,000
	less unrealised losses	-50,000	unrealised gain reserve	50,000
	Total assets	**250,000**	**Total liabilities**	**250,000**
as at 31/12/98	investments at cost	200,000	shareholders funds	150,000
	add unrealised gains	125,000	realised gain reserve	75,000
	less unrealised losses	-25,000	unrealised gain reserve	75,000
	Total assets	**300,000**	**Total liabilities**	**300,000**

Example of a balance sheet of a closed ended fund

The following table gives a description and explanation of each of the
lines normally to be found in the balance sheet of a closed ended CIF.

BALANCE SHEET ITEM	COMMENTS
Assets	
Fixed assets	*There are unlikely to be any fixed assets other than investments, unless the fund is self managed, in which case there may be some property and equipment*
Investments	*The investments will normally be marketable securities; there is no need to categorise these in detail on the face of the accounts. It will be more normal to show the portfolio by way of note. The key point is whether these investments are shown at cost or at market value – see above*
Current assets	
Cash and short term investments	*It is usual to include under this heading any investments with a life of less than twelve months, including bank deposits and short term paper. It is possible that some of these investments may be shown at market value*
Debtors	*The majority of these will be for amounts due from the market (brokers) for securities for which a sale has been contracted but not completed*
Dividends receivable	*Dividends declared or interest due but not received*
Liabilities	
Issued capital	*The amount of capital issued and paid; authorised but unissued capital can be shown by way of note*
Ordinary shares	*This figure will be the product of the number of shares in issue multiplied by their nominal value*
Reserves	
Share premium reserve	*The aggregate amount of premiums over the nominal value at which shares have been issued*
Capital reserves	*The balancing figure for any profit (loss) on sale of assets at a figure different from book value or from revaluation of assets to market value*
Retained profits	*Profits retained and not paid out as dividends*
Long term liabilities	*Debts which are due in more than 12 months*
Current Liabilities	
Creditors	*The majority are likely to be for payment due to the market (brokers) for purchases of securities contracted but not settled*
Bank overdraft	*Debts due in less than 12 months*
Taxation due	*Taxation due but not paid*

An open ended fund does not have a balance sheet as such, all the necessary information being conveyed by the statement of net asset value. But a way needs to be found to account for the issued shares or units whose number varies continuously.

13.5 Accounting for varying capital

The number of shares or units in issue in an open ended fund will vary from day to day. This is not an eventuality envisaged by most developing markets' company laws, which are designed for ordinary companies, which have a fixed amount of shares in issue for considerable periods of time, and by whom new issues of shares are infrequent. This can make open ended corporate funds impossible to operate in some markets, which is why many countries use the contractual form, based on the contract relationships often included in the section of the civil code relating to "trust" or fiduciary relationships.

Assuming that the hurdle of a company or joint stock company law, which does not recognise the possibility of a company continuously issuing and redeeming its own shares, can be overcome, standards will need to be set governing accounting for this changing capital. This can be achieved, as mentioned above, by accounting separately for the inflow and outflow of money resulting from purchases and sales, as shown in the statement of increase/decrease in holders' funds (page 289).

Every country has its own peculiarities with regard to company and contract law as well as different taxation and accounting: so while the principles outlined above generally apply, there are a wide variety of constraints which may affect the accounting outcome.

13.6 Relationship between tax and accounting

The taxation of CIFs and the accounting methods they use are intimately connected. The way in which capital and income are accounted for and shown will depend on the way in which each is taxed in the hands of the fund and in the hands of the holders. Depending on the tax treatment accounts may need to show:

13

- net capital gains realised of a taxable nature in the hands either of the fund or the holder

- net capital gains realised which are exempt from tax either in the hands of the fund or the holder

- income received of a taxable nature (different types of income – interest and dividends for instance – may attract different rates of tax)

- any tax credits resulting from tax already paid and offsettable against liabilities

The accounting system will have to be set up in such a way that all these different items can easily be recognised for the purpose of compiling tax returns. Different types of income and realised gains need to be presented to holders, and the certificate or statement which accompanies a dividend can be complex; it will have to show these items in a way which can be used by the holder to calculate his own tax liability if any. A detailed description of how income from different sources can suffer different tax rates can be found earlier in this Chapter.

Managing a CIF Manager

14

14.1 The business concept of an asset management company

This Chapter looks at the business aspects of running an asset management business: that is, a business which is set up to manage CIFs alone or CIFs in conjunction with other types of portfolio managed on behalf of institutional and retail clients. The business is very simple in theory. Income is derived from initial sales charges and annual management fees and redemption fees. Costs are largely those relating to salaries and office expenses. The difference between the two is profit. In practice though, however simple the profit and loss account statement appears to be, asset management businesses are not easy to manage, and it is as easy to make losses as it is to make profits. This is because, while almost all the costs, with the exception of marketing and advertising, are fixed, the income is both variable and hard to predict. This gives ample scope for management to be too optimistic about future business prospects and increase fixed costs which are not, in the event, covered by increased income; or to spend large sums on advertising a new CIF or service which does not live up to expectations.

The other aspect of any asset management business is that there are very significant economies of scale, particularly at the retail (CIF) end of the business. Massive investment in the technology of processing large numbers of small transactions can pay off handsomely if volumes increase, but can prove to have been an expensive mistake if the systems fail to perform adequately or volumes do not materialise.

14

14.1.1   Asset management is a highly valued business at certain times

The management of CIFs (and other types of institutional and private portfolios) is a business which, if it is well managed, can be a highly profitable one for its owners, not only in terms of current profitability and dividends, but also in terms of the future capital value of the business. This arises from the attribution of a capital value to the future streams of revenue derived from the contracts to manage CIFs, which in turn gives a CIF Manager a measurable market value. In recent times, the rule of thumb for this valuation in developed markets has tended to be between 2% and 4% of the value of funds under management. Thus, a CIF Manager with funds under management of 100 million would be valued at between 2 and 4 million.

The actual figures paid to acquire asset management businesses will depend on the structure of the business, the type of funds that it manages and the client base, as well as its actual or likely future profitability. Clearly an asset management business which only manages funds for its parent shareholder(s) and their affiliates would be worth less than one which has a broadly diversified client base. There has also been a tendency to value retail businesses more highly than ones which are predominantly institutional, since institutions can become nervous at ownership changes and start quickly to look around for a new manager, whereas CIF investors are more inert.

There are quite a number of CIF and other asset management companies which are listed on exchanges, and their prices can be used as a point of reference.

However, given their dependence on economic and financial factors outside their control, and in particular the health of securities markets, the profits from and the value ascribed to asset management businesses can be volatile. So there are some points in the economic cycle at which values ascribed to asset management businesses will be low.

14.1.2   Managing a CIF or asset management business is not as easy as it seems

In some respects, a CIF Manager appears a simple kind of company to manage. Conceptually it is. Revenues are derived from new sales of products or redemption fees and from annual management fees, while fixed costs are composed of wages and premises, and variable costs (confined mainly to marketing and sales) are completely within the control of the management company. The difference between revenues and costs is profit, which should continue to grow provided that funds under management continue to increase as a result of new sales and/or a rise in market values, and provided that costs are kept under control.

However, there are several reasons why the management task is not quite as simple as described in the last paragraph.

● the processes involved in CIF management all have to be integrated in terms of functions and systems, and all are time-critical with severe penalties for breakdowns and delays

● competition is very fierce, since the "retail" market is now regarded as the most interesting and consistently profitable area for investment management companies

● in the "institutional" market, those responsible for advising trustees and directors with whom to place their funds keep a sharp eye on performance and are quick to advise their clients to make a change, if performance or service deteriorates, for which there is usually no penalty to be paid or compensation for the manager

● compliance with increasingly tough regulations in different countries in which the company operates is expensive and complex

14.1.2.1 Forecasting is difficult

The main difficulty, however, is that, however easy it is to predict and control costs, forecasting and controlling the level of revenues is notoriously difficult. Revenues may depend on several relatively unpredictable factors:

- the level of securities markets will determine the amount of revenue from annual management charges – assuming that these are charged as a percentage of net asset value, the normal way of charging. Successful forecasting therefore will depend on being able to predict the level of different securities markets for as long ahead as the period for which budgetary forecasts are being made

- successful or unsuccessful investment performance will not only partially determine the level of funds under management but will also influence the ability of the manager to attract new clients or subscriptions; a consistently poor set of investment results will cause clients to withdraw their funds and look elsewhere for a better manager

- political and economic events and changes in taxation will encourage or discourage clients from investing or cause them to disinvest

It is also difficult for those responsible for managing the management company to determine what products and services should most appropriately be offered. Given the increasingly international nature not only of investing, but also of the investment management and CIF business, it is very tempting for larger management companies to try to offer every type of product and service everywhere; but just as is the case in any commercial company an excessively large range of products may produce the result that the efforts of the firm are spread too thinly and that none of the activities is as profitable as it should be.

The high level of leverage of asset management business

The above shows that if costs rise as revenues fall, profitability can be severely damaged.

14.1.2.2 Asset management businesses can easily find themselves wrongly positioned

Financial markets and fashions change quickly. It is easy for today's highly successful business segment to be tomorrow's problem child. Some real examples of possibly damaging decisions are as follows:

● who would have thought that the prominence and success of Japan's financial markets in the mid to late 1980s could have turned into a decade long bear market? Excessive commitment to either Japanese investments or Japanese clients would have turned out to have been a poor business decision

● the failure by most leading European asset managers to have an adequate presence in the US in the late 1990s during what has been called the "bull market of the century" is another example of bad strategic decision making

- it is also possible to waste large amounts of money in the expectation of developments which are much slower than anticipated; the integration of European markets was in sight in 1985 and still was by the turn of the millennium. Managers who had committed themselves to a major expansion in expectation of the development of a pan-European market would have suffered

- emerging markets often appear to have a bright future but can be a trap. In 1996-97 many regarded Russia an exceptional investment and business opportunity. Two years later the equity market had fallen by 90% and the government had repudiated its domestic debt. At least one heavily committed manager had virtually to close its almost valueless CIFs

While the difficulty of making predictions is a constant feature of the lives of managers of asset management businesses there is at the same time the fact that they must face strong competition. In the retail markets of developed countries competitive pressures have meant:

- fees and charges have been driven down, with a relentless pressure on profit margins, unless costs can be driven down too. This requires massive investment in technology and systems

- thinner margins require larger and larger funds under management for break even to be achieved

- the generation of sufficient sales requires a large commitment to advertising, marketing and customer service

The risk of failure is high.

14.2 Maximising the likelihood of success and minimising the risk of failure

As in any other business it is important for senior management to be clear about what it is trying to achieve. Its objective may depend on the objectives set by the owners of the management company. Examples of these objectives are:

- building up the value of funds under management as rapidly as possible by focusing on a particularly fashionable sector, regardless of immediate profitability, with a view to a sale of the business in the relatively near term

- building a sound, diversified business in the long term without immediate concern about creating short term value

- providing services to customers of the parent company or group, without too much regard for where the profit falls (this would typically be the aim of a bank or other financial institution with a wide range of products which it offers to its customers)

Whichever of these objectives (or others) is chosen, the mission statement will shape the plan and the budget. Failure to have a clear objective, as in any other business, will result in aimlessness and futile effort.

The broad objective will be coupled with a more specific "mission statement" which describes how the objective is to be reached. Possible examples of a mission statement for a CIF Manager include:

- to double funds under management over a period of five years by winning a growing share of sales through independent intermediaries based on good investment performance and high standards of service (possibly related to the first objective above)

- to become one of the top five CIF Managers by selling a value-for-money product range direct to the public (possibly related to the second objective above)

- to achieve a steady growth in funds under management by providing the parent company's customers with products designed to meet their needs (possibly related to the third objective above)

The definition of an objective and a route form the basis for the assessment of the company's ability to meet the targets and the steps necessary to do so.

CHAPTER

14

The ability to achieve the objective and fulfil the mission statement will be subject to obvious constraints, such as:

- the availability of capital resources to finance expansion – which in the case of management companies of CIFs will mean incurring losses initially

- the availability of competent trained staff

- the need to achieve profitability at some stage in the near future

- the external environment – investor confidence, availability of savings and competition

Above all success will depend on the ability of senior management to have a clear vision and to implement realistic plans.

14.3 Organisational structure

Clearly the way in which a business is organised, with defined responsibilities and reporting lines, is the basis for effective implementation and management.

A typical organisational structure

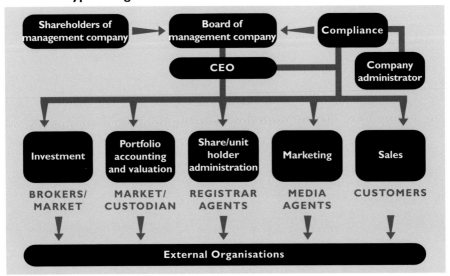

The functions carried out by each of the divisions and departments are described in greater detail in each of the sections of this book, but it is not merely the formal organisational and control structure which is important, rather it is the way in which successful integration and management of the range of relationships is achieved which is the key to effective delivery to the client and to cost control.

Within the internal organisation chart there are an important series of interdepartmental relationships which need to operate harmoniously. Among these are many which can give rise to tensions and problems. It is the duty of senior management to manage the organisation in such a way that tensions are minimised and the whole works harmoniously towards an agreed set of objectives, which are established in the planning and budgeting process. Anecdotally, some of the classic management problems may be found in the list below.

14.3.1 Investment management – portfolio accounting/administration – custodian/trustee

There is inevitably an important set of relationships between these two parts of the business, since the portfolio accounting department, in conjunction with the custodian or trustee, has to complete the transactions which have been initiated by the investment managers and then to ensure that the portfolio which is available to the investment managers is up to date. The following diagram illustrates the work flow and indicates some points at which problems may arise. For a more detailed work flow of the settlement process see section 8.6.

Administrative failure

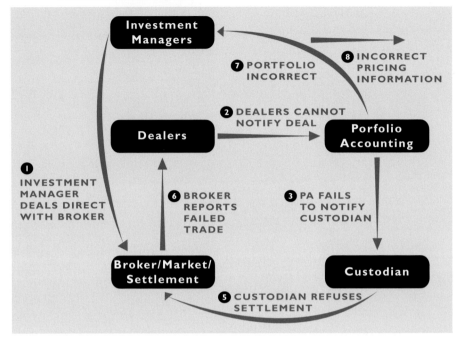

This diagram illustrates how a simple communication failure can turn into a serious problem:

1. the investment manager tells the broker to go ahead with a transaction without informing his dealers

2. the dealers cannot therefore inform his portfolio accounting department of the deal

3. the portfolio accounting department cannot tell the custodian or trustee to expect settlement

4. the custodian or trustee will therefore reject the settlement request from the broker

5. the broker will report to the dealer that a trade has failed (a trade of which the dealer has no knowledge)

6. the CIF's portfolio will therefore be incorrect (since the trade is valid having been agreed by a senior employee of the CIF Manager)

7. the investment manager will have an incorrect portfolio which does not show the purchase which he may or may not remember having agreed (as a result he may decide to buy the same security again)

8. the portfolio which forms the basis for valuation will be wrong and consequently the share/unit price will be wrong with serious compliance implications

Apart from potentially serious regulatory problems arising from allowing the investment manager to deal directly with a broker without reference to the CIF's dealers, there is an equally serious administrative problem which will arise from the failure to pass accurate and timely information along the chain of internal departments and external organisations. This diagram illustrates the effect right through the information chain; in reality failures may occur at any of the eight identified points.

One of the potential conflicts which will need to be managed can be identified in this chart, too: that is the unwillingness of investment managers, whose job is to grapple with complex market related decisions, to be constrained by administrative procedures.

14.3.2 Marketing and sales – investment management – share/unit holder administration

The following statements are always a feature of conversations with marketing and sales departments:

● the marketing department will never have a large enough budget to achieve its budgeted goals

● the range of products that the manager has on offer is not what the market wants

- the investment performance is poor relative to the competitors' and thus inhibiting sales

- the share/unit dealers are not providing good service to the customers

- commissions to sales agents and professional intermediaries are not high enough

In addition marketing departments will often fail to notify administrative departments of large impending marketing campaigns with the result that the administration is not prepared for a sudden increase in activity, does not know about the advertisements and is thus unable to answer questions about the offer or any special terms contained in it.

However, despite the many potential conflicts and complaints, marketing departments play a crucial role in the business of CIF Management, given that increasing sales and thus funds under management is one of the leading objectives of the business.

However the desirable build up in customer support for the products of a particular management company is not achieved by a series of smart advertisements. Success takes time, patience and organisation. Good co-ordination between departments has been stressed, but also good co-ordination between the different parts of a marketing and sales strategy will also make most effective use of the budgets that have been agreed. This book is not intended to be a textbook of financial marketing – there is already a large range of those available – but anyone setting out to manage a CIF business should be aware of the key issues, which are:

- consistent statements from everyone in the firm to all outside organisations, the customers and the media; everyone should be clear of the firm's main objectives and the principles it stands for

- consistent and recognisable style across the whole range of a firm's published material – prospectuses, contract notes, reports, advertisements, the Internet site

- dissemination of information to all who may be in contact with outside organisations or the customers; all staff should be aware of the range of products and their characteristics

- good and open relations with the key journalists who write or broadcast about personal finance

- accessibility and responsiveness to customers who want information or want to complain; willingness to admit errors rather than cover them up

The aim of senior management in managing the marketing department is to ensure that sales are maximised for the minimum expenditure and that money is not wasted on harebrained marketing schemes.

14.3.2.1 Consistent presence in the market

One of the hardest decisions for senior management to take is when to increase the spend on marketing and when to reduce it. In periods when financial and securities markets are in decline and sales are hard to make, an obvious reaction is to cut the spend on marketing and advertising, the one major variable cost in a CIF Manager's profit and loss account. This is relatively painless in that it does not usually involve many unpleasant redundancies.

But experience has shown that to disappear from the market place, however beneficial that may be for short term profits, may not be the best long term strategy for a number of reasons:

- the market forgets quickly

- customers become concerned that their managers are going out of business

- sales agents recognise that the company has ceased to support their efforts and will turn elsewhere

- it is expensive to re-enter a market once abandoned

The most successful asset management businesses are always visible through good times and bad, although in bad times they will be spending significantly less than when they can achieve an immediately profitable return on its marketing expenditure.

Effective senior management will have the vision to resist the inevitable attempts by their company finance director to kill expenditure at the first sign of a downturn.

14.3.3   Share/unit holder dealing, administration and servicing

This department is at the front line between the company and its customers. As such its standards and services will be those by which the whole firm is judged. In common with any organisation which is processing and recording large amounts of data there is considerable scope for error, given that a major CIF Manager may have millions of share/unit holders carrying out thousands of transactions a day.

Given that this part of the business is dependent on IT and systems and requires an increasingly large investment into those, particularly if the firm is international in its scope, it has become increasingly attractive for all but the very largest CIF Managers to outsource part or all of this function to specialist firms which are able to achieve economies of scale and continue to invest in the very latest equipment and systems. Their operations do not need to be located in expensive city centre locations and therefore most such companies are based in cheap out-of-town locations, where not only rents but also salaries are lower. The very largest suppliers of administrative services will offer a complete package which will include:

- share/unit dealing

- issue and redemption

- registration

- portfolio accounting

- preparation and dispatch of reports to share/unit holders

- pricing

- compliance reporting

The very largest companies, which may be owned by banks, may also offer, subject to local regulatory sanction, and within a different department, the custody, trustee or depositary services as well.

As will be seen later, use of an outsourced service will permit, to some extent, fixed costs to be turned into variable ones and thus a reduction in the critical break even point of the management company.

14.3.4   Finance

In addition to all the other accounting and bookkeeping functions which are present in a CIF Management company, dealing with portfolio accounting and share/unit holder reports, the CIF Manager will need its own books of accounts to be kept. Accounting for the CIF Manager, planning and budgeting are vital management control functions, which not only record the progress of the company in financial terms but also provide the tools for responding to the budgetary requests from different departments and for allocating the available resources between them.

It has already been pointed out that budgeting and forecasting the likely revenues of a CIF Manager is difficult. This is true in the context of an established business in a known market. It is doubly difficult when a decision is taken to enter a new market (in the business not in the investment sense), in which there will be a number of variables and uncertainties which are outside the experience of the senior management.

To some extent, entering a new market, while it can be analysed logically using the same tools as those applied to forecasting in a more familiar market, is an act of faith. It will involve losses until the faith is justified by new customers and sales, and may not end up having been the right decision at all. Strong nerves, deep pockets and a committed board and major shareholder are needed for this kind of expansion, which is why merger or acquisition may be the preferred option.

A strong finance department is an asset to any business, particularly to a business as international and complex as CIF Management.

14.3.5 Compliance

In the increasingly international context in which CIF Managers operate, compliance with laws and regulations is no longer simply a matter of knowing and obeying the law of one country. It is one of the major concerns of senior management to ensure that the CIF Manager remains in compliance since the consequences of failure to do so, with the result that the CIF Manager is fined or publicly censured, can not only be expensive but extremely damaging to the reputation and hence future profitability of the CIF Manager.

There is always a conflict between the compliance department and all other parts of the business; compliance usually comes up with the answer "no" to any question like "can we do this" and is thus regarded by operational departments as an unreasonable drag on their pursuit of legitimate business and profit.

In the organisation chart shown above the compliance department is shown as reporting directly to the Chief Executive, which is a measure of its importance and its need to be seen as independent from other line operating departments. Its function is twofold:

- to ensure that the CIF Manager remains in compliance with all relevant legislation and files reports regularly with the proper authorities

- to ensure that the internal organisation and operation of the CIF Manager is such as to ensure that it can and does comply with the relevant regulations and that staff are fully aware of their regulatory responsibilities

Among the tools it will use to fulfil its functions are:

- internal procedural manuals for all relevant departments, which set out in detail the functions that need to be performed and the correct and compliant way of performing them

- written undertakings by staff that they have read and understood the company's internal rules of conduct as applied to their particular jobs

- regular staff training to keep relevant departments up to date with changes in legislation and regulation or with the regulatory requirements of new markets which the CIF Manager proposes to enter

- internal compliance inspections designed to ensure that correct procedures laid down in internal manuals are being followed

- maintenance of a register of complaints from customers and regular analysis of this to ensure that complaints are dealt with and that there is not a regularity in the pattern of complaints which points to some systematic weakness

- regular review of the CIF Manager's publicity material, advertisements, prospectuses and reports to ensure that they have all the required contents and do not make statements which are misleading or incorrect

- regular meetings with a compliance committee of senior managers from different parts of the firm to report problems and agree solutions

The director of compliance and his department are the first point of contact for the Securities Regulator, and one of the duties will be to maintain a good and open relationship with the relevant people there. The department will also be in the front line if the Securities Regulator decides to conduct an inspection or an investigation.

14.4 Planning

The basis of a strategic plan is the objectives of the shareholders of the business. Generally, the owners of a CIF Manager will want to increase the funds under management to the maximum extent possible as rapidly as possible. This will enable them theoretically to increase profits rapidly and to sell the business, if they wish, at a good price.

Key elements of the plan are as follows.

14.4.1 Analysis

External factors will have a major influence on the company's ability to meet its goals. Factors that should be considered, together with any dangers they present to the company and opportunities they present, include:

14.4.1.1 Prospects

- how much do people save? Is the ratio rising or falling?

- does the public have confidence in CIFs? What could happen to improve or reduce confidence?

- what products does the public prefer? What might make them change their preferences? Do taxes currently give individuals incentives to use or avoid CIFs and is this likely to change?

14.4.1.2 The economy

- is the legal regime for joint stock companies and CIFs firmly established? Are major changes likely? If so what would be the effects?

- what is the nature of existing markets for securities? Are there likely to be improvements in security, clearing systems, listing procedures, stock exchange membership, or corporate governance that would increase public confidence in markets?

- how stable is economic policy? Are stop-go policies or a high rate of inflation possible? Are short-term interest rates likely to be raised in defence of the currency exchange rate?

- what scenarios appear most likely for the performance of the domestic stockmarket? What are the implications of very poor and very good performance?

14.4.1.3 Competition

- which competitors appear likely winners over the next few years? Why? What elements of their strategies could be worth imitating?

- what new entrants to the market are likely in the foreseeable future? Will they have large capital resources or captive distribution? Could they cut existing operators off from a significant number of potential customers?

- what gaps are there in the market for products or methods of reaching prospects?

14.4.2 Current status

This analysis of the external environment then leads on to a similar analysis applied to the company itself. Here the answers should be more precise and specific, especially in terms of any perceived threats or opportunities.

14.4.2.1 Customers

- who are the existing or potential customers?

- what are their characteristics in terms of gender, family, age, income, geography, wealth, affiliations, employment, etc?

- what are customers' views of the company or its parent company? its image? its products? their performance? the service?

- is the situation of the customers, in terms of income, employment and wealth, improving or deteriorating? Will this change?

14.4.2.2 Ownership

- does the company have stable ownership for the foreseeable future?

- does the company have sufficient capital for its current needs? Is more capital available if needed?

- what return on capital is required and how soon? What proportion of profits do the owners wish to withdraw?

14.4.2.3 Brand

- does the company have a brand image?

- is it well known for any particular characteristic or policy?

14.4.2.4 Distribution

- does the company have partners to assist in distribution?

- are these arrangements stable?

- is there potential for new partnerships?

14.4.2.5 Skills

- how does the company rate its skills in marketing, investment, administration and customer care?

- how does it compare with its nearest rivals?

14.4.2.6 Products

- how do the company's products compare with those of competitors in terms of design, performance and charges? How does the average performance of its products compare with rivals'?

- how quickly is the company capable of launching a new product?

- is the existing range of products adequate in terms of the needs of existing customers? in terms of the needs of prospects?

This part of the analysis should involve as many people as possible and can be undertaken on a departmental basis and down to the smallest functional unit within a department. If employees are involved in this analysis, it will be much easier to persuade them to 'own' the budget that emerges from the planning process and this in turn will make the budget far more accurate.

14.5   Creating the budget

The planning process is intended to produce a budget that shows in money terms the effect of the company's moves to meet its objectives.

The senior management of a CIF Management company will have a number of specific concerns in creating the budget.

14.5.1   Stability of earnings

The greatest potential weakness of a CIF Manager is the fluctuation of revenues and profits in response to market movements. In particular, CIF Managers with a large volume of open ended funds are exposed to a market fall in two ways: the decline in the value of the assets reduces management fees and revenues, and the fall may encourage more investors to sell their holdings, thus further reducing revenues.

For many CIF Managers, building a portfolio that includes closed ended as well as open ended funds is therefore a desirable strategic objective. Even though the value of closed ended funds also falls in falling markets, investors cannot exit the funds, so revenues are more stable.

Opportunities to launch closed ended funds will depend on the supply/demand situation, since it is virtually impossible to launch new closed ended funds at times when existing closed ended funds are trading at wide discounts to their net asset values.

CIF Managers therefore need to have an overall objective in terms of the balance of open and closed ended funds and to take advantage of market conditions to achieve this.

14.5.2   The need to grow funds under management

Economies of scale have a profound influence on the CIF business. They give CIF Managers strong incentives to expand funds under management, since costs should rise by only a small amount and a very high proportion of the extra revenues therefore represents profit. This results in two principal trends, the launch of many new funds and a steady move to larger business units.

In most markets, more CIFs are launched than there is room for in the market. But because the extra costs in running a small CIF are also small, there is little pressure on managers to reduce the number of funds. In fact, many large CIF Managers go through periods when the number of CIFs they manage increases, followed by periods of consolidation and fund mergers as precursors to new waves of expansion. This is particularly true in the case of closed ended funds, whose shares are listed and traded. When there is oversupply their shares trade at a large discount and become attractive to predators, who buy at prices well below net asset value and then move to liquidate the company or convert it into an open ended fund when they will be able to redeem their shares at full asset value.

14.5.3   Factors which will affect revenues and costs

The main factors affecting the levels of revenues and costs are explored below.

14.5.3.1 Revenue

The revenue of the management company of a CIF is principally dependent on the amount of funds managed on which annual fees are earned, expressed as a percentage of the total value of funds managed, and on the amount of new sales which will either themselves bring an immediate contribution to profits through the retention of part of the initial sales charge or which will add to the total of funds managed.

The construction of a budget and the accuracy of the prediction of the outcome will therefore depend crucially on two factors:

- the predicted level of and the returns produced by the various markets in which the funds under management invest – bond, money markets and equity markets at home and abroad

- the amount of new sales (less redemptions) that are expected during the budget period

This is the most difficult part of the budget process. The prediction of the behaviour of financial markets is an inexact science. But in order to produce any kind of budget it is necessary to make an attempt. The alternative, which is less satisfactory, is to assume a scenario in which only sales, less redemptions, are taken into account, and there is an assumption of no market movement.

In trying to predict market movement, the following factors will need to be taken into account.

14.5.3.2 The overall economic outlook

The disciplines and analysis applied here will be very similar to that used by the CIF Managers' macro economic analysts, who work with the investment specialists.

14.5.3.2.a The rate of inflation

The higher the level of inflation, the higher interest rates will be.

Except in conditions of hyper inflation, higher interest rates normally exert a depressing effect on the value of shares, but may provide good opportunities for offering products based on deposits or products based on bonds. But when both inflation and interest rates are high, and the share market is depressed, equity investments can be seen as being good value and the source of substantial gains in the future.

14.5.3.2.b Foreign exchange rates

Many factors influence foreign exchange rates. In principle, relative rates of economic growth, relative inflation rates and trade flows (imports and exports) are considered the principal factors, but in recent times, the flow of capital has been more decisive. Unfortunately, this factor is the most difficult to assess or predict. A steadily weakening exchange rate is likely to lead to individuals wanting to invest abroad, while a steadily strengthening exchange rate is likely to result in individuals investing more at home.

The exchange rate will also be a significant factor in translating any revenues from subsidiaries abroad into the home currency for accounting purposes.

14.5.3.2.c The rate of growth (or decline) in GDP

This will affect the growth and profitability of enterprises, the dividends they pay and the level of stock market prices. It will also affect consumers' attitudes, their propensity to spend and save and hence their willingness to invest.

14.5.3.2.d Industry and customer factors

Consumers' responses to changes in the levels of inflation, interest rates and the stock market are not always predictable. There is no reliable formula which can predict consumers' choices of where to place their savings in any given combination of economic and political eventualities.

The likely impact – positive or negative – of tax measures designed to encourage or discourage saving in a particular way needs to be taken into account.

The range of products available to meet the needs which are predicted based on the macro and micro economic factors, the performance and reputation of those products or the new products which will need to be introduced to meet changing needs should be considered.

14.5.3.2.e Competition

The ability of competitors to attract the available pool of savings and to compete with them for an adequate share of the pool will depend on:

- the number of competitors in the market – if the market is very overcrowded it may be harder to meet ambitious targets

- the strengths and weaknesses of the competition in relation to marketing, administration, customer service and product range

14.5.3.3 Costs

While the future revenues of a management company of a CIF are very difficult to predict for the reasons given above, and their variance around any central assumption is likely to become greater the further into the future the prediction is made, the costs are relatively predictable and controllable. In principle, they are also almost all fixed costs. So most management companies make great efforts to turn fixed costs into variable costs and to ensure that any fixed costs that they cannot deal with in this way are kept as low as possible.

14.5.3.3.a Turning fixed costs into variable costs

The key fact about the structure of CIF profitability is that a significant portion of costs are relatively fixed and do not alter quickly in direct proportion to changes in sales volumes or in response to increases or decreases in the market value of funds managed. Thus a management company's profits are subject to considerable "operational leverage". If costs remain relatively constant and funds under management grow, profits will rise faster than the increase in funds under management. The opposite is also true. A decline in the value of funds under management will cut revenues much faster than costs. This is illustrated in the *graph*, from which it can be seen that profits are powerfully leveraged by fixed costs. It is relatively hard to change the fixed costs of the management company quickly.

Outsourcing

The desire for greater adaptability and flexibility has led some CIF Managers in developed countries to subcontract (or 'outsource') large parts of their administration to specialists.

Specialist administrators are also usually prepared to agree to a mix of fees and charges, which are partially fixed and partially variable. They may be partly based on transaction volumes, for example. A management company is thus able to transfer part of the risk resulting from fluctuations in markets or sales to another organisation which is prepared to assume some of that risk.

Typically the companies which offer such specialist services have grown out of either shareholder registration operations or from custodians. In developed markets, such companies increasingly tend to offer a comprehensive package so that a customer can outsource to one company rather than to a number of outside suppliers.

Variable pay for senior executives and investment managers

Another way to turn fixed costs into variable costs that is common in the investment management business is to remunerate senior staff in ways other than through fixed salaries. This enables fixed salaries to be kept down. Because they require the staff of the company to share the risks and rewards that result from volatile market conditions, such remuneration systems may also help to attract more dynamic and enterprising people into the organisation. Some of these methods are:

- bonuses related to the overall profits of the management company: these are usually appropriate to the most senior people who can actually have a major effect on the profits

- bonuses related to the investment results or returns of the funds managed: these are usually appropriate for investment managers

- bonuses related to sales targets: these are appropriate for internal sales and marketing staff

- share options which grant participants the opportunity to buy shares in the management company at some point in the future at a fixed price

Sales and marketing commissions

Apart from the bonuses related to sales targets mentioned in the previous paragraph, it is possible to convert sales costs in part to variable costs through the payment of commissions expressed as a percentage of sales value achieved. Typically those who can be paid in this way will be prepared to work on a "no sale, no payment" basis. and include:

- individual direct salesmen

- firms of independent financial advisers and brokers

- branches of the parent company

Of course the management company cannot rely totally on the efforts of these organisations, but will need to maintain a centrally planned marketing and advertising budget which will be a variable cost. The extent to which this expenditure is pruned in difficult times is the subject of much debate. It is always tempting for senior managers to minimise the effect of a market fall on profits by cutting out all advertising expenditure, using the justification that it is not going to produce immediate sales; but as section 14.3.2.1 points out, ongoing visibility is important to investor confidence.

Subcontracting investment management

It is rare but not unknown for CIF Management companies to subcontract investment management as well as all the other functions described in this section. There are plenty of independent investment managers eager to undertake investment management for a fee related to the value of the funds: they too have fixed costs and the addition of third-party contracts of this kind is very attractive for them. A CIF Manager might consider this option in respect of new CIFs investing in foreign countries in which it has no expertise of its own. Using such a subcontractor would avoid incurring extra fixed costs in the form of new hirings of investment managers of its own.

14.5.3.3.b Controlling fixed costs

Clearly, depending on the extent to which subcontractors are used, the management company may be left with a substantially reduced proportion of overhead costs in relation to total costs. Fixed costs can be controlled in the normal ways by efficiency and good information.

If a CIF Manager took advantage of all these opportunities to outsource specialist functions, it could create a "virtual" management company which carried out no day to day functions at all, but simply provided the entrepreneurial skill, the capital and perhaps the brand name. Such virtual management companies do exist, usually created by an organisation with an existing customer base and a strong brand name – a major retail chain for example.

14.6   The budget in practice

The next chart shows a budget for a CIF Manager. The budget assumes a start up business with no funds under management at the beginning of the period shown.

The budget format used here is an accounting and not a cash flow format. For example, the payments of the annual charges by the CIFs may be spread unevenly through the year; payments for the office leases may be quarterly in advance, etc. These cash flow factors will need separate consideration, especially in relation to their impact on capital adequacy.

The Growth Fund Management Company Budget

YEARS	1	2	3	4	5	6
Gross sales[1]	860.00	1000.00	1200.00	1500.00	1750.00	2000.00
Initial charge[2]	43.00	50.00	60.00	75.00	87.50	100.00
Cost of sales[3]	25.80	30.00	36.00	45.00	52.50	60.00
Net retained charge[4]	17.20	20.00	24.00	30.00	35.00	40.00
Net investment[5]	100.00	150.00	200.00	250.00	300.00	350.00
Less initial charge	5.00	7.50	10.00	12.50	15.00	17.50
Invested[6]	95.00	142.50	190.00	237.50	285.00	332.50
Adjusted for market[7]	99.75	149.63	199.50	249.38	299.25	349.13
Closing fund[8]	99.75	259.35	484.79	782.64	1160.15	1625.29
Annual fee[9]	1.00	3.49	7.18	12.19	18.65	26.69
Gross profit[10]	18.20	23.49	31.18	42.19	53.65	66.69
Expenses[11]	6.00	7.00	9.00	12.00	15.00	19.00
Profit before tax[12]	12.20	16.49	22.18	30.19	38.65	47.69

Notes

[1] As shown in sales forecast in 14.6.1

[2] Initial charge assumed to be 5%

[3] Commission to sales agents assumed to be 3%

[4] Line 2 – line 3

[5] As shown in sales forecast in 14.6.1

[6] Amount invested after deducting initial sales charge

[7] Market values increase by 10% per annum

[8] Cumulative total value

[9] Fee assumed to be 2% per annum is calculated on the formula which provides for a charge on half the value of net sales which are assumed to occur evenly through the year

[10] Line 4 + line 10

[11] Management and other expenses

[12] Line 11 – line 12

The next Chart shows the actual result and illustrates that in a real world, sales do not rise steadily and that markets and costs do not rise by a neat 10% per annum. It is possible for things to go wrong.

The Growth Fund Management Company Actual Results

YEARS	1	2	3	4	5	6
Gross sales[1]	860.00	1000.00	1100.00	500.00	1000.00	1500.00
Initial charge[2]	43.00	50.00	55.00	25.00	50.00	75.00
Cost of sales[3]	25.80	30.00	33.00	15.00	30.00	45.00
Net retained charge[4]	17.20	20.00	22.00	10.00	20.00	30.00
Net investment[5]	200.00	100.00	200.00	100.00	400.00	500.00
Less initial charge	10.00	5.00	10.00	5.00	20.00	25.00
Invested[6]	190.00	95.00	190.00	95.00	380.00	475.00
Adjusted for market[7]	190.00	99.75	199.50	99.75	399.00	498.75
Closing fund[8]	190.00	308.75	539.13	469.30	484.50	1103.90
Annual fee[9]	1.90	4.80	8.17	11.78	13.38	14.68
Gross profit[10]	19.10	24.80	30.17	21.78	33.38	44.68
Expenses[11]	6.00	7.00	9.00	12.00	15.00	19.00
Profit before tax[12]	13.10	17.80	21.17	9.78	18.38	25.68

[1] As shown in sales forecast in 14.6.1
[2] Initial charge assumed to be 5%
[3] Commission to sales agents assumed to be 3%
[4] Line 2 – line 3
[5] As shown in sales forecast in 14.6.1
[6] Amount invested after deducting initial sales charge
[7] Market values increase by 10% per annum
[8] Cumulative total value
[9] Fee assumed to be 2% per annum is calculated on the formula which provides for a charge on half the value of net sales, which are assumed to occur evenly through the year
[10] Line 4 + line 10
[11] Management and other expenses
[12] Line 11 – line 12 – Note due to unexpected market conditions, profit is much lower than budgeted

The two examples shown above of a budget and actual results are illustrative only and very crude to the extent that they are summaries of what would be much more detailed schedules of sales and costs which would lie behind such a summary. The example below shows the format for a typical sales forecast. In reality this would not be expected to look further ahead than the next financial year.

14.6.1   Budget methodology

This is a 'macro' budget; each functional unit within the company should also have its own 'micro' budget. The creation of the company's budget is through a combination of 'top-down' strategic direction from the directors and 'bottom-up' planning for implementation by managers of the business units.

The chart below shows one example of a budget from a functional unit, probably the most significant for budgetary purposes, the sales department.

Budgeted sales and redemptions for the next financial year

QUARTERS	1	2	3	4	TOTALS	
Growth Fund						
Sales	20	30	20	10	80	
Redemptions	0	20	15	5	40	
Net	20	10	5	5	40	
Income Fund						
Sales	20	30	50	30	130	
Redemptions	50	50	50	50	200	
Net	-30	-20	0	-20	-70	
Bond Fund						
Sales	200	100	200	150	650	
Redemptions	100	70	150	200	520	
Net	100	30	50	-50	130	
				Totals	Sales	860
					Redemption	760
					Net	100

Of course it is likely that each of the funds above, the Growth Fund, the Income Fund and the Bond Fund will have different charging and sales commission structures, so the predicted sales patterns and volumes will have implications for the budgetary lines which deal with income from initial and annual charges and sales commissions. The Bond Fund is likely to have lower charges so the high sales predicted will have less effect on the bottom line than if the high sales had been of the Growth Fund which is likely to have higher charges.

In practice each of the business unit's budgets have to be co-ordinated since none can be set independently. The common starting point is sales and income from initial and annual charges. Any given increase (or reduction) from previous levels should have similar effects throughout the organisation. The managers of business units then need to work through the implications in terms of personnel, premises, systems, etc.

Through effective use of technology, draft budgets can be widely distributed and co-ordinated. Senior managers should have access to the detailed budgets of the smallest business units so that they have a firm grasp of costs and the changes (or lack of changes) in costs resulting from any increase (or decrease) in sales.

14.6.2   Budget control

Conventional budget control is through feedback. Performance is recorded and measured against budget. Variances from the budget lead to action. Constant monitoring of performance against budget is used to keep senior managers informed of the state of the company.

The problem with this is that in the CIF business, change can be very rapid. By the time the data has been analysed and presented to managers, opportunities may have been missed. So ideally feedback should be supplemented by 'feed forward', whose objective is to react to change as it happens, to anticipate events and to adapt plans continuously.

In a sense this merely recognises that there is a continuum of possible outcomes for the sales/revenue line in the budget, and that the likelihood of a figure set at the start of the year being achieved is quite low. One answer adopted by many CIF Managers is to produce a set of budgets based on different sales/revenue lines. For example, if the projection was for sales of 800,000, budgets would also be produced for sales of 600,000 and 1,000,000. Producing these would give senior managers clear ideas about what would be necessary, so that action could be taken quickly if the decision was made to switch the budget basis at any point during the year.

While budgets are necessary, they must not be too rigid, and must be capable of being reviewed, revised and over ridden during the course of a year.

14.6.3   Using the budget as a management tool

The usefulness of the budget as a management tool depends on the extent to which people throughout the organisation are committed to the budgeting process. Managers can to a large extent sabotage the process by building slack into their budgets. They may, for example, exaggerate costs in order to be able to accommodate pressure for cuts. This will actually be a rational solution for individual managers to adopt if the following circumstances prevail:

- there is great pressure not to overspend budgets, and sanctions are applied to those who do so

- there is no system for reviewing or adapting budgets during the year

- senior managers are excessively concerned with meeting the budget rather than dealing with the problems faced by the cost centres

- budget holders are dealt with in isolation, individually, so that the budget process is seen as a game between the individual and the company

It is therefore the responsibility of senior managers to convince managers throughout the organisation that it is worth co-operating and producing realistic figures. Careful thought should be given to incentives to encourage managers to adopt the right attitudes, in particular bonuses based partly on departmental targets and partly on the success of the company as a whole.

14.7 The search for size – domestic and multinational mergers of CIF Managers

Although this Chapter endeavours to give an insight into the way profitability can be achieved by the managers of CIFs, and the way in which the managers think about their business, there are some other bigger trends which need to be understood.

There is a belief that size is a benefit in management of CIFs, and as a result there has been a trend for managers of CIFs to grow by acquisition. This trend is particularly accentuated at the point at which CIF Managers have reached a limit to their growth in one market and this in turn has led them to seek to become multinational.

Multinational operation requires the possession of investment management capability spanning all world markets, and in many cases this means offices in several countries at least. There is an incentive to spread these costs over the largest possible volume of assets. The attractions are:

- the costs of enhancements in systems can be spread over a larger volume of funds, which generate greater revenues (see below)

- the CIF Manager can resell products developed for a domestic market internationally in much larger volumes

- similar funds can be merged to form larger ones

- economies in staffing, offices, advertising and marketing and administration can produce cost savings

- the diversification of distribution and a customer base across several continents can produce greater stability in revenues

- synergies can result from cross-marketing

All of these factors provide a powerful incentive to amalgamate.

There is however still a place for small specialist managers, and the case for massive size is yet to be proven. In particular, the risk of contamination needs consideration. A problem with operations in one part of the world may lead to loss of confidence in other countries. Securities Regulators now co-operate far more actively internationally. If they become concerned about one aspect of a company's international operations, this may lead to pressure from regulators in other countries as well.

14.8 Financial conglomerates aim to provide a range of services

The largest CIF Managers are now part of integrated investment management groups which also manage pension and other institutional funds, and which in turn are owned by multinational and multifaceted financial groups within which there are banks, insurance companies and other financial service providers. This conglomerate approach stresses the need to provide a whole package of financial services which can meet all the needs of a particular customer in a "one stop shop".

CIF Managers are seen as desirable components of financial conglomerates because their earnings are relatively stable, compared with revenues from investment banking and corporate finance. As compared with pension funds, which require regular briefings and presentations from investment managers, CIFs and their individual investors are undemanding clients in respect of investment managers. So the retail sector has become increasingly fashionable.

For this reason, stockmarket-listed CIF Managers receive high share ratings compared with banks, though their shares also show more volatile movements reflecting the fact that their earnings are directly affected by movements in share prices generally. Given the operational gearing inherent in the CIF business, it is perhaps not surprising that in both the US and the UK, individual investors would have enjoyed far superior returns from 1980 to 1998 by owning the shares of listed CIF Managers rather than even the best of the CIFs they managed over the same period.

Glossary

A

Accrued Income

The income of a CIF which is held pending distribution and included in the net asset value

Accumulation

Adding income to capital, instead of distributing it as dividends, thus increasing the CIF share or unit price. See 'reinvestment' for alternative method

Active management

The management of a portfolio through analysis of fundamental economic and corporate trends (versus 'passive management', see later)

Annual fee

Recurring fee paid annually for the management of a fund

Appraiser

The valuer of illiquid fund assets (required by regulation)

Ask price

See 'offer price'

Asset allocation

The process of diversifying a fund portfolio between asset classes – typically cash, bonds or equities

Asset value

The value of assets which comprise the portfolio of the fund, valued at market prices or by an appraiser if illiquid

Auditor

Organisation required to undertake an annual independent audit (and sometimes a check on valuation and pricing)

Back end load

　　　See 'exit fee' under 'Charges'

Bearer security

　　　A security, for which the only evidence of ownership is possession

Bid price

　　　Price at which a CIF unit or share is able to be sold back to the CIF
　　　Management (also 'repurchase' or 'redemption' price): see also 'offer price'
　　　and 'spread'

Blue chip

　　　A high quality investment. Term usually applied to equities

Bond

　　　Any interest bearing or discounted government, municipal or corporate
　　　security that obliges the issuer to pay the bondholder a specified sum of
　　　money, usually at specific intervals and/or to repay the principal amount of
　　　the loan on maturity. A secured bond is backed by collateral; an unsecured
　　　bond (or debenture) is backed by the credit of the issuer but not collateral

Book value

　　　For CIFs, the original cost of the asset, modified by subsequent transactions

'Bottom up'

　　　Type of investment analysis that emphasises fundamental data on companies
　　　rather than macroeconomic or market data. See 'top down'

Broker

　　　Individual or institution which introduces the two parties to a transaction to
　　　each other. Brokers do not take positions in securities for themselves

Cancellation

　　　See 'liquidation'

Capital

　　　For CIFs, this term is used to signify the cost or market value of CIF assets as
　　　opposed to the income (dividends, interest, rental) generated by them

Capital gain (loss)

　　　The profit (or loss) made on the sale of a capital asset

Capital reserves

　　　The reserves created on the passive side of the balance sheet to reflect
　　　changes in the value of closed ended CIF assets. They may take the form
　　　either of realised or non-realised reserves

Cash fund

Used here to describe a fund which seeks to attract cash investment, rather than privatisation vouchers or other entitlements

CDT

Term used in this book to refer to any of three types of organisation (custodians, depositaries, trustees) which carry out similar functions for CIFs

Central Depositary

A term used variably to describe an entity which may simply be the central registrar for all listed or quoted securities; or for an organisation which may also undertake clearing and settlement functions for such securities

Certificated share or unit

A share or unit for which an ownership certificate is issued. Certification may or may not be a legal requirement

Charges

Entry fee ('initial charge' or 'front end load') levied upon purchase of units or shares in a CIF; annual fee (see 'annual fee' above) or exit fee ('redemption charge' or 'back end load') levied upon sale of units or shares in a CIF. Entry or exit fees may be added to or deducted from, the NAV of the unit or share. Also see 'no load'

CIF

Collective Investment Fund

CIF Manager

Company or organisation responsible for the management and administration of one or more CIFs

Clearing

The process of matching trades for clearance and settlement

Closed End(ed) Fund

A fund which has a fixed number of shares or units in issue

Collective investment scheme

Generic name for investment funds

Commission

Fee payable to agents or salespeople who sell CIF shares or units to clients: normally a percentage of the amount invested in the CIF by their customers. May also refer to commission paid to a broker for making securities transactions for the CIF's portfolio

Compensation

Issue of vouchers or other entitlements to compensate for loss of property in former command economies. In some cases these can be exchanged for holdings in CIFs or other assets

Compensation fund

A fund designed to compensate investors for losses incurred through fraud or malpractice by licensed entities

Conflict of interest

The term used to describe the situation where an individual or company may have a commercial or financial involvement in a transaction, but a legal or fiduciary duty to act in a way which would be prejudicial to their own commercial advantage

Contractual fund

A fund formed under the law of contract or Civil Code (eg Germany Investmentfond or Russian unit investment funds). May be open ended, interval or closed ended

Corporate fund

A fund formed under joint stock company law (eg American mutual funds or Russian shareholder investment funds). May be open ended, interval or closed ended

Coupon

Interest rate on a debt security (bond) which the issuer promises to pay to the holder until maturity, expressed as an annual percentage of face value. Also used in privatisation to refer to vouchers (eg Czech and Slovak Republics) used to buy privatising assets

Creation

In CIF terms, the act of creating additional shares or units in an open ended or interval CIF. Achieved by depositing with the fund the value of the shares or units to be created and increasing the number of shares or units in the fund in proportion to the value deposited

Custodian

Licensed entity responsible for safekeeping of CIF assets (it may also be responsible for a range of other tasks. Also referred to as (Specialised) Depositary

Customer database

Record (list) of customers which enables all transactions and holdings of a management company's CIFs by one individual to be identified; often contains other marketing data

Dealer

An individual or organisation which buys and sells securities which it owns for its own account

Depositary (Specialised)

See 'Central Depositary' and 'Custodian'

Dilution levy

Sum paid into a CIF by a buyer or seller to compensate ongoing investors for the effect of transaction costs in diluting NAV

Discount

In relation to a closed ended CIF, the difference between net asset value of a share or unit in the fund and the market price of that share or unit, when the market price is lower than net asset value: expressed as a percentage of net asset value

Diversification

The division of a capital sum among a wide range of investments in order to reduce risk

Dividend or Distribution

The amount paid out by a company or CIF to the holders of its preference, ordinary and deferred shares; usually on a six monthly basis

Distribution

Also used to refer to means of reaching potential CIF customers

Dual pricing

CIF pricing system whereby investors purchase units or shares at one price ('offer price') and sell at a lower price ('bid price'). See 'single pricing'

Efficient Portfolio Management (EPM)

A technical term meaning, essentially, the use of derivatives by a CIF in order to reduce risk, reduce cost, or generate additional capital or income with little, or an acceptably low, level of risk as compared with a traditional portfolio of securities

Emerging market fund

CIF whose objective is to invest in the securities of countries whose markets are relatively new and riskier than established markets

Equity

The risk capital of a company: shares (also referred to as "equities" or in the US "common stock")

Expenses

Costs levied on CIFs other than entry, annual and exit fees; for example, audit fees

Face value

The value stated on the security, also known as 'nominal' or 'par' value. See 'par value'

Forward pricing

Where transactions to buy or sell shares or units in a CIF are done at the price product at the next valuation after the order is received. Thus the price for the transaction is fixed in the future. See 'historic pricing'

Front end load

See 'charges'

Front running

Purchase of a security by the investment manager (or an associate) of a CIF in advance of a larger purchase by a CIF

Fund of funds

A CIF whose portfolio consists of the shares or units of other investment funds. Not the same as an umbrella fund

Gearing (UK) or Leverage (USA)

The process whereby capital growth and income to shareholders are increased by borrowing, which provides scope for additional investment to be made but which carries a fixed liability. The return on the extra investment, minus the cost of the borrowing, gives the shareholder an enhanced, or "geared" profit (loss)

Growth fund

A CIF whose most significant objective is to increase the value of the capital assets

Hedge fund

Speculative investment vehicle, usually located offshore, often constructed as partnerships

Historic pricing

Where transactions to buy or sell shares or units in a CIF are done at the price produced at the most recent valuation prior to receipt of the order. Thus the price for the transaction is fixed in the past. See 'forward pricing'

Income

Revenue to a CIF – ie, dividends, interest or income – earned by its assets

Income fund

A CIF whose most significant objective is to generate a high and growing income which can be paid out as dividends to investors

Index

A mathematical compilation of the prices or rates of securities, currencies or commodities, which gives an average of the price movements of a market or sector, consumer prices or currency, against which the performance of a CIF may be compared

Index fund

A CIF whose portfolio is constructed in such a way that it will replicate as closely as possible the performance of a specific index

Initial charge

See 'charges'

Insider dealing

The use of privileged, non-publicly disclosed information to trade advantageously in securities

Institutional investor

Institutions whose prime function is to gather the savings of individuals and give them financial protection through insurance, pensions or the spreading of risk. Usually refers to pension or insurance funds, or CIFs, or their managers

International fund

A CIF whose objective is to invest its assets in securities of countries other than that in which it is domiciled; either in a number of different countries or in a single country

Interval fund

A CIF where the number of shares or units in issue is not fixed but which only opens for issue and redemption at stated intervals, the minimum usually being once a year

Investment and borrowing powers

Also known as composition and structure of assets. Regulation which defines the types of asset which are and are not permitted to be held by a particular type of CIF; the maximum percentages of the portfolio which may be invested in any class of asset or single asset; the maximum ownership of the issued capital of any one issuer which may be held by any one CIF or group of CIFs operated by the same management company; ability for the CIF to borrow and limitations on such borrowing in terms of purpose, amount and duration

Investment committee

Group of individuals responsible for investment management process within a CIF Manager

Investment company

Used here to refer to a corporate form CIF (and not a CIF Manager)

Investment fund

Generic name for all types of CIF. See also 'collective investment scheme'

Investment manager

The individual or company responsible for the management of one or more CIFs

Issue

Used here to refer to the creation and sale of new shares or units in a CIF

Leverage

See 'gearing'

Licensing

The process by which a regulator approves an entity to conduct regulated business

Liquidation

The removal from existence of a number of shares or units in a CIF or company. The required number of shares are cancelled and their value paid out from the assets of the CIF or company. Also refers to the winding up of a CIF and distribution of assets to holders

Liquidity

Characteristic of a security with enough units or shares in circulation to allow large transactions to take place without a substantial change in price. Also refers to the ability of an investor to convert assets into cash quickly

Listed company/quoted company

A company whose shares have obtained a listing or quotation on a recognised stock exchange. The phrase is confined to full listing and not generally extended to a company whose shares are traded (see 'traded') on an unlisted securities market (USM) or an over the counter market (OTC)

Load

See 'charge'

Lump sum investment

The investment of a single sum of money into shares or units of a CIF (as opposed to regular savings schemes)

Mass privatisation programme (MPP)

A programme whereby ownership of companies or other assets is transferred in bulk from the State to the private sector, usually done through the issue of privatisation entitlements to citizens which are often called "vouchers" or "coupons" or "certificates", for which they pay nothing or a small administrative charge. These entitlements may be (in different countries in different combinations) sold for cash ("tradable"); exchanged for shares or units in privatisation funds or for shares of privatising companies; or used to acquire property

Merger

The process by which two or more CIFs or companies are amalgamated into a single CIF or company

Money market fund

A CIF which invests in short term debt instruments including negotiable certificates of deposit, commercial paper, bankers acceptances, treasury bills, etc. Not the same as a 'cash fund' for the purposes of this book. See 'cash fund'

Mutual fund

The name applied to corporate form collective investment funds in the USA; sometimes used to refer to investment funds generally

Net asset value (NAV)

The value of the assets of a CIF, net of its liabilities

Net asset value per share or unit

The assets of a CIF, net of its liabilities, divided by the number of shares or units of the CIF in issue

No load fund

A CIF which levies no entry fee (front end load). See 'charges'

Nominal value

See 'face value' or 'par value'

Non-certificated shares or units

Shares or units for which a certificate of ownership has not been issued

Offshore

Generic term for financial centres with lower taxes and often more flexible or lower standards of regulation than most countries; used as a domicile for CIFs

Open end(ed) fund

A CIF where the number of shares or units in issue is not fixed and in which units or shares can be issued or redeemed either daily or frequently (usually a minimum of once in every two weeks)

Ordinary share

The risk capital of a company, often called the equity capital, hence ordinary shares being referred to as "equities". Also called "common stock" in the USA

Over The Counter (OTC) market

A market where securities are not traded outside a formalised exchange (eg telephone trading based on screen-based prices)

Par value

The nominal price of a share, debenture or loan stock. The par value bears no relation to the market value of that security, which depends entirely upon supply and demand in the market. Consequently, a security may stand in the market either at par (equal to nominal price) or above or below par. See 'face value' and 'nominal value'

Participations

Term sometimes used to describe units in contractual form CIFs

Passive management

Describes the process of managing an index. See 'index fund' and 'active management'

Portfolio

Chosen selection of securities or other assets which together form the assets of a CIF

Portfolio management

The management by a professional manager of the portfolios of a group of investors, either individual or institutional

Preference shares

Shares which carry the right to a (normally fixed) dividend which ranks before the payment of a dividend to ordinary shareholders, but behind the claims for interest by debenture and loan stock holders

Premium

In relation to closed ended CIFs, the difference between the net asset value per unit or share and the market price of that unit or share, where that price is higher than the net asset value; expressed as a percentage of net asset value. See 'discount'

Pricing

The calculation of a price at which a share or unit of an interval or open CIF is sold or redeemed; it is based on the net asset value of all assets in the portfolio, divided by the number of shares or units in issue

Privatisation (Investment) fund (PF or PIF)

Used in this book to describe a CIF which seeks to raise primarily vouchers or privatisation entitlements, rather than cash

Property

Used in this book to refer to "immovable assets" – ie buildings or land ("real estate" in the USA)

Prospectus

> A legal document detailing the terms of the offer being made of a CIF's units or shares which is required to contain all the information about a CIF or company that the prospective purchaser needs to know in order to reach an informed decision as to whether to buy or not

Recognised market

> Internationally, a market on which securities are traded "recognised" by a Securities Regulator as meeting certain standards of transparency and disclosure

Recognised quotation

> In Russia, a quotation of a security by a recognised (ie licensed) trade organiser

Recognised trade organiser

> In Russia, refers to a trading system or exchange which holds a licence for such activity from the securities regulator

Redemption

> Used in this book to refer to the buying back or repurchase and cancellation (see 'liquidation') by the management company of a share or unit from a CIF investor

Register

> The official record of investors in a CIF or company

Registrar

> A legal entity licensed to create and maintain the register of a CIF or company

Regular savings scheme

> A method whereby small sums are invested in a CIF on a regular (often monthly) basis (as opposed to 'lump sum investment', see above)

Reinvestment

> Describes the process of using net income (ie dividends or distributions) from a CIF to buy additional shares or units in that CIF. See 'accumulation' for alternative method

Repurchase

> See 'redemption'

Return

> See 'total return'

Risk

> In portfolio theory, risk is defined as the variability or volatility or an investment as measured by standard deviation or variance

S

Sales agent

Term used in this book to describe an individual or an entity (which is not the manager nor the custodian of the CIF) which is authorised to promote the sale and repurchase of CIF shares or units. Such entities may, or may not, be required to be licensed

Securities regulator

Term used in this book to describe the organisation charged by law with administering the laws relating to securities and CIFs and making rules within that law

Self managed fund

Term used to describe a CIF which directly employs its own personnel to undertake its management functions; thus it does not have an external management company

Self regulation

A system in which the main regulator delegates certain regulatory duties and powers to a particular sector of the financial industry, which is thereby permitted to regulate itself through a specially formed regulatory organisation referred to as an 'SRO'

Settlement

The making of payments for the purchase of, or receiving money, from the sale of securities at the same time as delivery or receipt of those securities

Share

A security which represents ownership of a portion of a company or CIF. See 'ordinary share' and 'preference share'

Shareholder fund

See 'corporate fund'

Single pricing

Pricing system for CIFs where both purchases and sales take place at a single price which is net asset value, plus or minus any charges. See 'dual pricing'

Spread

The difference between the buying price ('offer' or 'ask' price) and the selling price ('bid' price) or a share or unit. See 'dual pricing'

Stock market

General term referring to the organised trading of securities through exchanges or OTC markets

Suspension

Temporary cessation of trading of a security on a stock market also applied to temporary cessation of issue and redemption of CIFs

glossary

T

Tail end underwriting

Use of one or more CIFs to absorb the unwanted securities offered by an affiliate of the CIF Manager

Top down

Method of investment analysis where primary market decisions are made on the basis of macroeconomic factors. See 'bottom up'

Total return

The annualised return from an investment combining income and capital growth

Trade association

An organisation formed by companies in the same sector whose purpose is to promote the interests of its members. This can include information gathering and provision, lobbying and public education as well as media relations

Trade organiser

In Russia, refers to organisations or systems where securities are traded

Trail commission

Ongoing commission payment to agents or salespeople based on a percentage of the value of their customers' ongoing investments

Total Expense Ratio (TER)

The total of the annual costs of operation of a CIF, expressed either in cash terms or as a percentage of average net asset value (TER does not include entry or exit fees)

Tradable

Used in this book for vouchers or privatisation entitlements that may be sold for cash

Traded

Used in this book to describe securities which are bought and sold on a recognised market

Trust companies

A term variably used to mean a CIF which operates under trust law or under trust management provisions. Sometimes also used for management companies of trust type funds

Trustee

Individual or company who holds the assets of a CIF on behalf of its investors, who are the beneficiaries of the trust. See 'unit trust'

Trusts

Used in this book to refer to CIFs operated under trust law